Energy Security Cooperation in Northeast Asia

Drawing on cutting-edge research from leading scholars, this book investigates state preferences for regime creation and assesses state capacity for executing these preferences in Northeast Asia's energy domain, defined as the geographical area comprising the following countries: Russia, Mongolia, China, Japan, South Korea and North Korea. It examines questions pertaining to how states perceive the need and necessity for establishing a regime when it comes to the issue of energy and how much commitment they make to the effort in Northeast Asia.

The book analyzes the factors that shape each country's fundamental energy interests in the region, how these interests impact their attitudes toward engaging the region on energy security and the way they carry out their regional engagement. Based on countries' interests in promoting institutionalized regional energy cooperation and their capacity for forging that cooperation, the collection assesses each state's role in contributing to an energy regime in Northeast Asia. It then concludes with a critique on the decade-plus quest for energy security cooperation in Northeast Asia and suggests ways forward for facilitating regional energy security cooperation.

This book will be of great interest to scholars and students of environmental policy, energy policy, security studies, Asian studies and international relations.

Bo Kong is ConocoPhillips Petroleum Professor of Chinese and Asian Studies and Assistant Professor of International and Area Studies at the University of Oklahoma College of International Studies, USA.

Jae H. Ku is Director at the U.S.–Korea Institute at Johns Hopkins University, USA.

Routledge Explorations in Environmental Studies

Nuclear Waste Management and Legitimacy
Nihilism and responsibility
Mats Andrén

Nuclear Power, Economic Development Discourse and the Environment
The case of India
Manu V. Mathai

Federalism of Wetlands
Ryan W. Taylor

Governing Sustainable Urban Renewal
Partnerships in action
Rory Shand

Employee Engagement with Sustainable Business
How to change the world whilst keeping your day job
Nadine Exter

The Political Economy of Global Warming
The terminal crisis
Del Weston

Communicating Environmental Patriotism
A rhetorical history of the American environmental movement
Anne Marie Todd

Environmental Justice in Developing Countries
Perspectives from Africa and Asia-Pacific
Rhuks Temitope Ako

Climate Change and Cultural Heritage
A race against time
Peter F. Smith

Energy Security Cooperation in Northeast Asia

Edited by Bo Kong and Jae H. Ku

LONDON AND NEW YORK

First published 2015
by Routledge
2 Park Square, Milton Park, Abingdon, Oxon OX14 4RN

and by Routledge
711 Third Avenue, New York, NY 10017

First issued in paperback 2017

Routledge is an imprint of the Taylor & Francis Group, an informa business

British Library Cataloguing-in-Publication Data
A catalogue record for this book is available from the British Library

Library of Congress Cataloging-in-Publication Data
Energy security cooperation in Northeast Asia / edited by Bo Kong and
Jae Ku.
pages cm
1. Energy security—East Asia—International cooperation.
2. Energy policy—East Asia. 3. East Asia—Foreign economic relations.
4. East Asia—Foreign relations. I. Kong, Bo. II. Ku, Jae H.
HD9502.E182E555 2015
333.79095—dc23
2014042488

ISBN 13: 978-1-138-30802-2 (pbk)
ISBN 13: 978-1-138-78530-4 (hbk)

Typeset in Goudy
by Swales & Willis Ltd, Exeter, Devon, UK

Contents

Illustrations

Contributors

Carla P. Freeman is Associate Director of the China Studies Program at John Hopkins School of Advanced International Studies. She previously served as programme officer for civil society and community development with a focus on sustainability at The Johnson Foundation; was a political risk analyst for China, Japan, Korea, Taiwan and Vietnam; and has held various academic positions, including director of the Program in Global Studies and International Affairs at Alverno College in Milwaukee and visiting scholar at the University of Wisconsin-Milwaukee.

Mikkal E. Herberg is Research Director of the National Bureau of Asian Research Energy Security Program at the University of California. He is also a senior lecturer on international and Asian energy at the Graduate School of International Relations and Pacific Studies, University of California, San Diego. Previously he spent 20 years in the oil industry in senior planning roles for the Atlantic Richfield Company, where from 1997 to 2000 he was Director for Global Energy and Economics. He also headed country risk management and his previous positions include Director of Portfolio Risk Management and Director for Emerging Markets.

Llewelyn Hughes is a senior lecturer at the Australian National University's Crawford School of Public Policy. Prior to joining faculty at the ANU he was an Assistant Professor of International Affairs at the Elliott School of International Affairs at George Washington University (GWU) in Washington DC, and before that a research fellow in the Consortium for Energy Policy Research at the John F. Kennedy School of Government, Harvard University.

Charles Krusekopf is Director of the School of Business and Associate Professor of International Business at Royal Roads University in Victoria, British Columbia. He is the founder and Executive Director of the American Center for Mongolian Studies, an American Overseas Research Center based in Ulaanbaatar, Mongolia. He has worked as a researcher and consultant for numerous organizations on projects related to Mongolia, including the U.S. State Department, World Bank, Soros Foundation, GLG and Albright Stonebridge Group.

Jae-Seung Lee is a professor at Korea University's Division of International Studies. He was also a visiting scholar with the Korean Studies Program at Stanford University for the 2011–12 academic year. Before joining the faculty of Korea University, he served as a professor at the Institute of Foreign Affairs and National Security (IFANS) and at the Ministry of Foreign Affairs and Trade.

Adam N. Stulberg is Associate Professor and Co-Director of the Center for International Strategy, Technology, and Policy (CISTP) in the Sam Nunn School of International Affairs at Georgia Tech. Previously he served as a political consultant at RAND from 1987 to 1997, and as a senior research associate at the Center for Nonproliferation Studies (CNS), Monterey Institute of International Studies (1997–8). Dr Stulberg was a post-doctoral fellow at CNS (2000–1) and a policy scholar at the EastWest Institute, and has been a consultant to the Carnegie Corporation of New York and the Office of Net Assessment, Office of the U.S. Secretary of Defense.

Suyuan Sun is a senior fellow, School of Advanced International and Area Studies, East China Normal University, and a researcher associated at BRICS Studies Center, Fudan University. Previously, she was a research fellow at the Shanghai Institute for International Studies from 2001 to 2005, followed by a position as a visiting scholar at Vrije Universiteit Brussel during the 2008–9 academic year and at the University of California San Diego School of International Relations and Pacific Studies in the 2012–13 academic year.

Editors

Bo Kong is the ConocoPhillips Petroleum Professor of Chinese and Asian Studies and Assistant Professor at the University of Oklahoma's College of International Studies. He is also a senior fellow of the Foreign Policy Institute of the Johns Hopkins University School of Advanced International Studies (SAIS), Senior Associate in the Energy and National Security Program of the Center for Strategic and International Studies (CSIS), member of the Advisory Board for the Revenue Watch Institute, member of the International Editorial Board for the Universiti Kebangsaan Malaysia (UKM) journal – *Jebat: Malaysian Journal of History, Politics & Strategic Studies*, and member of the ChinaFAQs Expert Group.

Jae H. Ku is the Director of the U.S.-Korea Institute at SAIS. Before joining the U.S.-Korea Institute, he was the Director of Human Rights in North Korea Project at Freedom House. He has taught at the Johns Hopkins University School of Advanced International Studies, Brown University, Yonsei University Seoul, Korea, and Sookmyung Women's University, Seoul. He has been a recipient of both Fulbright and Freeman fellowships and has researched at various think tanks, including the Center for Strategic and International Studies, Washington, DC, the Korean Institute of International Studies, Seoul, and the Institute for International Relations Hanoi, Vietnam.

Acknowledgements

Launched in 2008 as an outgrowth of a conference Jae H. Ku and I organized in Shanghai, this volume on energy security cooperation in Northeast Asia has been long overdue and gone through multiple complications. We sought to produce a book that goes beyond headlines and examines the fundamental assumptions about preferences of Northeast Asian states for institutionalized regional energy security cooperation and their ability to produce such a regime. But the task proved more challenging and the distance between conference papers and coherent book chapters turned out to be longer than we had anticipated. In the course of the ensuing six years, we had to turn to two different contributors for chapters on both Russia and Japan and three for the chapter on South Korea. We also had to forgo one chapter completely after having spent a large amount of time and effort. Meanwhile, the energy and geopolitical landscape of the region kept changing, with China's rise, the Fukushima nuclear disaster in Japan, the shale gas revolution in North America, Russia's pivot to the east and the 2014 Ukraine crisis. As a result, we had to ask the contributors of the edited volume to make multiple changes and updates.

In the midst of all these complications, keeping the project alive and sustaining its momentum tested our patience and commitment. But the generous support and invaluable trust afforded to us from the institutions, individuals and our loving families are the most important reasons that carried us through the project. To be specific, the National Nuclear Security Administration (NNSA) of the U.S. Department of Energy and the U.S.–Korean Institute (USKI) at the Johns Hopkins University School of Advanced International Studies (SAIS) provided the funding for both organizing the conference and carrying out the book project. Further, the ConocoPhillips Petroleum Chair in Chinese and Asian Studies at the University of Oklahoma, which I assumed beginning from June 2013, enabled me to continue the project after my departure from the Johns Hopkins University SAIS. To all of them, we would like to express our gratitude.

Our thanks also go to many individuals who are integral to our endeavour. We sincerely appreciate all of our chapter contributors for their patience, understanding and support. Despite our repeated requests for seemingly endless editorial changes during the constant delays, our contributors have always given us a vote of confidence and the best response we could hope for. Their cooperation has not only inspired our admiration and respect, but also solidified our commitment to the book project. Next, Jenny Town at the USKI was the go-to person for everyone involved in the project. She also played an indispensable role in organizing the conference from which the book project originated and a follow-up writers' retreat that rekindled its momentum when it was mired in the above-mentioned complications. In addition, Eliza Notides, Charlotte Chiang and John Langdon provided me with excellent research assistance during their time as MA candidates at the Johns Hopkins University SAIS. At the University of Oklahoma, Andrew Fox and Derek Steiger also provided me with outstanding research support. Derek Steiger deserves my special thanks for his prompt, reliable and invaluable support, which proved critical in helping me meet the submission deadline.

On the editorial front, we would like to thank Louisa Earls, albeit no longer with Routledge, for encouraging us to submit the proposal and setting a deadline for seeing it in print. We are also thankful to Beth Wright, our editorial assistant at Routledge, for being supportive and understanding. Our thanks also go to Judy Arginteanu, our independent editor, for her timely and efficient editorial assistance, which helped us consummate the project with a peace of mind.

Finally, I would like to dedicate the book to my wife Wei Wang and my two daughters—Shiangyi Claire Kong and Shiangcheng Hanna Kong—and express my deep gratitude to them for their love, support and sacrifice when I had to use family time to work on the book. My special appreciation goes to my newborn daughter Hanna for being so remarkably cooperative for postponing her arrival by one week. She was born on 21 October, which was also the due date of the manuscript.

Bo Kong
Norman, Oklahoma
21 October 2014

1 Introduction

Bo Kong and Jae H. Ku

This volume has a simple purpose: to understand state preferences for regime creation and assess state capability to implement these preferences in Northeast Asia's energy domain, defined as the geographical area comprising the following countries: Russia, Mongolia, China, Japan, South Korea, and North Korea. Specifically, it aims to answer the following questions pertaining to how states perceive the need and necessity for establishing a regime, that is, a set of "principles, norms, rules, and decision-making procedures around which their expectations converge" (Krasner, 1983), in the issue area of energy, and how much commitment they make to the effort in Northeast Asia. The questions are: What shapes each state's fundamental energy interests in the region? How have these interests impacted their attitudes toward engaging the region on energy security and the way they have carried out their regional engagement at different levels—government, industry, and the so-called epistemic community level? Based on their interests in promoting institutionalized regional energy cooperation and their capability to forge that cooperation, how do we assess each state's role in contributing to an energy regime in Northeast Asia?

Northeast Asia's twin energy policy puzzles

These questions go to the heart of the supply side of regime formation. A deep understanding of them will help shed light on two empirical policy puzzles in Northeast Asia's energy domain: (1) Why haven't the common energy security challenges confronting the region's consumer countries spawned collective responses or a formalized regime? (2) Why haven't the abundant complementarities between energy-consumer and -producer countries in the region provided fertile ground for the formation of regional cooperation featuring a communal approach to energy security?

On the one hand, viewed from energy-consumer countries' point of view, Northeast Asia faces a set of common challenges that in theory should have galvanized the region into some sort of collective action. Because its per capita energy endowment is below world average, the region relies heavily on imports. In fact, it is home to some of the world's leading importers of fossil fuels—No. 2, No. 3, and No. 6 oil importers (China, Japan, and South Korea, respectively);

No. 1, No. 2, and No. 4 coal importers (China, Japan, and South Korea); and No. 1 and No. 2 liquefied natural gas (LNG) importers (Japan and South Korea). This dependence is most acute when it comes to oil. For example, China, Japan, and South Korea each obtain 50 percent, 80 percent, and 90 percent of their imported crude oil from the volatile Middle East. As a result, three common challenges arise. First, this overwhelming Northeast Asian dependence on the Middle East, which is also replicated across the entire Asia-Pacific region, has helped give rise to the historical "Asian premium" for Persian Gulf crudes, a surcharge in the 1980s and 1990s. However, this premium began to disappear in the new millennium, especially with industrializing economies in Asia driving the global demand for oil and the Middle East becoming ever more dependent on the Asian demand. Nevertheless, Northeast Asia's oil import from the Persian gulf means massive wealth transfer from Northeast Asia to the Middle East; this high dependence also subjects Northeast Asia's energy security well-being to the vicissitudes of the internal politics and external relations of the Middle East. The volatilities plaguing the region, as evidenced by the enduring Palestine–Israel conflict; the frequent occurrence of "hot wars," such as the Iran–Iraq War and the two Gulf wars; the on-and-off latent crises, such as the Iran nuclear crisis; the outbreak of "black swan"-type incidents, such as the recent Arab Spring Movement; and the ongoing Syria crisis, are constant reminders of the imperative for the Northeast Asian economies to diversify their energy imports and the danger of supply disruptions to their imported energy.

The risks of supply disruptions are of even more concern than those at the source of supply in the Middle East and include those threatening Northeast Asia's imported energy in transit. Specifically, its imported energy has to traverse some of the world's most challenging sea lines of communications (SLOCs), that is, "choke points" such as the Strait of Hormuz and the Strait of Malacca. While the open passage of the former is frequently taken hostage by the Iranian nuclear crisis and likely to become collateral damage in the case of an escalating military confrontation, the latter is prone to risks of piracy, terrorism, collision (i.e., with another seagoing craft), and oil spills. Consequently, Northeast Asia's reliance on the two choke points not only aggravates the supply vulnerabilities of its imported energy from the Middle East, but also risks increasing its energy import expenditure due to the associated transit risk premiums.

Considering that these common challenges threaten all of Northeast Asia's major consumer countries' energy security and economic well-being, one would expect that they could have triggered a series of collective and concerted policy responses. These might include some sort of consumer countries' alliance designed to collectively bargain with their Persian Gulf exporters to eliminate the Asian premium or coordinate their attempts to reduce their vulnerabilities to supply disruption, price fluctuation, and transit risk. This coordination could take the form of building shared strategic petroleum reserves, synchronizing efforts to develop projects abroad and promote alternative energy as well as energy efficiency at home, or jointly patrolling and protecting the SLOCs. In terms of cost-benefit analysis, these collective policy responses would undoubtedly yield higher collective energy security dividends at a lower cost than uncoordinated self-help practices.

On the other hand, part of the solution to this threefold energy security challenge is actually embedded in the structural complementarities integral to the Northeast Asian region. While the region is populated by some of the world's leading energy importing nations, it is also home to the world's largest exporter of energy—Russia. With the largest natural gas reserves in the world, the eighth-largest reserves of oil, and the second-largest reserves of coal, Russia is the world's largest natural gas exporter, second-largest oil exporter, and third-largest coal exporter. In light of its geographical proximity to the leading energy importing economies in Northeast Asia, Russia is thus well positioned to play a significant role in meeting their import demand. As far as oil is concerned, Russia's impressive resource base offers China, Japan, and South Korea an option to diversify away from their dependence on the Middle East, bargain down the Asian premium, and cut down their transit reliance on the Strait of Hormuz and the Strait of Malacca.

This synergy is accentuated by the fact that adopting this eastward strategy would actually enhance Russia's energy and developmental interests. First, Russia needs Northeast Asian consumer countries' help to maintain its status as a world-leading energy exporter. Its oil fields in West Siberia are depleting fast, whereas those in East Siberia and the Russian Far East (RFE), although estimated to contain vast reserves, will need a vast amount of capital to develop the necessary infrastructure to tap the reserves. With deep pockets and ties to their state-owned financial institutions, state-owned energy companies from China, Japan, and South Korea would have little problem financing the energy development in East Siberia and the RFE. Next, Russia's hydrocarbons production in these new territories would be closer to its Northeast Asian neighbors than to its traditional European market. Considering the depressed energy outlook in the European market due to the lingering euro crisis and many European countries' efforts to promote renewable energy, as well as to diversify away from Russia in the aftermath of the Russia–Ukraine gas dispute, an eastward move would help Russia gain security of the demand for its energy. Finally, the development of these reserves would also assist the Kremlin in revitalizing East Siberia and the RFE, whose economic development and demographic trends stand in contrast to those in neighboring China and consequently raise geopolitical and security concerns in Moscow.

In addition to Russia, the substantial resource endowment and the strategic location of Mongolia add two more complementarities to the synergy between the energy-importing and -exporting nations in Northeast Asia. First, the country could in and of itself become a major fuel exporter to the major energy-consuming countries in the region. In fact, it has already surpassed Australia as the leading coking coal exporter to China. Once it completes the proposed Erdenet-Moron railway, it will be able to supply the entire Northeast Asian market, including China, Russia, Japan, and South Korea, and even export to India.

Second, strategically situated between Russia and its Northeast Asian neighboring economies, Mongolia could become a transit country for land-based pipelines that supply Russian oil and gas to China, Japan, and the two Koreas. There is even a possibility of the country exporting its own oil and gas to its Northeast Asian neighbors. According to the Petroleum Authority of Mongolia (PAM), and the latest positive geological and geophysical data, reports of oil seeps throughout the sedimentary basins, recent discoveries of oil, and the geologic similarity of hydrocarbon basins of Mongolia to adjacent Chinese producing basins all suggest the high probability of finding substantial petroleum reserves in Mongolia.

In light of the structural complementarities between, on the one hand, the energy-producing countries (Russia and Mongolia) and, on the other, the energy-consuming countries (China, Japan, and South Korea), one would expect to see regional collaboration that improves everyone's energy security, from either a supply security or demand security point of view. At a lower level, this regional energy security cooperation could take the form of jointly building energy infrastructure that pipes Russian oil and gas, and ships Mongolian coal to all consumer countries in Northeast Asia, including North Korea. At a higher level, this regional energy security cooperation could take the form of harmonizing energy governance across countries in terms of energy trade, investment, and transit.

Contrary to expectations, neither the common challenges confronting Northeast Asian energy consumer countries nor the synergy between energy-consuming and -producing countries in region has led to any effort resembling a regional energy regime. Instead of providing consumer and producer countries in Northeast Asia with the occasion to work together, they have pulled them apart. Indeed, they have prompted the region's consumer countries to engage in competitive rivalries for the perceived scarce and strategic energy commodities and to resort to state intervention in intraregional energy transactions, which has not only raised the stakes for each in the politicized competition, but also accentuated their impulses for self-interest practices featuring rivalry and nationalistic responses. Meanwhile, Russia, as the region's only net hydrocarbons exporter, cannot resist the impulse to seize the opportunity to play consumer countries against each other to maximize its gains. Its practices have only accomplished the opposite effect, however: Instead of proving itself a reliable player and trustworthy partner, Russia has heightened the investment risks in its energy sector its Northeast Asian neighbors face. As a result, its goal of revitalizing the RFE with the use of Northeast Asian capital remains ever more elusive. Consequently, these self-help-driven responses have not only stoked regional mutual mistrust and misgivings, but also poisoned the atmosphere for facilitating regional energy security cooperation and establishing an energy regime. Pursuits of individual national energy interests have threatened to tear apart rather than stitch together the regional fabric.

Unsatisfactory explanations

There are two conventional explanations for the twin energy policy puzzles in Northeast Asia. Some attribute the lack of cooperation to the disparities among countries in the region. They argue that energy regime creation in a region that shares more differences than similarities among its member states is too difficult a task. Indeed, member states in Northeast Asia differ on almost every important factor affecting energy cooperation—political systems, stages of economic development, integration into the international system, and energy governance systems. For example, Thomson (2006) argues, in the broader context of an *East* Asian institutional framework, that the imbalances in trade and level of development between Northeast and Southeast Asia reduce incentives for greater cooperation.

Others are quick to point to the long-observed historical and institutional problems plaguing the region. Indeed, despite its accelerating intraregional economic interdependence after the end of the Cold War, the region still remains a geographic construct riddled with precarious geopolitical fault lines that, if not handled well, could jeopardize the region's peace and prosperity. These fault lines are for the most part historical legacies that have been compounded by the recent uneven economic development among countries in the region and its resultant changing configuration of the balance of power, which now favors China over both Russia and Japan in the region. They manifest themselves in specific "leftover" issues, such as the lingering enmity between South Korea and North Korea and a series of thorny territorial disputes between Russia and Japan, Japan and China, Japan and the two Koreas, the two Koreas and China, and the two Koreas themselves. Their manifestations are also found in the lack of an overarching organization—or the well-known "organizational deficit" (Chung, 2000; Wada, 2006)—in the region that could mitigate the classic anarchical syndrome, such as the lack of mutual trust and the permeation of security dilemma. With these fault lines configuring Northeast Asia's geopolitical and strategic context, skeptics question any attempt to promote security cooperation in the region, including in the issue area of energy (Choo, 2006; Thomson, 2006; Zhao, 2008; Choi, 2009).

But neither of these explanations is completely satisfactory. If the region's disparities and its organizational deficit were to have such strong deleterious effects on attempts to foster a sense of community in Northeast Asia, they should not be confined to the issue area of energy. However, the issue area of trade and finance has seen so much regional interdependence and integration that it has prompted two scholars to declare that the making of Northeast Asia is actually happening (Calder & Ye, 2010).

Although using a different definition of Northeast Asia (Russia, Japan, South Korea, China, and Taiwan), Calder and Ye have provided four perspectives on Northeast Asian regionalism: (1) Three full-fledged critical junctures—the Korea War, the 1997–1998 Asian financial crisis, and the 2008–2009 global financial crisis—have provided stimulus and momentum for the formation of the Northeast Asian community; (2) the expansion of transnational networks, including bureaucracies, corporations, epistemic communities, and even military actors, has embraced a Northeast Asian identity and led the integration process; (3) this integration is distinct from the clear-cut and legalistic European style; instead, it has primarily relied on policy-oriented yet informal epistemic networks for

performing important and increasingly substantive regional-governance functions; and (4) small but strategic "middle powers," such as South Korea, have
played the critical role as catalysts for integration among their larger neighbors
(Calder & Ye, 2010, pp. 258–64).

While offering some hope on Northeast Asian regionalism, the explanatory
power of this analysis needs further empirical test and is called into question by
the recent deterioration of Japanese–Chinese and Japanese–South Korean ties
in the political and diplomatic realm. Specifically, attributing the growing economic integration and interdependence to the contribution of the strengthening
of transnational policy networks in Northeast Asia is debatable. Considering the
strong role of the state in these Northeast Asian economies, it is entirely plausible their governments would have adopted a pragmatic and utilitarian approach
to deepening ties in the area of trade and finance, where the transaction cost
entailed to forge the necessary cooperation is low and pales in comparison with
the resultant concentrated benefit. In this sense, instead of following the lead of
these transnational policy networks, states may have merely used them as a strategic channel and instrument to better promote their economic interests. If this
were true, the economic integration would not extend to the diplomatic, political, and security realm. Indeed, this appears to be the case in Northeast Asia.
Tokyo's arrest of a Chinese trawler boat captain after a collision with Japanese
naval vessels in September 2010, and the tensions over Tokyo's attempt to buy
the disputed Diaoyu/Senkaku Islands, have contributed to a recent deterioration
of Japanese–Chinese bilateral relations. This, in combination with the deterioration of South Korean–Chinese relations as a result of Beijing's attitude toward
North Korea when it allegedly sunk the South Korean naval vessel *Cheonan* in
March 2010, as well as South Korean–U.S. joint military exercises in the Yellow
Sea, further illustrate the tenuous role of transnational policy networks in performing regional-governance functions. It is especially questionable whether
integration in the economic realm can cause ripple effects in the area of high politics. Furthermore, given the U.S. "pivot toward Asia" and desire to construct the
Trans-Pacific Partnership (TPP), it is too early to conclude that the integration
in Northeast Asia is likely to exclude the United States, which remains the security guarantor of the region. In fact, many contributors to the body of literature
on the prospects for multilateral cooperation in Northeast Asia argue that, given
these hurdles, such cooperation is not possible without the United States playing
a substantial role, either through leadership or in support (Chanlett-Avery, 2005;
Wada, 2006; Choi, 2009; Kim, 2014).

Furthermore, to the extent "the making of Northeast Asia" is happening in
the area of trade and finance, it is doubtful the above-mentioned four contributing mechanisms can be replicated in the energy domain. The critical junctures
one can think of in the energy context—the first oil shock in 1973, the second
oil shock in 1979–1980, or the recent "commodity super-cycle" between 2001
and 2010, when oil prices rose more than fivefold—have not led to any regionalism in the issue area. Neither is there any evidence that the transnational policy
networks focused on energy security have come of age and played any substantive

role in shaping or leading regional energy governance. Nor have the "middle power" South Korea or Mongolia managed to play a catalyst role in accelerating energy regime creation.

Contribution of this volume

Thus, the empirical policy literature is unable to satisfactorily explain why neither the common energy security challenges faced by Northeast Asia's consumer countries nor the structural complementarities between its energy consumer and producer countries have led to little progress toward institutionalized regional energy security cooperation in the region. It leaves many questions unaddressed. This volume aims to fill this vacuum by considering the following possibilities that could have contributed to this lack of progress. First, member states in Northeast Asia do not perceive the need and necessity for institutionalized energy security cooperation because they believe they can handle their energy security challenges sufficiently on their own. Second, they see the need and necessity but are uninterested because they perceive the costs of forming such a regime to be much higher than the benefits such a regime could deliver. Third, they see the need and necessity, but worry about the unequal distribution of collective energy security dividends. Fourth, fundamental trust required for forming such a regime is lacking, and this lack of trust is caused by their early experiences in dealing with each other or with the international system. Fifth, powerful domestic champions are also lacking—champions such as policymakers, bureaucrats, and policy experts inside member states that could give legitimacy and support to the idea of forming such a regional energy regime. Finally, the mode of promoting regional energy security cooperation thus far has neither been the most effective nor the most conducive to energy regime formation. Simply, this volume studies the perceptions, interests, intentions, and capabilities of member states in Northeast Asia with regard to institutionalized energy security cooperation or energy regime formation.

In doing so, this volume considers these explanations for the lack of regional regime creation through the lens of the three primary schools of thought. First are power-based theories, focusing on the impact of power distribution. Theorists such as Grieco (1988) and Mearsheimer (1995) argue that regime creation and enhanced cooperation are unlikely due to the problem of relative versus absolute gains. Second are interest-based theories, emphasizing the constellation and allocation of interest. For example, Keohane and Nye (1977) emphasize the complexity of actors and processes involved in creating a more cooperative environment. Additionally, Lisa Martin's 1992 work highlights the value of multilateral institutions as a solution to dilemmas of strategic interaction and highlights the types of coordination problems, discussed at length this volume, that states face in creating new institutions. Third are knowledge-based theories, highlighting the role of knowledge dynamics, communication, and identities. Hasenclever *et al.* (1997) highlight, for example, that the need for regimes is based on actors' perceptions of a problem, which are based on their causal and normative beliefs, which are at least partially independent of their material environment. Additionally, Hemmer and Katzenstein (2002) posit that the poverty of multilateral institutions in Asia is a result of a lack of shared identity within the region. The contributors to this edited volume have brought their own ontologies into the analyses, each considering the questions they ask through one of these lenses.

Structure of the book

This volume begins with an overview of energy competition and cooperation in Northeast Asia, followed by case studies of China, Japan, South Korea, Mongolia, and Russia, and concludes with a chapter that examines what it would take to build an energy cooperation regime in Northeast Asia. In Chapter 2, Mikkal Herberg, who is a seasoned expert on energy policy globally and especially on East Asia, lays out the fundamental trend that has militated against energy cooperation in Northeast Asia: the strengthening of state intervention in markets and active energy diplomacy. In order to access precarious future energy supplies transported over uncertain energy supply routes, Northeast Asian countries "have together driven a regional propensity towards a state-dominated mercantilist national competition over control of energy supplies and transport routes which has, in turn, become another source of regional tension." This trend is further complicated by strategic regional rivalries over territory and history, as well as the meteoric rise of China's geopolitical importance and energy demands, which have contributed to the "zero-sum" atmosphere.

In Chapter 3, Suyuan Sun, an expert on Chinese energy policy and senior researcher in China, examines China's perception of and its role in energy cooperation. Sun defines China's energy security as having two aspects: the acquisition of fossil energy resources from a producing country and how the consuming country uses the fossil energy efficiently and in an environmentally friendly manner. China approaches these twin goals in a similar manner through bilateral relations, albeit with different sets of partners. In the former, that is, acquisition of resources, China's diplomacy, based on the logic of self-help, cooperates almost exclusively with Russia, the producer; in the latter, China cooperates with Japan and South Korea to acquire energy-saving technologies. In both cases, however, cooperation is made more difficult by the factors outlined in Chapter 2: Russia's manipulation and energy consumers' mutual competition and distrust, which have made it unlikely that those multiple bilateral arrangements can be integrated into a single multilateral agreement.

Llewelyn Hughes, an expert and leading researcher on Japanese energy policy, writing about Japan in Chapter 4, sees a more nuanced approach to energy security cooperation. Hughes argues that simply looking for state-to-state cooperation in energy security misses the point; the fact that the Japanese government's attempts to diversify the geographic sources of its fuel imports and its strengthening of competitiveness of the domestic firms have enabled a significant degree of cooperation between Japan, China, South Korea, Russia, and other countries. Regional energy security cooperation occurs in spite of the lack of inter-state cooperation in many cases because the market-based activities of Northeast Asia promote substantial cross-border cooperation.

In Chapter 5, Jae-Seung Lee, one of the top scholars on Korean international affairs and energy security policy, assesses South Korea's approach to energy security. Lee states that there are two dimensions to South Korea's perception of energy security: energy security as an "objective" to guarantee a stable supply, and energy security as a means to achieve a higher security goal. For South Korea, the former involves long and tedious negotiations with Russia for the provision of oil and natural gas, and the latter involves instituting a peace-building mechanism on the Korean Peninsula that would provide energy security to North Korea in return for North Korea's good behavior in terms of international relations. In both cases, a spiral of competition and geopolitical tension has prevented real progress in energy cooperation and a creative agenda-setting to maximize regional public-goods is necessary.

Charles Krusekopf, who is director of his department and is an expert on Mongolia, writes in Chapter 6 that Mongolia has the potential to play a more important role as a supplier of energy for the region and a potential corridor for Russian energy exports to China. This potential role, however, is hampered by the competition from its wealthier neighbors, namely China and Russia, which are vying for Mongolia's natural resources (coking and thermal coal, uranium, oil, and renewable energy such as wind and solar). As a result, Mongolia's objectives in energy security—to develop its domestic energy resources to become less dependent on Russia and to expand its export market beyond China—have been negatively impacted by the vagaries of Sino-Russian competition and cooperation.

In Chapter 7, Adam Stulberg, who is one of the leading scholars on Russian politics and energy policy, characterizes Russia's energy foray into Northeast Asia as both concerted and befuddling. On the one hand, Russia has invested large sums in infrastructure-building, such as the Eastern Siberia–Pacific Ocean (ESPO) pipeline, to connect vast resources in oil production with China and Japan. However, at the same time, Russia has been hesitant to fully commit to the level of production desired by the region, because of fears it will become merely a resource appendage, especially for China. Further, such expansion has stoked anxiety and fear among the energy-consuming countries in the region; similarly, countries outside of the region are also more anxious because of Moscow's intervention in the Ukraine crisis and the subsequent threats to shift oil and gas away from Europe to Asia. Stulberg argues that Russia's primary goal is not to seek cooperation but to stimulate "energy development in the RFE (Russian Far East) to undergird Russia's competitive advantages—commercially and strategically—across the region." The upshot, he argues, "is that distinct balances of market and institutional conditions in respective oil and gas sectors have created powerful incentives for commercial and strategic posturing, thus restricting Moscow's capacity to play a prominent role in Northeast Asian energy governance, irrespective of shifts in strategy for developing the RFE."

In the final case study in Chapter 8, Carla Freeman, who is an expert on Chinese politics and East Asia in general, inventories and assesses the functional elements and features of existing international institutions that govern energy cooperation. She concludes that while "there is broad interest across the region in enhancing the regional environment for energy security," there exists serious fragmentation "among countries in the region linked to broader security and geo-political issues, level of economic development, and type of economic system." One possible remedy, she proposes, is to embrace a "harder" institutionalization that sets aside states' obsession with sovereignty and noninterference—an insti-tutionalization achieved through cooperation around energy delivery systems, increased investments, and expanding the membership of countries in the region in existing international institutions.

Finally, we conclude by distilling the message from our volume's contributors to provide a comprehensive picture of the ongoing search for energy security cooperation in Northeast Asia. After analyzing the backdrop against which the search emerged and how it is rationalized, it provides a critique of the region's endeavor and investigates why the search has remained elusive over the past decade or so. Specifically, it adopts a supply and demand framework to assess the prospect for a regional energy security cooperation regime in Northeast Asia. It concludes that member states do not demand energy security cooperation when engaging the region on energy and pursuing their discrete national energy inter-ests. An energy security cooperation regime is further unlikely due to the region's inability to supply the necessary institutional framework. It also suggests moving beyond energy security cooperation and focusing rather on the existing energy complex as well as market regimes that tackle shared concerns of energy govern-ance in the region.

References

Calder, Kent and Ye, Min. 2010. *The Making of Northeast Asia*. Stanford, CA: Stanford University Press.

Chanlett-Avery, Emma. 2005. *Rising Energy Competition and Energy Security in Northeast Asia: Issues for US Policy*. CRS Report for Congress, February.

Choi, Hyun Jin. 2009. Fueling Crisis or Cooperation? The Geopolitics of Energy Security in Northeast Asia. *Asian Affairs* 36(1).

Choo, Jaewoo. 2006. Energy Cooperation Problems in Northeast Asia: Unfolding the Reality. *East Asia: An International Quarterly* 23(3).

Chung, Ok-Nim. 2000. *Solving the Security Puzzle in Northeast Asia: A Multilateral Security Regime*. Brookings Institution, September. Online: www.brookings.edu/research/papers/2000/09/01diplomacy-chung (accessed June 4, 2014).

Grieco, Joseph M. 1988. Anarchy and the Limits of Cooperation: A Realist Critique of the Newest Liberal Institutionalism. *International Organization* 42(3).

Hasenclever, Andreas, Mayer, Peter, and Rittberger, Volker. 1997. *Theories of International Regimes*. Cambridge: Cambridge University Press.

Hemmer, Christopher and Katzenstein, Peter J. 2002. Why is There No NATO in Asia? Collective Identity, Regionalism, and the Origins of Multilateralism. *International Organization* 56(3), June.

Keohane, Robert O. and Nye, Joseph S. 2001. *Power and Interdependence: World Politics in Transition* (3rd edn). Boston, MA: Little, Brown.

Kim, Younkyoo. 2014. *Rethinking Energy Security in Northeast Asia.* Berkeley, CA: Nautilus Institute for Security and Sustainability.

Krasner, Stephen D. 1983. Structural Causes and Regime Consequences: Regimes as Intervening Variables. In Stephen D. Krasner (ed.) *International Regimes.* Ithaca, NY: Cornell University Press.

Martin, Lisa L. 1992. Interests, Power, and Multilateralism. *International Organizations* 46(4), Autumn.

Mearsheimer, John. 1995. The False Promise of International Institutions. *International Security* 19(3).

Thomson, Elspeth. 2006. ASEAN and Northeast Asian Energy Security: Cooperation or Competition? *East Asia: An International Quarterly* 23(3).

Wada, Haruki. 2006. Envisioning a Northeast Asian Community: Regional and Domestic Factors to Consider. In Edward Friedman and Sung Chull Kim (eds.) *Regional Cooperation and its Enemies in Northeast Asia: The Impact of Domestic Forces.* New York: Routledge.

Zhao, Suisheng. 2008. China's Global Search for Energy Security: Cooperation and Competition in Asia-Pacific. *Journal of Contemporary China* 17(55).

2 Energy competition and energy cooperation in Northeast Asia

Mikkal E. Herberg

Asia is now at the center of global energy markets as demand has grown rapidly in the wake of decades of high economic growth. The region's rising energy demand has been centered in China but extends across developing Asia. Although energy demand growth has slowed over the past decade in Japan and South Korea, both countries remain virtually totally dependent on imported energy. As a region, Northeast Asia possesses a relatively modest energy resource base that inevitably means that dependence on imported energy is rising dramatically. China is a significant oil and natural gas producer but demand has outrun domestic production. East Siberia in Russia has become an important oil and gas production and export source, and Central Asia has begun supplying China via new large, long-distance pipelines. Nevertheless, the distribution of the energy resources that Northeast Asia needs in order to continue fueling its economic growth is very uneven, and a rapidly rising volume of Northeast Asia's future petroleum needs will need to be imported longer distances from the Persian Gulf, Africa, and even Latin America, historically unstable regions of the world.

Deep and growing energy import dependence has led to a profound sense of insecurity in the region over the reliability and costs of future petroleum supplies and fears that shortages, disruptions, or severe price spikes could become major bottlenecks to continued economic growth. For most of these governments, particularly China, economic performance and job creation are seen as ensuring the bedrock for political legitimacy and stability.

For Northeast Asia, energy security has increasingly become a matter of "high politics" of national security and no longer just the "low politics" of domestic energy and economic policy. Energy security is now a perennial concern for the strategic and economic agendas of all the major Asia-Pacific powers, most importantly China, Japan, and South Korea. The *perception* of energy insecurity remains the foundation of U.S. energy policies even as the unconventional oil and gas revolution rapidly reduces U.S. oil and gas import needs. While energy security has been a critical issue since the oil shocks of the 1970s, the stunning rise in oil prices from 2003 to 2008 and the return of high prices following the global recession have seriously aggravated these fears.[1]

This chapter argues that the major Northeast Asian powers have, up to the present, sought to strengthen their control over imported energy supplies and costs largely by resorting to increasingly muscular state intervention in markets and active energy diplomacy. This is rooted domestically in the state-dominated approach to energy industries in each country as it interacts with the specter of precarious future access to energy supplies and uncertain energy transport routes. Ironically, each of the Northeast Asian states is working to reform domestic energy markets, introduce more competition, lower energy costs, reduce subsidies, and improve efficiency. But this has had only a limited impact on how they approach their external energy dependence.

Regional strategic rivalries have further amplified a competitive atmosphere over access to imported energy as the states of Northeast Asia contend over maritime territorial disputes, unresolved historical grievances, and control of regional sea lanes. China's rise is central to this as it gradually reshapes the regional strategic order and intensifies the security dilemma of all the powers in the region. These factors have together driven a regional propensity toward state-dominated mercantilist national competition over control of energy supplies and transport routes, which has, in turn, become another source of regional tensions. An increasingly "zero-sum" vicious circle has resulted as energy security has become increasingly politicized. Northeast Asia has looked to Russia to potentially become a large new, nearby energy supplier to the region but, until recently, it has been largely disappointed. Moscow has been slow to shift its energy export strategy away from slow-growing Europe toward faster-growing Northeast Asia. Hence competition over control of energy, both among the consumers themselves, as well as between the consumers and exporters, has added fuel to the region's strategic rivalries.

Despite this competitive atmosphere, there have been many efforts over the past 20 years to improve regional energy cooperation. Major initiatives have been pursued through APEC (Asia-Pacific Economic Cooperation), the East Asia Summit (EAS) process, and the Association of Southeast Asian Nations (ASEAN)+3 or (APT). There is much bilateral energy cooperation over renewables, improved energy efficiency, and collaboration on developing energy technology to reduce greenhouse gas emissions. Much of the push on energy cooperation has come from Japan, which is deeply concerned about its energy vulnerabilities, particularly in the post-Fukushima era, and South Korea, which geographically is situated where regional cooperation could greatly enhance its energy diversification. But, so far, national and competitive approaches have predominated as each state has been largely unwilling to share decision making over its energy security interests with other regional powers. The important question going forward is whether regional efforts will be able to make greater headway in the future forging more consistent regional energy cooperation in response to their common energy security dilemmas.

The United States has an important interest in how Northeast Asia responds to its energy challenges and insecurities. The U.S. acts as the key regional balancer in an area that lacks a regional architecture and institutions to manage conflict. Asian stability is central to U.S. prosperity and security. Thus, whether energy security remains a source of regional tensions or can be shaped into a force for regional cooperation needs to become a conscious and carefully crafted dimension of Washington's regional strategy. The recent boom in U.S. oil and gas production opens up the opportunity for the United States to become a major energy exporter to Northeast Asia and become a source for strengthening the region's energy security and cooperation.

The goal of this chapter is to analyze the Northeast Asian states' recent responses to their energy security anxieties and examine whether, in the future, they are likely to choose a path of greater regional energy cooperation or continued competition over energy access. The discussion is divided into three sections. The first section discusses the roots of increased state intervention in energy markets, trade, and investment, focusing on the region's rising dependence on imported energy, global energy industry trends, major regional strategic shifts, and how these changes have impacted domestic and external energy strategies in Northeast Asia. The second section analyzes how each of the key energy players in Northeast Asia has responded to its anxieties over secure access to energy supplies, reflecting different state approaches, resource endowments, and perceptions. The final section discusses prospects for the future and whether energy can be reshaped into a force for regional cooperation.

Energy security and state intervention

There are a number of common threads that have shaped the pursuit of energy security in Northeast Asia and the balance between energy competition and cooperation. These reflect the convergence of sharply tightening markets and prices over the past decade, the traditionally strong role of the state in domestic and regional energy markets in Northeast Asia, global energy industry changes, and the strategic dynamics in the region.

The enormous increase in energy demand, import dependence in Asia broadly, and high prices for oil and liquefied natural gas (LNG) are at the root of the growing state concerns over energy security. In Asia this boom in demand and import dependence has been centered on China as well as Southeast and South Asia. Over the past two decades developing Asia, not members of the Organisation for Economic Co-operation and Development (non-OECD Asia), accounted for 70 percent of the entire rise in global oil demand. China alone accounted for nearly one-third.[2] Asia's booming oil demand was the key factor in the sharp oil price rise to nearly $150 per barrel in mid-2008 and deeply aggravated the sense of energy "scarcity" across the region. Dependence on imported oil rose to nearly 60 percent in China by 2013, while Japan and South Korea remained 100 percent dependent on imported oil, natural gas, and coal supplies. The huge rise in oil prices and rising LNG prices, along with the specter of future supply scarcity, catalyzed a renewed state focus on supply security in Beijing, Tokyo, and Seoul. Alternatively, for Russia, as the largest oil and gas exporter in the world, the huge price and revenue windfall reinforced the Kremlin's impulse to retake control of the oil industry and reduced the incentives to expand energy exports to Asia. Hence, Asia's demand boom, the 2008 price shock, and supply insecurity touched off a renewed focus on supply security among Northeast Asia's importers while limiting Moscow's interest in regional energy investment or cooperation.

Domestically, among the importers, the price shock and supply uncertainties reinforced traditional impulses toward interventionist domestic approaches to energy markets and energy security. China, Japan, and South Korea each have highly centralized energy industries with either outright state ownership or very tight coordination and collaboration between government and the energy industry. China's oil and gas industry is dominated by three major state-owned oil companies, in South Korea the industry is dominated by three state monopolies (KNOC, KOGAS, and KEPCO), and in Japan the international oil and gas sector is largely the creation of the Ministry of Economy, Trade and Industry (METI), originally under the umbrella of the Japan National Oil Company (JNOC) and more recently evolved into the Japan Oil, Gas and Metals National Corporation (JOGMEC), INPEX, and other quasi-government companies, or through the large trading houses such as Mitsui and Mitsubishi, which work closely with METI. The arguments for stronger state intervention to secure energy supplies in each country have, perversely, been reinforced in response to stronger state intervention by other major states. Those advocating reliance on open and flexible energy markets and stronger regional energy cooperation have faced very strong nationalist headwinds.

These two drivers have converged with two other long-term oil industry developments to reinforce a more interventionist approach to energy security in the region. First, the oil and gas industry globally has increasingly come to be dominated by state-owned national oil companies (NOCs), which has increased the political nature of decision making and accentuated the state-to-state, strategic dimensions of the search for energy security. This began with the rise of the Organization of Petroleum Exporting Countries (OPEC) in the early 1970s and the creation of large, state-owned NOCs in the large oil- and gas-producing and -exporting countries. This represented a historic shift in ownership and control of the world's oil resources driven by the producers' interest in gaining control over the exploitation of their oil resources in order to better serve their national economic and social development goals. Their NOCs were to become key engines of economic development. Presently, the ten largest oil and gas reserve holding companies in the world are producer NOCs. According to the U.S. Energy Information Administration (EIA), NOCs controlled 78 percent of the world's proved oil reserves and 58 percent of oil production in 2012.[3]

The role of the traditional international oil companies (IOCs), such as ExxonMobil, BP, Royal Dutch Shell, and Total, remains important in many of the world's largest and most technically complex oil and gas projects, but their dominance has been gradually eroded by the rise of these state producer leviathans.[4]

More recently, NOCs have been on the rise among the large consuming and importing countries, a trend led by Asia's large oil and gas importers.[5] As Asia's oil and natural gas demand and import dependence has accelerated, the major regional importers have responded by strengthening national control over overseas oil and gas supplies by building stronger, more globally competitive national oil companies. Importing governments in the region have been unwilling to leave energy security entirely to the markets, private international oil companies, or regional cooperation. Each capital, therefore, has subsidized and promoted its own NOCs to invest in oil and gas supplies abroad as an important instrument to pursue a range of national energy security goals. The extent and character of state influence over these NOCs varies considerably by country, and most of the NOCs retain a great deal of autonomy in their day-to-day investments and operations. Some are far more commercially capable than others. The state–NOC relationship is more a matter of collaboration and convergence of interests in the commercial competitiveness of the companies. The perceptions among the political leadership are that promoting their companies' successful investments fundamentally strengthens the country's energy security. This has become a competition among China, Japan, and South Korea to build "national champions" in the oil industry—nationally controlled oil companies that can compete globally to access and develop oil and gas resources but also respond to state purposes. In Asia, this is reinforcing the impulse among Asia's major powers toward an increasingly politicized, competitive, and nationalistic approach to energy security. In this zero-sum, nationalistic atmosphere, it has been extremely difficult to forge regional efforts to cooperate on energy security goals.

Second, the economic and strategic rise of China in tandem with China's enormous developing impact on global oil and energy markets is also influencing the trend toward an increasingly politicized regional energy security environment. For the United States, Japan, South Korea, and other countries in the Asia-Pacific region, the rise of China promises to profoundly reshape the region's geopolitical, economic, and strategic order. China's enormous and rapidly growing energy demand and rising dependence on imported energy, combined with its active, state-centered reach outward to secure control of oil and gas supplies through its NOC investments, financial support, and various trade and aid emoluments in key energy exporting regions, has the potential to reshape the global energy security order as much as it will the global and strategic economic order. China's emergence as a major force in global energy has reinforced the energy security angst of other Asian powers that fear that China's voracious and seemingly endless appetite and quest for oil and gas abroad could undermine their future access to energy supplies. Whether this is sensible or not, these powers are reacting with their own competitive efforts to secure future energy supplies. The U.S. has sought to redirect Chinese energy security policies toward cooperation and collaboration in multilateral energy security institutions such as the International Energy Agency (IEA), G-20, and elsewhere.[6]

Asia's energy insecurity, centralized energy industries, the state-dominated shape of the global petroleum industry, and China's geopolitical and energy rise help account for the predominance of a zero-sum atmosphere toward energy security in Northeast Asia. Energy competition and suspicions are spilling over into strategic competition and aggravating broader strategic relations among the region's major powers. Conversely, strategic suspicions spill back into energy competition and add a toxic element to any efforts to promote a more cooperative regional approach to energy security. Energy competition among the key Asian powers mirrors the existing major strategic rivalries in the region. This is being played out across a range of arenas of energy investment, trade, and maritime and pipeline transportation.

Different cases of state intervention

Among the big three Northeast Asian oil importers—China, Japan, and South Korea—responses to their common challenges have been similarly intervention-ist, but there are significant national differences as well. Japan was the early mover in adopting overseas energy access as a strategic goal in the wake of the oil shocks of the 1970s that severely damaged the Japanese economy. South Korea moved later, beginning in the late 1980s, as oil and gas demand skyrocketed during the hyper-growth phase of Korean industrial development. China moved decisively as its oil import dependence mushroomed after the late 1990s. Beijing's push overseas has been orders of magnitude larger and more comprehensive than those of Japan or Korea. In fact, Tokyo's and Seoul's fears that the expansion of China's NOCs and Beijing's energy diplomacy since 2000 could undermine their future access to overseas oil and gas supplies have played an important role in reinvig-orating their overseas efforts. All three have similarly sought to strengthen their NOCs' overseas investment success through active energy diplomacy, boosting state low-cost financing and investment funds, and offering infrastructure invest-ment and low-cost loans to resource producers. Each has also sponsored various, often competitive, oil and gas pipeline projects, seeking to channel oil and gas directly to their countries. Each has aggressively asserted sovereignty claims to disputed areas potentially containing large oil and gas deposits in the South and East China seas. The other regional energy players, Russia and the United States, have different approaches. The U.S. has sought to reinforce the effectiveness of transparent and integrated market approaches to energy security as an antidote to the statist approach of the Northeast Asian states. And Russia sees energy secu-rity in profoundly divergent terms as an oil and gas exporter. Resource national-ism has increasingly been the theme of the Kremlin.

China

As suggested earlier, China has been a major catalyst for much of the region's focus on state solutions for energy security. China's particular evolution has reflected its rapid and largely unanticipated transition from oil self-sufficiency until the early 1990s to the role of a major oil importer. China will become ever more heavily dependent on OPEC and the major Gulf exporters for its future oil needs despite Beijing's strong efforts to diversify supplies from Eurasia, Africa, and Latin America. The vast majority will have to transit long distances through vulnerable maritime choke points from Africa, by pipeline and rail from Russia, and by pipeline from Central Asia. Within 15 years, three-quarters of China's

total oil needs will likely have to transit the Malacca Strait and the sea lanes of
the Indian Ocean and Southeast Asia.

Beijing's energy security angst is rooted in the leadership's concerns that oil
supply disruptions or skyrocketing prices could undermine economic growth and
the job-creating machine that underpins social and political stability. Beijing's
strong intervention in pursuit of energy and oil security has reflected the highly
centralized nature of its energy industry rooted in state ownership of the three
national oil companies, the China National Petroleum Corporation (CNPC),
China Petroleum and Chemical Corporation (Sinopec), and China National
Offshore Oil Corporation (CNOOC). These three companies dominate both
the upstream and downstream industry in China. Of the three Northeast Asian
energy-importing states, given the legacy of its socialist history, China has the
strongest level of state intervention in the energy industry and energy remains
one of the most closely managed industries by Beijing's leadership and mandarins.
Energy planning, pricing, allocation, and investment are all strongly influenced
by the government. Hence, it has been quite natural for the government to work
closely with its three NOCs to pursue its energy security goals and promote future
national access to oil supplies and to reduce the potential impact of price shocks.
This has been shaped in the so-called "go-out" strategy and is embodied in
energy, commercial, and financial diplomacy by Beijing's leaders, along with the
commercial growth of China's NOCs making equity investments in overseas oil
and gas fields. China's NOCs have now acquired a range of large equity oil stakes,
long-term crude oil and LNG supply contracts, and oil and gas pipeline projects
in virtually every major energy-exporting region. Most recently, China has also
been putting its large foreign exchange reserves to use by providing investment
capital to its NOCs and cheap loans to cash-strapped oil producers in return for
long-term guaranteed oil supplies.[7]

Beijing's energy security strategy is ideologically strongly rooted in the historic
impulse toward self-sufficiency and national control. Beijing has focused heavily
on ownership and physical control of barrels along with future access. Mistrust of
global energy markets is deeply ingrained. There is also a prevailing view among
Beijing's leadership that global oil markets are controlled or powerfully influenced by the United States, which seeks to exploit China's energy weakness as
part of its broader strategy of containment. This sense of vulnerability to U.S.
pressure on its energy access is accentuated by U.S. strategic power in the Persian
Gulf, the U.S. Navy's control over critical energy transport sea lanes, and what is
thought to be U.S. power over the global oil industry and institutions. Concerns
over U.S. strategic power and ability to potentially deny China access to energy
supplies in a crisis sharply differentiate the roots of China's approach to energy
security from that of Japan or South Korea.

At the political leadership level, these factors help explain what has so far
been a strongly interventionist character to Beijing's energy security strategies.[8] It
has also promoted an image of "China Energy Inc." in Tokyo, Seoul, New Delhi,
and Washington. The reality, however, is much more complex. Beijing leads less
and its approach is far less strategic than is commonly portrayed. Most of China's

NOCs' investments abroad have strong commercial and competitive roots, and it is often very unclear whether the state or the NOCs are in charge, or who is leading whom. It is probably better viewed as collaboration based on the convergence of the competitive/corporate interests of China's NOCs in global expansion that converges with a strategic view among Beijing's leadership, rightly or wrongly, that state financial and diplomatic support for their NOCs investments abroad serves China's energy security interests. In many ways this is as much industrial policy as energy security policy. But other countries in the region, such as Japan, South Korea, and India, feel they are competing with a coordinated and very formidable Chinese energy investment package of competitive oil industry strengths of China's three NOCs, combined with extensive state economic, financial, and diplomatic support.

China has pursued energy security on a wider scale and in more areas around the globe than have any of the other Northeast Asian states. Beijing has strongly supported large investments and supply contracts by CNPC, Sinopec, and CNOOC in virtually all of the major oil exporting regions. Most of the large investments and contracts have been supported by extensive Beijing diplomacy, a wide array of cheap financing, and a range of trade and aid deals, and, most recently, have been backstopped by huge government-to-government loans from Chinese state banks. All three companies have become major players in the Middle East oil patch. Iran has become China's third-largest source of oil imports, and CNPC, Sinopec, and CNOOC have options for major new oil and gas investments. The Saudis are now China's largest single source of imported oil, recently surpassing 1 million barrels per day (mmbd) (Mouawad, 2010). China's NOCs are also now the largest investors in Iraq's enormous post-war program for oil field development and rehabilitation. Beijing and its NOCs have also been expanding rapidly in Central Asia. China's NOCs are now large oil producers in Kazakhstan and have built a large oil pipeline to western China and a complex of large gas pipelines from Turkmenistan. Energy relations with Russia have been less productive, but this has recently begun to change. Russia had been shipping 250 thousand barrels per day (mbd) of oil to China by rail in recent years, but plans to build the Eastern Siberia–Pacific Ocean (ESPO) oil pipeline, to bring much larger oil supplies to China, was delayed for years as Russia dithered over development of the pipeline and as Japan sought to use its own financial diplomacy to alter the planned route of the pipeline to the Pacific coast. Finally in late 2009, in the wake of China's state banks providing $25 billion in cheap loans to Russia's cash-strapped Transneft and Rosneft, Russia moved ahead to complete the pipeline to bring 300 mbd to northern China and a further supply to the Pacific coast. Recent agreements could raise that to 1 mmbd over the longer term. In a major breakthrough Russia and China finally agreed in mid-2014 to a long-term contract for Russian pipeline natural gas exports that had been under negotiation for over a decade (Anishchuk, 2014).

Beijing has also used extensive state diplomacy, aid, and low-interest loans to support its NOCs in building a growing oil investment position in Africa and the Americas as well. China's largest operations have traditionally been in

Sudan, but this production has been badly disrupted as a result of the Sudan–South Sudan war, followed by civil war in South Sudan. China's NOCs are also increasingly active in highly productive West Africa, with major new investments in large offshore oil fields in Angola and Nigeria, and new investments in East Africa. CNPC has sizeable investments in Venezuela, as well as planned joint refinery projects in China that would be designed to process Venezuelan crude. Venezuela has been the recipient of two large multibillion-dollar loans from China, the latest one $20 billion in mid-April 2010, to support expanded heavy oil development (*Bloomberg News*, 2010). Brazil is also now on the path to becoming a significant oil producer and exporter, and China has quickly moved to secure several future long-term guaranteed oil supply contracts from Petrobras (*Bloomberg News*, 2010). Beijing's NOCs have also become major investors in oil shale development in Western Canada (*China Daily*, 2009; Jones, 2010; Guo & Loon, 2012). In Southeast Asia, CNPC and CNOOC have substantial equity investments in oil and LNG production in Indonesia and Australia. The importance that China's government attaches to these various components of its international oil and gas strategy is illustrated by the $30 billion loan facility that the China Development Bank agreed to provide CNPC in 2009 (Lau & Dyer, 2010; *Oxford Analytica Daily Brief*, 2010). China's NOCs had overseas investments of nearly $200 billion in 50 countries by 2014 (Andrews-Speed, 2014).

Japan

Other Northeast Asian energy importers, as well as the United States, have fueled the interventionist atmosphere in the region but each has reacted in ways that reflect domestic politics and state–industry relations. Japan, which is 100 percent dependent on imported oil, natural gas, and coal supplies, has pursued a somewhat more balanced approach to its energy security since the oil shocks of the 1970s. While Tokyo retains a strong interventionist role in the pursuit of energy security, it has also pursued a more market-oriented approach than China has. Domestically, the government responded to the oil and energy shocks of the 1970s with a mix of stronger intervention, as well as the development of markets and new supplies to fashion a new energy security strategy. There have been effectively two factions within the government—one advocating reliance mainly on strengthening global and regional energy markets and multilateral cooperation, which we might call the "internationalists," and a more "statist" group centered in METI that advocated strong state intervention and the importance of energy security as a strategic necessity.

For example, Japan was a founding member of the IEA, helped pioneer the development of multilateral energy cooperation through strategic oil stocks under the IEA, and has led in domestic energy efficiency and energy policy reforms to reduce oil consumption. Tokyo has also been a leader in largely unsuccessful efforts to promote greater regional energy cooperation and reliance on energy markets through APEC, the ASEAN+3, and the East Asia Summit (EAS).

Nevertheless, the interventionist impulse has remained strong. Tokyo's capacity to pursue Japan's access to energy supplies is extensive, but its use of more interventionist measures has ebbed and flowed depending on the period. In response to the early 1970s' oil shocks, Japan rapidly boosted its direct state support for JNOC in order to secure control of overseas oil supplies. JNOC funded a number of smaller oil exploration companies, including INPEX and JAPEX (Japan Petroleum Exploration), to expand Japan's oil acquisition capabilities.[9] However, the historical results of Japan's efforts were relatively disappointing in securing control of oil supplies abroad. Japan's overseas equity share of oil imports has remained stable, at around 15 percent of oil supplies. In 2000, Japan lost its largest oil concession abroad, the Arabian Oil Company (AOC) in the Neutral Zone of the Persian Gulf, which many saw as a symbol of an unproductive policy.

Under Prime Minister Junichiro Koizumi, from 2001 to 2006 there was a shift away from an interventionist and public ownership approach to a more mixed private–public oil industry approach. Domestic energy reforms sought to boost markets and competition, and lower energy costs, which were among the highest in the world. In the reorganization of Japan's upstream oil industry, Tokyo dissolved the troubled JNOC in 2002 and in 2004 created JOGMEC to better assist Japanese oil and gas companies in their exploration and production projects abroad. But with the end in 2006 of the Koizumi years of economic and energy market reforms, rapidly rising oil and LNG prices, and Beijing's emergence as an aggressive acquirer of and competitor for overseas oil supplies, Tokyo shifted emphasis back toward seeking nationally controlled oil supplies, so-called "Hinomaru oil."[10] In the New Basic Energy Policy Act of 2006, the government raised its target for the volume of oil imports by Japanese companies from the 2006 level of about 15 percent to a target of 40 percent of oil imports by 2030. The Japan Bank for International Cooperation (JBIC) also has been mandated to expand its loans and financial assistance to Japanese companies in advancing their international equity oil and gas projects. In 2010, in revisions to the Basic Plan, the government approved the Strategic Energy Plan of Japan, which set a target of raising overall energy self-sufficiency from 18 percent to 36 percent by 2030, which implied an enormous increase in Japanese investments overseas in new oil and LNG projects (METI, 2010).

The March 2011 earthquake and Fukushima nuclear disaster have deeply accentuated Japan's energy security anxieties. The shutdown of virtually the entire nuclear power generation fleet by mid-2012 and uncertainty about when and how much nuclear power will be restored has forced a huge increase in imported oil and LNG to meet minimum electricity needs. In the context of sharply rising global oil and LNG prices during 2012–13, this has created a sense of deepening national energy crisis. This is being addressed mainly through reducing and effectively rationing electricity consumption domestically and a much greater emphasis on efficiency and safety, and development of renewable energy supplies. However, the crisis has also reinforced the commitment to stronger "resource diplomacy" by Tokyo to secure oil and LNG supplies and greater longer-term investment efforts by Japan's oil- and LNG-importing companies.

Japan's recent overseas drive to secure oil and gas supplies has met with several notable setbacks and, in several cases, has brought it into direct competition with China, which has accentuated the overlap of energy competition and strategic rivalry.[11]

The most prominent example of Japan's frustrations was its long effort to secure development rights to Iran's large Azadegan oil field. INPEX negotiated with Iran for several years to secure a development contract but was caught between Tokyo's energy security goals of controlling an equity stake in such a large oil field and its strategic alliance with the United States. There was enormous U.S. pressure to get Japan to cancel a deal to develop the field, citing potential damage to the U.S.–Japan Alliance. In the end, U.S. pressure, combined with Iran's onerous investment terms, led INPEX to largely withdraw from the project. Much to Japan's chagrin, and as many in Tokyo predicted, China's CNPC eventually took over the deal, although it is still unclear whether CNPC will proceed.

In another frustrating case for Japan, Tokyo intervened late in China's negotiations with Russia on a large oil pipeline that was to be built to northern China, with an offer of a large financial package to develop Russia's East Siberian oil fields and build the oil pipeline to the Pacific coast at Nakhodka, where the oil could be shipped to Japan. Russia played China and Japan off against one another for several years as Moscow dithered over the various issues of the field and pipeline development. Ultimately, China secured the deal with a $25 billion oil-backed loan to Rosneft and Transneft in 2009. But Moscow eventually did extend the pipeline to the Pacific coast, making an additional volume available to Japan and South Korea.

A third case illustrates the fraught nature of the energy security competition between Japan and China involving a natural gas field development in the East China Sea. China has been developing a modest-sized natural gas field offshore China, the Chunxiao field, which lies close to the median line claimed by Japan as the boundary of its Exclusive Economic Zone (EEZ). Moreover, the field is not far from the disputed Senkaku/Diaoyu Islands. Japan has argued that the gas field may extend across the EEZ median line, in which case Japan claims a right to a part of the field's production. China has rejected this claim and argues that, based on the extension of China's continental shelf, the EEZ demarcation line is much further east and the gas field is nowhere near what China defines as the EEZ line. This escalated quickly to the point where Chinese gunboats were used to force Japanese seismic vessels out of the area. After several years of haggling, Japan and China in 2008 came to a general agreement in the Japan–China East China Sea agreement to negotiate some form of joint development in the area, but this has so far not been completed and negotiations seem to have collapsed; more recently, the situation has deteriorated as the territorial tensions have escalated and spilled on to the gas field negotiations. In late 2009, Japan's Coast Guard arrested a Chinese fisherman close to the Senkaku/Diaoyu Islands, charging him with violating Japan's EEZ. This set off a furious diplomatic reaction in Beijing and demonstrations in front of the Japanese Embassy. China's official protests were backed up by an unofficial cutoff of exports of rare earth minerals to Japan.

China also canceled scheduled meetings to discuss the East China Sea gas field disagreement (Ryall, 2010; *The Telegraph*, 2010). Efforts continued to try to find a cooperative energy relationship with China. In meetings between Japanese Prime Minister Noda and Chinese Premier Wen Jiabao in December 2011, Japan and China agreed to build a framework to facilitate discussions on the East China Sea gas field (Sekiguchi, 2011). However, the intensifying 2013–14 confrontation between Japan and China over the Senkaku/Diaoyu islands has completely shut down efforts to find a more cooperative relationship over energy in the East China Sea.[12]

In other areas, Japan's stepped-up support for its oil companies, now largely under the rubric of JOGMEC and INPEX, has had some success. Despite the problems with the ESPO pipeline, JOGMEC has acquired some modest exploration rights in East Siberia, and Japan retains a significant interest through Mitsui and Mitsubishi in the huge Sakhalin-2 LNG project, put together by Shell but now majority-controlled by Gazprom. Two Japanese companies also are involved in a proposed new LNG project slated for Vladivostok recently announced at the Vladivostok APEC meeting in November 2012. Also, INPEX controls roughly 100 mbd of oil production in Indonesia, and a separate consortium, JODECO, has a 200 mbd equity stake in the United Arab Emirates (UAE) oil production. JOGMEC is also spearheading Japanese upstream efforts in Venezuela and Brazil. Moreover, Japan has been much more successful in securing control over LNG supplies on which it is 100 percent import-dependent. Japanese companies virtually invented the LNG business during the 1960s and 1970s, and Mitsubishi, Mitsui, and Marubeni are major stakeholders in a range of LNG projects in the Asia-Pacific region, as well as in the Persian Gulf in Qatar and UAE. Japanese companies are deeply involved in investing in proposed large U.S. LNG export projects based on booming unconventional shale gas production.

South Korea

South Korea's energy dilemmas closely resemble those of its neighbor Japan and, consequently, many of Seoul's responses to its energy security anxieties have been similar as well. Korea is also 100 percent import-dependent for its oil and natural gas supplies, as well as for much of its coal needs, and has pursued two parallel energy security paths similar to Japan. On the cooperation side, Korea became a member of the IEA in the early 1990s and holds a 90-day supply of strategic oil stocks as part of its IEA obligations to be able to release stocks during potential oil supply disruptions. And Seoul has been a strong promoter of regional energy cooperation, particularly efforts—ultimately unsuccessful—to develop a regional natural gas pipeline project that would bring Russian gas from East Siberia through North Korea to the south.

Along the mercantilist track, Seoul has promoted overseas oil and gas supply development by its state oil company, the Korea National Oil Corporation (KNOC), since 1977. Currently, various projects are underway in more than 40 countries. But although the Korean government has invested in the order of

$5 billion in supporting efforts to secure control over global oil supplies, as of 2009 only about 4 percent of Korea's oil consumption was met with equity oil controlled by Korean companies. Oil and gas imports from Korean-controlled companies accounted for just 9 percent of combined oil and gas imports (Nam, 2010).

Korea's most successful recent opportunities have been in Yemen, Argentina, Peru, the North Sea, and the United States, along with new fields under development in Iraq, Colombia, Kazakhstan, Venezuela, Libya, and Vietnam. Despite these limited results, in its most recent *Overseas Energy Development Plan* (2010) the Korean government has raised its 2019 target for the share of oil and gas consumption to be met by Korean overseas equity production to 30 percent (IHS Global Insight, 2010); for historic background see Ryu (2009) and commentaries by Calder and Herberg (2009). Seoul recently has set up a special government funding account for overseas resource development project, the Energy Project Special Account (Jung-Won, 2008). Moreover, Seoul projected raising energy-related guarantees and loans via the Korea Trade Insurance Corp. and the Export-Import Bank to $7.3 billion in 2013 from 2010's $4.5 billion. Korean companies have not faced direct investment competition with Chinese companies as often as Japan, but this is changing. In mid-2009, KNOC lost out in bidding against China's Sinopec to acquire a large, London-based oil company, Addax, which had sizeable production in Nigeria, as well as in the Kurdish region of Iraq (Winning, 2009). KNOC is handicapped in competing with Chinese NOCs because available state financing is much more limited, and KNOC is expected to earn market returns for its investments, unlike, in some cases, Chinese NOCs, which are focused only on adding production. Nevertheless, KNOC has successfully made several large acquisitions, including UK-based Dana Petroleum PLC for $2.9 billion and Hunt Oil's Canadian assets for roughly $500 million.

United States

The United States, while not a strictly Northeast Asian state, has contributed substantially to the zero-sum energy security atmosphere in the region with the constant drumbeat of nationalistic rhetoric coming from Congress, the Pentagon, and conservative think tanks about China's energy strategy. The U.S. does not have national oil companies and, instead, has based its energy security strategy mainly on promoting open global energy markets and private investment. The U.S. has encouraged investment in new global oil supplies, promoting new oil production from as wide a group of countries and companies as possible, and development of strategic petroleum reserves through the IEA and other multilateral energy cooperation efforts.[13] Also, for four decades the United States has been deeply engaged at a strategic level in key producing areas, most importantly the Persian Gulf, in order to try to enhance political stability and the uninterrupted flow of oil and gas to global markets.

From this perspective, many in the U.S. political establishment, particularly on Capitol Hill, have viewed China's aggressive state-centered strategy of securing national control over oil and gas resources as a kind of predatory, hoarding response that threatens to limit access to these supplies for other major energy importers.[14] While this notion doesn't make any sense in a global market such as oil, the perception remains strong in Washington as well as in capitals across the region. Many in the United States also believe that U.S.-based oil companies are at a severe competitive disadvantage facing the highly subsidized competitive bidding from China's NOCs for new oil and gas exploration and development opportunities. These perceptions, and tensions in U.S.–China energy relations, reached their peak in 2005 when China's CNOOC attempted to acquire the U.S. oil company Unocal, which led to a firestorm of criticism and opposition to the deal in Congress and several months of serious bilateral tensions. CNOOC ultimately withdrew its offer, recognizing that the acquisition could not succeed in the face of widespread political opposition in Washington. It was not until 2010 that another attempt to acquire U.S. oil company assets occurred, when CNOOC acquired a minority share in Chesapeake Energy Corporation's shale gas leases in Texas for $1.08 billion and, in early 2011, expanded its stake in two other Chesapeake shale gas properties (Winning & Yang, 2011). Several other new minority investments by Chinese NOCs have followed similarly in the U.S. shale gas sector. More recently, CNOOC's acquisition of Canada's Nexen included about 10 percent of Nexen's assets located in the United States, mainly offshore Gulf of Mexico fields, including one sizeable field in which Nexen is the operator. Perhaps reflecting a more balanced attitude toward Chinese NOC oil investments, there was a much more muted reaction among those in the United States suspicious of China's NOCs and their investment intentions. The investment was eventually approved by the Committee on Foreign Investment in the United States (CFIUS), the inter-departmental committee set up to review the national security consequences of foreign investments in the United States, although CNOOC was still required to relinquish operating rights in many of the Nexen blocks it acquired in the U.S. Gulf of Mexico (Rampton, 2012).

The unconventional oil and gas revolution in the United States that has gathered pace in the last half of the 2000s has profoundly altered the 40-year rise in dependence on imported oil and gas and is beginning the change the underlying context of U.S. energy strategy. Tight crude oil production has risen from 5 mmbd in 2007 to an expected 9.3 mmbd in 2015 (U.S. Energy Information Administration, 2013). Shale gas production has risen fifteen-fold since 2006. Dependence on imported crude oil has dropped from 12 mmbd in 2005 to just 6 mmbd in 2014, the lowest level in two decades. Forecasts suggest that, by 2020, net U.S. oil imports are likely to be near zero when net exports of oil products are taken into account. At the same time, the U.S. is on the way to becoming a major exporter of natural gas (in the form of LNG) to Asia by 2020. Hence, the United States will increasingly become a source of energy supplies to Asia to help strengthen the region's energy security. Declining oil import needs will increasingly free up global supplies for Asian buyers and ease pressure on global oil markets. There is even a growing debate in the U.S. about the possibility of allowing crude oil exports that have been banned since the 1970s' oil shocks. The debate in the United States over energy security policy is thus beginning to evolve from one dominated by import

dependence and energy scarcity to a narrative of energy abundance. The implications of this for U.S. energy strategy are only beginning to take shape, and the old
scarcity foundation of policy remains powerful and widespread.[15] But for Asia the
production boom and exports of LNG promise to ease energy security constraints
and potentially make energy cooperation in Northeast Asia more possible. It will
also loosen the hold that large exporters such as OPEC and Russia have over oil
and LNG markets and help diversify supplies to the region.

Russia

Russia and East Siberia have loomed to the north as a key and potentially growing
regional oil and gas supplier. Since the opening up of the former Soviet Union,
China, Japan, and South Korea have looked to Russia to become a critical nearby
source of oil and gas to help the region diversify and shift from its dependence on
seaborne imports, mainly from the Middle East and Africa.

However, the promise of regional energy cooperation and large new supplies from the region to Asia has not materialized so far on the scale many had
expected. There are several underlying explanations. Similarly to other large oil
and gas exporters, Russia's primary reference point has been resource nationalism,
that is, strong national control over oil and gas resource development and limited
foreign involvement or influence in its energy affairs. Despite Moscow's frequent
rhetoric about regional energy cooperation, the Kremlin is suspicious of potential
regional energy schemes that could limit its ability to extract the maximum benefits from energy exports to Northeast Asia on a project-by-project basis. Bilateral dealings that maximize Russia's bargaining power are preferred. So resource
nationalism consistently trumps regional energy cooperation. These instincts to
drive an extremely hard bargain over its resources have made it difficult to craft
regional oil and gas export proposals that make real economic sense for Asia.

The progressive strengthening of intervention in the energy industry also
reflects a powerful shift in Russian domestic politics with the rise of Vladimir
Putin. During the 1990s, under the Yeltsin administration, the promise of private
investment and new supplies for Asia was initially very strong. The Russian oil
sector was increasingly controlled by new private sector Russian companies such
as Yukos and LukOil, and some of the oil majors such as BP, Exxon, and Shell.
Three major oil and gas supply sources were planned to serve Northeast Asian
markets. One was a large potential oil field development near Angarsk in East
Siberia that was initially planned to pipeline oil to China and the Pacific coast.
Second, there were plans for a huge natural gas pipeline from the huge Kovykta
field in the same area of East Siberia to China and on to South Korea and, possibly, even on to Japan. Third were two large projects at Sakhalin Island led
by Exxon (mainly oil at Sakhalin-1) and Shell (mainly natural gas as LNG at
Sakhalin-2). However, following the election of Vladimir Putin at the end of the
1990s, resource nationalism returned with a vengeance, and the trajectory for
Russia's oil and gas industry was shifted sharply toward recentralizing control over
the industry in the Kremlin, reshaping ownership and control toward Russian

state companies, and reducing the role of private and foreign oil companies. The Kremlin under Putin also deeply fears becoming a resource appendage of China and its huge energy appetite, which has also limited its willingness to negotiate major new oil and gas export deals with China. The environmental impact of potential large pipeline developments across environmentally sensitive regions of East Siberia has also added a layer of resistance to new oil and gas pipelines to Northeast Asia. In East Siberia there is resistance to exporting natural gas due to a desire to use it locally to drive economic development in the poor and isolated region. With oil development, there is uncertainty driven by unresolved local pressures to get a share of tax revenues from oil development. Although Russian energy is beginning to flow to Northeast Asia, progress has been extremely slow and tortuous. And the bilateral nature of Russia's approach tends to aggravate the atmosphere of competition among Northeast Asia's energy importers as they vie with one another for scarce opportunities to do business with the Russians.

Until recently only the two large Sakhalin projects, negotiated during the mid-1990s under the Yeltsin administration, have moved forward, with roughly 250 mbd exported to Asia from Exxon's Sakhalin-1 project in the mid-2000s and Shell's huge 9.8 million-ton-per-year LNG project finally coming online in 2010 to supply Asian LNG markets. The East Siberian oil project did finally materialize as the ESPO pipeline running to northern China with 300 mbd. However, the logjam on this was only broken by China's offer of $25 billion in loans to Rosneft and Transneft to complete the project. In late 2012 the extension of the ESPO pipeline to the Pacific coast was completed, which allowed the added 300 mbd being moved by rail to the coast to be diverted to the pipeline and exported largely to Japan and South Korea. Completion of the expansion of the pipeline, slated to be in the range of 1 mmbd to the Pacific coast, is planned for 2016, but this has been slowed by limited volumes of East Siberian crude.

The proposed East Siberia gas pipeline project remained bogged down for a decade by indecision in the Kremlin and at Gazprom about making the large natural gas infrastructure investments in East Siberia that would be required to pipe gas to China and South Korea, gas pricing disagreements with China's CNPC, and lingering strategic reluctance in Moscow to the resource appendage problem with China. However, in the wake of the 2014 Ukraine crisis and Western sanctions on Russia, Putin has turned his attention east and finally broke the logjam on the gas pipeline deal.[16] In May 2014, China and Russia finally signed the long-term gas deal for a 38 billion cubic meters (bcm) per year volume to be completed by 2020. Given the growing pressure on Russia from the West, Putin has become heavily dependent in the future on oil and gas markets in the east, especially China. The revival of Rosneft under Igor Sechin has also spurred progress on new LNG projects in the east to supply Asia. There are proposals for three LNG projects, one at Vladivostok, another Rosneft/ExxonMobil project based on Sakhalin-1 gas, and an added third LNG train at the Sakhalin-2 project. Rosneft has also signed new deals with CNPC to increase oil exports to 1 mmbd by the end of the decade. So, after a decade of disappointment, Russia seems likely to finally emerge as a much more significant supplier to Northeast Asia.

Future regional energy dynamics: competition or cooperation?

Whether Northeast Asia's energy security future will be characterized by national competition and rivalry or market-based multilateral cooperation remains uncertain.

The confrontational path is easy enough to outline based on recent history. A continuation of the recent drift toward mistrust and national competition over markets, described earlier, would have potentially ominous implications both for regional stability and for global energy markets. The more interventionist energy security strategies of the Northeast Asian powers, and Russia's rigid statist approach to exporting energy, combined with the U.S. perception that the statist energy security strategies across the region threaten to undermine free market investment and U.S. access to oil and gas resources, has deeply politicized the region's energy security dynamics.

Moreover, a number of tensions will probably continue to bedevil regional energy relationships, and these tensions will need to be carefully managed. U.S.–China energy relations face a legacy of distrust and suspicion, such as China's energy relations in problem states such as Iran and Sudan. The current U.S.–China Strategic and Economic Dialogue includes an energy working group, but the Dialogue has only recently begun to focus on energy security in a strategic context.[17] Energy relations between China and Japan continue to be buffeted by chronic strategic and maritime territorial disagreements between the two key Northeast Asian powers, most recently a serious confrontation over the Diaoyu/Senkaku Islands. The East China Sea gas field controversy has festered without any recent progress.[18] Japanese–Russian territorial disputes over the Northern Islands also have historically undermined energy relations between these two countries. However, the recent Russian shift toward Northeast Asian energy markets in the wake of the Ukraine crisis and Western sanctions has opened new possibilities for LNG projects in the east that would bolster Northeast Asian LNG supplies. Nevertheless, regional energy cooperation and building energy transport infrastructure has made slow and halting progress.

The alternative of a more collaborative and market-oriented regional energy security environment would build on the past 40 years since the oil shocks of the 1970s, during which world energy markets have become increasingly globalized, integrated, efficient, and flexible, and during which multilateral energy cooperation has grown. This has been reflected in the development of efficient futures markets, spot markets and prices, more transparent data on global supply and demand, highly flexible oil and gas supply contracts, and a widening development of new supply sources from new countries. Periods of oil supply shortages now lead to higher prices, but at the same time markets rapidly sort out supply movements so that there are no real physical shortages, as happened in the 1970s. Oil is always available in the market at a price. It cannot be hoarded effectively on a sufficient scale by national authorities. The market is now too big, integrated, dynamic, and transparent. With the development of an integrated, flexible, and transparent global oil market, OPEC's job has become more difficult, and it can only influence prices indirectly and often ineffectively. Globalized and integrated oil markets have reduced the power of OPEC and increased the influence of market supply, demand, and investment. The new boom in U.S. tight oil and shale gas production has also brought huge new supplies and eased the potential impact of supply disruptions in the Middle East and elsewhere.

The industrial countries, including Japan and South Korea, strengthened multilateral energy cooperation by creating the IEA to collectively manage supply shocks by forging a system of strategic oil stocks and emergency management. Energy security has regularly been on the agenda of the G-8, and now the G-20, to work toward cooperative management of global energy supplies. Japan was a pioneering member of the IEA in the 1970s, pushed by those in the government who saw markets and multilateral cooperation as key means of ensuring Japan's energy security. South Korea joined the IEA after it entered the OECD in the early 1990s. Alternatively, the reticence of the new, large oil consumer/importers China and India to engage very seriously with the IEA is clear evidence that they continue to see energy security in more national rather than multilateral terms.

The negative, interventionist future path described above for Northeast Asia could be avoided by finding ways to turn energy into a source of regional cooperation and integrated markets rather than national competition and politicized markets.[19] The major oil consumers and importers in Northeast Asia have fundamental common energy security interests in stable global energy markets, secure and free access to energy supplies, reasonable prices, and reliable and flexible energy transport routes and infrastructure. The region could work toward building trust, managing the impulse toward competition, and working together to promote new supplies and build new regional energy infrastructure.

This would require strong leadership and reordering of strategic priorities in Tokyo, Seoul, Washington, and Beijing to promote regional energy cooperation, along with an effort to manage likely areas of tension over energy. The fact is that the most recent national energy plans of the big three Northeast Asian states—China, Japan, and South Korea—all contain among their key goals the strengthening of regional and global energy cooperation. There are in each case significant factions of the leadership that see multilateral cooperation as a key part of their energy security calculus. In this light, the region should approach energy cooperation at many levels—regional, multilateral, and bilateral.

The United States can play an important role in a regional energy dialogue on common energy concerns; the U.S. is both the strategic superpower in Asia and an energy superpower globally. Moreover, as a result of the boom in U.S. shale natural gas production and tight oil production, the United States, along with Canada, is on the cusp of becoming a significant LNG and oil exporter to Northeast Asia. This shift brings important energy security benefits for Asia. More U.S. supplies of LNG are likely to help cool LNG prices and bring a new hub-based LNG pricing influence into the rigid oil-linked pricing system that has dominated in Asia. The sharp decline in U.S. oil import needs likewise will take some pressure off tight global oil markets and free up supplies to meet rising Asian oil import needs. This makes the U.S. an important player in the region's energy security dynamics. At the same time, China is becoming a global energy power; Japan is the third-largest oil importer in the world and the global superpower of energy efficiency; and South Korea is a growing consumer located at the nexus of potential large regional flows of oil and natural gas. Russia should be part of these efforts as the key potential new supplier to the region if its impulse for tight national control and bilateral negotiations can be moderated.

Confidence-building and improving mutual trust should be the goal; it should focus on common interests in global energy market stability and sustaining market competition for access to supplies rather than state-led exclusive energy deals. In a globalized energy market, no country can achieve energy security unilaterally. Over time this dialogue could potentially strengthen regional oil and natural gas production and pipeline developments. Multilaterally, the region should have a goal of bringing China and India more directly into the global institutions such as the IEA. Today the world's global emergency oil management system doesn't include China or India, two of the world's six largest oil-consuming countries. Involvement in the IEA would provide expertise on energy efficiency, demand management, technology, and policymaking that could accelerate the "learning curve" of energy policymakers in China. It would also help forge a stronger sense among the Northeast Asian states of their common energy security challenge. Technically China or India cannot join the IEA without being a member of the OECD, so this would require some creative institutional engineering. Recently, China has discussed with the IEA the possibility of an "associated" membership, along with India, Russia, and several other countries. But Beijing also tends to see the IEA as a U.S.-dominated organization and would rather consider the G-20 or other regional groupings such as the Shanghai Cooperation Organization (SCO) to pursue regional energy security cooperation.

Another potential source of strengthened energy cooperation could evolve from growing bilateral, regional, and global cooperation on the development of renewable energy, new technologies, and collaboration on promoting improved energy efficiency. For example, China and Japan have a bilateral energy dialogue that promotes cooperation on energy efficiency and technology. Japan is the global leader in energy efficiency, and partnerships with China are seeking to help China improve its energy efficiency, a key Beijing goal as it struggles with China's severe air pollution problems. Collaboration on technologies to reduce greenhouse gases could be an important bridge to broader energy cooperation. China, the United States, and others have a vital interest in the development of carbon capture and storage technologies, as all are major consumers of coal for power generation. There are a number of cooperative efforts here among the major energy consumers.

Another recent driver for greater regional energy cooperation arises, ironically, from the post-Fukushima impact on regional LNG markets and Japan's energy security. As Japan's LNG imports have mushroomed to replace lost nuclear generation capacity, the rise in LNG prices and supply anxieties has promoted a push toward greater cooperation between Japan and South Korea in acquiring supplies and contracting. Japan has also inaugurated the first LNG producer–consumer dialogue to promote greater cooperation both among consumers and also between consumers and the large LNG suppliers (Platts, 2012).

Regionally, there has been a lengthy and strong interest in Asia in developing regional energy security arrangements that would reflect the region's common interests as large oil and gas importers, and each of the major regional groupings has its own initiatives. Japan has been at the forefront of forging these efforts, along with South Korea. For the most part these efforts have been fragmented, diluted, and spread over many initiatives, none of which has raised energy security to a sufficiently high level to address the deep politicization of energy security competition in the region. APEC has had an energy security initiative, established in the mid-1990s and administered largely through its Energy Working Group (EWG).[20] The EWG has been instrumental in promoting common dialogue, particularly on natural gas issues, but APEC as an organization is too large, diverse, and preoccupied with trade issues to provide an effective forum for crafting a common energy security strategy at a state leadership level. Its efforts have largely focused on market transparency, emergency preparedness, and long-term green energy initiatives. But ASEAN+3 (APT) developed its Energy Partnership beginning in 2002–3, which has sought to focus on energy security, emergency oil stocks, oil markets, natural gas, and renewable energy (see, for example, Anon., 2008). The East Asia Summit (EAS), which includes India, Australia, and New Zealand, also developed its own East Asia Summit Energy Security Declaration, announced in 2007, which promised to focus on energy efficiency and environment, reducing fossil fuel use, encouraging open and competitive regional and global energy markets, reducing greenhouse gas emissions, and promoting new private investment in energy supplies and infrastructure. Hence, there clearly is a strong impulse in the region to strengthen regional energy cooperation.

However, in reality each of the organizations is generally occupied with seeking solutions to larger strategic challenges and tensions, as in the case of APT and EAS or, as in the case of APEC, much more driven by trade issues. The organizations have been long on process and short on actual projects to work together on key energy security problems. Perhaps the best that can be said is that they remain potentially important confidence-building mechanisms and useful for regional exhortations of common concerns and intent. It may be that Northeast Asia's energy security challenges, and the toxic zero-sum political atmosphere surrounding oil and energy need to be addressed more directly and through a separate dedicated process. The most effective way to address this is by forging a new Northeast Asian regional energy forum or dialogue that would bring together the six key regional powers in a confidence-building process of focusing directly on collaborative regional solutions to the region's energy security concerns. It should include both the large importing countries China, Japan, South Korea, and the United States, but also Russia as a key supplier. This principle was behind a meeting that Beijing convened in 2006 called the Five-Country Energy Ministers Meeting, which brought together the five large oil importers of Asia (China, India, the United States, Japan, and South Korea) to discuss common energy security concerns. In this case India was included but Russia was not. Another meeting was held in 2008, but the effort has atrophied into another exercise of discussion without high-level involvement due to lack of commitment among the leadership.

Hence, a new dialogue is needed to air important differences and seek common ground. It is vital that this be supported by the leadership of each country as an important dimension of energy security efforts. Previous efforts described above have been fragmented and diffuse, and have lacked senior leadership engagement. This initiative should occur on an annual basis, rotating among the capitals and chaired by senior bureaucrats engaged in energy security policymaking. It should also have a side track of an oil company working group that brings both private IOCs and NOCs into the same process. It is unlikely that this will result quickly in major new investments or transport infrastructure, but a lengthy period of trust-building among the regional powers is necessary before more concrete results can be expected. Common energy security concerns need to be discussed in a setting that is conducive to building confidence to tackle common problems, such as the lack of access to major producer country reserves. This forum could also be the place to discuss possibly developing Northeast Asian regional emergency oil stocks. It is far more economical to build and maintain regional stocks than each country in the region holding its own. This could address the possibility of collaborative release of stocks during oil supply disruptions. Further, this could help instill the "habit" of thinking regionally about energy security solutions.

Conclusions

Northeast Asia's rapid economic growth is driving an enormous surge in energy and industrial commodity consumption that is fundamentally altering global market and prices for these products. In the context of Asia's competitive strategic context and the lack of regional institutions to mediate regional tensions, an increasingly competitive and nationalistic atmosphere has developed over national strategic control of energy and some other raw materials. These tensions are increasingly spilling into the strategic dynamics in the region, adding a toxic element to regional geopolitics and aggravating key bilateral rivalries. Although all the major states, including the United States, are major energy importers and, therefore, have common interests in working together to help stabilize global energy and commodity markets, those forces in each country advocating cooperative regional energy efforts have been less able to carry the day.

It will take strong and courageous leadership by advocates of greater energy cooperation in the region's key capitals to turn these competitive and destructive dynamics into more cooperative and productive dynamics. Hence, the outlook is for a mixed approach, with modest cooperative efforts through the IEA, G-20, the various Asian regional organizations, and through bilateral energy dialogues co-existing uncomfortably with a strong nationalist and interventionist overlay. Currently there does not seem to be a critical mass to forge ahead with creating a regional energy security forum, which would be the single most effective way to begin to significantly strengthen regional energy cooperation. The Obama administration, while pursuing a strong long-term "green" energy agenda, does not seem to have an interest in engaging Northeast Asia in a near-term strategic energy security dialogue and remains deeply preoccupied with ending two wars, deepening fiscal constraints, and the general political dysfunction in Washington. Beijing seems comfortable paying lip-service to multilateral energy cooperation but largely continuing along its NOC-based, bilateral energy security strategy. Tokyo and Seoul seem much more interested in promoting regional energy security cooperation, but Tokyo has much deeper problems coping with the energy impact of the tragic earthquake, tsunami, and extraordinary nuclear disaster, and Seoul cannot lead this effort on its own.

Without stronger and more visionary leadership, the region faces a future of more unstable energy and commodity markets, higher and more volatile prices for key determinants of their economic prosperity, greater risks of damaging supply disruptions, and deepening intraregional political tensions. The region is likely to face a further period of rising oil and gas prices as global oil markets tighten with rising Asian oil demand and the gradual global economic recovery. This is likely to further aggravate energy security concerns and risks, intensifying the zero-sum atmosphere that already exists. The problem of choosing between cooperation or national competition will return even more virulently as energy prices and national anxieties rise.

Notes

1 Average annual dated Brent prices over the three years 2011–13 were $112.40, seven dollars higher than the previous annual peak price in 2008 (BP, 2014).
2 See International Energy Agency (2013).
3 See www.eia.gov/energy_in_brief/article/world_oil_market.cfm.
4 For the best recent work on this, see Marcel and Mitchell (2006), Victor *et al.* (2012), and also James A. Baker III Institute for Public Policy (2007).
5 On Asia's NOCs, see Herberg (2007) and Mitchell and Lahn (2007).
6 For a full discussion of these issues, see Herberg (2011); from a Chinese perspective, see Daojiong (2010).
7 See Downs (2011).
8 There is a deep literature on the roots of China's energy security policies. For some of the best work, see Zweig and Jianhai (2005), Daojiong (2006), Downs (2006), Houser (2008), and Kong (2010). For an overview of China's energy security policies from a Chinese institutional perspective, see Shixian (2009), along with commentaries by Yishan and Wu (2009).
9 For further historical background, see Herberg (2004).
10 For an excellent discussion of Japan's more recent energy security policies, see Takeishi (2009).
11 On the state of Sino-Japanese energy security competition, see Calder (2006), Jiang (2006), Conference on Japan's Contemporary Challenges (2007), Itoh (2008a), and Liao (2008a, 2008b).
12 For a thorough analysis of recent developments, see Drifte (2014).
13 For an excellent discussion of U.S. energy security policy, see Pumphrey (2009).

14   There is an extensive literature on U.S.–China energy relations, including Lieberthal
      and Herberg (2006), Daojiong and Weixing (2007), Zweig (2010), and Andrews-
      Speed *et al.* (2002), p. 115.
15   Two recent studies suggest the range of possible U.S. responses to its growing raw
      energy power of oil and gas production. See Jones *et al.* (2014) and Ladislaw *et al.*
      (2014). For another vision from more of an energy-industry viewpoint, see Mitchell
      (2013) and Emerson (2014).
16   There is a large literature on these developments; see Poussenkova (2007, 2008), Itoh
      (2008b, 2010), Perovic and Orttung (2009), and Downs (2010).
17   For a good summary, see Pumphrey (2007); see also Christoffersen (2010).
18   For a good summary, see Yoshimatsu (2011).
19   See Herberg (2008).
20   See APEC (n.d.).

References

Andrews-Speed, P. 2014. *When Will China's National Oil Companies Rationalize their
    Overseas Investment Portfolios?* Online: www.andrews-speed.com (accessed February
    20, 2014).
Andrews-Speed, P., Liao, X., and Dannreuther, R. 2002. *The Strategic Implications of
    China's Energy Needs.* London: International Institute for Strategic Studies.
Anishchuk, A. 2014. As Putin Looks East, China and Russia Sign $400 billion Gas Deal.
    Reuters, May 21.
Anon. n.d. Online: www.spp.nus.edu.sg/ips/docs/LeeYY_2008-AEC-011.pdf (accessed
    June 8, 2010).
APEC. n.d. APEC *Energy Security Initiative.* Online: www.ewg.apec.org/energy_security.
    html (accessed May 12, 2014).
Bloomberg News. 2010. China Lends Venezuela $20 Billion, Secures Oil Supply. *Bloomberg
    News,* April 19.
BP. 2014. *BP Statistical Review of World Energy.* London: BP.
Calder, K. 2006. Simmering Sino-Japanese Rivalries. *Foreign Affairs,* April–May.
Calder, K. and Herberg, M. 2009. Commentaries. In F. Fesharaki, N. Kim, and Y.H. Kim
    (eds). *Energy Security in the North Pacific.* Ulsan-si: Korea Energy Economics Institute,
    pp. 320–33.
China Daily. 2009. Brazil Sells Oil to China, Expects $10 Billion Loan. *China Daily,*
    February 20.
Christoffersen, G. 2010. U.S.–China Energy Relations and Energy Institution Building in
    the Asia-Pacific. *Journal of Contemporary China* 19(67).
Conference on Japan's Contemporary Challenges. Yale University, March 9–10, 2007.
    Sino-Japanese Energy Relations: Prospects for Deepening Strategic Competition. New
    Haven, CT: Yale University.
Daojiong, Z. 2006. China's Energy Security: Domestic and International Issues. *Survival,*
    Spring: 179–90.
Daojiong, Z. 2010. *Oiling the Wheels of Foreign Policy? Energy Security and China's
    International Relations.* Singapore: S. Rajaratnam School of International Relations.
Daojiong, Z. and Weixing, H. 2007. Promoting Energy Partnership in Beijing and
    Washington. *Washington Quarterly* 30(4), Autumn: 105–15.
Downs, E. 2006. *China, Brookings Foreign Policy Energy Security Series.* Washington, DC:
    Brookings Institution.

Downs, E. 2010. Sino-Russian Energy Relations: An Uncertain Courtship. In B. Womack (ed.) *The Future of China-Russia Relations*. Lexington, KY: University of Kentucky Press, pp. 146–56.

Downs, E. 2011. *Inside China, Inc.: China Development Bank's Cross Border Energy Deals*. Washington, DC: Brookings Institution.

Drifte, R. 2014. The Japan-China Confrontation Over the Senkaku/Diaoyu Islands: Between "Shelving" and "Dispute Resolution." *Asia-Pacific Journal: Japan Focus* 12(30), July 28.

Emerson, S. 2014. The Myth of Petroleum Independence and Foreign Policy Isolation. *Washington Quarterly* 37(1): 21–34.

Guo, A. and Van Loon, J. 2012. Cnooc Buys Nexen in China's Top Overseas Acquisition. *Bloomberg News*, July 23.

Herberg, M. 2004. Asia's Energy Insecurity: Cooperation or Conflict? In Ashley J. Tellis and Michael Wills (eds) *Strategic Asia 2004–05: Confronting Terrorism in the Pursuit of Power*. Seattle, WA: National Bureau of Asian Research, pp. 354–7.

Herberg, M.E. 2007. *The Rise of Asia's National Oil Companies*. Seattle, WA: National Bureau of Asian Research.

Herberg, M.E. 2008. Energy Security in the Asia-Pacific Region and Policy for the New Administration. In The Asia Foundation (eds.) *America's Role in Asia: Asian and American Views*. San Francisco, CA: The Asia Foundation, pp. 131–44.

Herberg, M.E. 2011. *China's Energy Rise and the Future of U.S.–China Energy Relations*. Washington, DC: New America Foundation.

Houser, T. 2008. The Roots of Chinese Oil Investment Abroad. *Asia Policy* 5, January: 141–66.

IHS Global Insight. 2010. South Korea to Triple Energy Self-Sufficiency Over 2009–2019. *IHS Global Insight*, December 22.

International Energy Agency. 2013. *World Energy Outlook 2013*. Paris: International Energy Agency.

Itoh, S. 2008a. China's Surging Energy Demand: Trigger for Conflict or Cooperation with Japan. *East Asia: An International Quarterly* 25(1), March.

Itoh, S. 2008b. Russia's Energy Diplomacy Toward the Asia-Pacific: Is Moscow's Ambition Dashed? *Energy and Environment in Slavic Eurasia*, May. Slavic Research Center of Hokkaido University.

Itoh, S. 2010. The Geopolitics of Northeast Asia's Pipeline Development. *Pipeline Politics in Asia*, September.

James A. Baker III Institute for Public Policy. 2007. *The Changing Role of National Oil Companies in International Energy Markets*, Baker Institute Policy Report, No. 35. Houston, TX: James A. Baker III Institute for Public Policy, Rice University.

Jiang, W. 2006. History Aside, Chinese-Japanese Conflict Now Plays Out Over Gas and Oil Reserves in the East China Sea. *YaleGlobal*, April 25.

Jones, B., Steven, D., and O'Brien, E. 2014. *Fueling a New Order: Geopolitical and Security Consequences of Energy*. Washington, DC: Brookings Institution.

Jones, J. 2010. Sinopec Makes China's Biggest Canada Oil Sands Deal. Reuters, April 12.

Jung-Won, S. 2008. South Korea Aims to Triple KNOC Assets by 2012. *Dow Jones Newswires*, June 12.

Kong, B. 2010. *China's International Petroleum Policy*. Santa Barbara, CA: Praeger/ABC Clio.

Ladislaw, S.O, Leed, M., and Walton, M.A. 2014. *New Energy, New Geopolitics*. Washington, DC: CSIS.

Lau, J. and Dyer, G. 2010. PetroChina Secures $30bn State Loan to Fund "Go Global" Strategy. *The Financial Times*, September 10, p. 1.

Liao, J.X. 2008a. The Politics of Oil Behind Sino-Japanese Energy Security Strategies. *Asia Papers*, March, p. 66.

Liao, J.X. 2008b. Sino-Japanese Energy Security and Regional Stability: The Case of the East China Sea Gas Exploration. *East Asia: An International Quarterly* 25(1), March: 57–78.

Lieberthal, K. and Herberg, M. 2006. China's Search for Energy Security: Implications for U.S. Policy. *NBR Analysis* 17(1), April: 10–15.

Marcel, V. and Mitchell, J.V. 2006. *Oil Titans: National Oil Companies in the Middle East.* London: Chatham House.

Ministry of Economy, Trade and Industry, Japan (METI). 2010. The Strategic Energy Plan of Japan: Meeting Global Challenges and Securing Energy Futures. Tokyo: METI.

Mitchell, J.V. 2013. *U.S. Energy: The New Reality.* London: Chatham House.

Mitchell, J.V. and Lahn, G. 2007. *Oil for Asia: the Rise of Asian National Oil Companies.* London: Chatham House.

Mouawad, J. 2010. China's Growth Shifts the Geopolitics of Oil. *New York Times*, March 19.

Nam, I.-S. 2010. Korea to Improve Energy Self-Sufficiency. *Wall Street Journal*, December 22.

Oxford Analytica Daily Brief. 2010. China: Energy Companies Change Strategic Tack. *Oxford Analytica Daily Brief*, April 26.

Perovic, J. and Orttung, R.W. 2009. Russia's Role for Global Energy Security. In A. Wenger, R. Orttung, and J. Perovic (eds) *Energy and the Transformation of International Relations.* Oxford: Oxford University Press, pp. 117–57.

Platts. 2012. Japan to Gather LNG Producers, Consumers for Public Forum in September. *Platts Latest News Headlines*, May 14. Online: www.platts.com/latest-news/natural-gas/tokyo/japan-to-gather-lng-producers-consumers-for-public-7602560 (accessed April 10, 2013).

Poussenkova, N. 2007. *The Wild Wild East.* Moscow: Carnegie Moscow Center.

Poussenkova, N. 2008. *All Quiet on the Eastern Front: Russia's Energy Sector between Politics and Business.* Zurich/Bremen: Center for Security Studies (CSS), ETH Zurich/Research Centre for East European Studies, University of Bremen.

Pumphrey, D.L. 2007. *U.S.–China Relationship: Economics and Security in Perspective.* Washington, DC: U.S.–China Economic and Security Commission.

Pumphrey, D.L. 2009. U.S. Perspective on National Energy Security. In F. Fesharaki, N. Kim, and Y.H. Kim (eds) *Energy Security in the North Pacific.* Ulsan-si: Korea Energy Economics Institute, pp. 118–44.

Rampton, R. 2012. U.S. Lawmaker Asks for Conditions on CNOOC-Nexen Deal. Reuters, July 30.

Ryall, J. 2010. Tensions Between China and Japan Rise Over Disputed Gas Field. *The Telegraph*, September 17.

Ryu, J.-C. 2009. Korea's Perspective on Energy Security. In F. Fesharaki, N. Kim, and Y.H. Kim (eds) *Energy Security in the North Pacific.* Ulsan-si: Korea Energy Economics Institute, pp. 290–319.

Sekiguchi, T. 2011. Japan's Noda Reaffirms Cooperation with China. *Wall Street Journal*, December 25.

Shixian, G. 2009. China's Perspective on National Energy Security. In F. Fesharaki, N. Kim, and Y.H. Kim (eds) *Energy Security in the North Pacific.* Ulsan-si: Korea Energy Economics Institute, pp. 149–79.

Takeishi, R. 2009. Japan's Energy Security Strategy. In F. Fesharaki, N. Kim, and Y.H. Kim (eds.) *Energy Security in the North Pacific*. Ulsan-si: Korea Energy Economics Institute, pp. 208–56.

The Telegraph. 2010. China Demands Japan Takes Steps to Resolve Dispute Over Territorial Waters. *The Telegraph*, September 16.

U.S. Energy Information Administration (EIA). 2013. *Annual Energy Outlook 2014*, early release. Washington, DC: EIA.

Victor, D., Hults, D., and Thurber, M. (eds). 2012. *Oil and Governance: State-owned Enterprises and World Energy Supplies*. Cambridge: Cambridge University Press.

Winning, D. 2009. KNOC Loses Race for Addax, But Has Edge on China Peers. *Dow Jones Newswires*, June 25.

Winning, D. and Yang, J. 2011. CNOOC and Chesapeake Agree on Deal. *Wall Street Journal*, January 31.

Yishan, Xia and Wu, Kang (2009) Commentaries. In F. Fesharaki, N. Kim, and Y.H. Kim (eds.) *Energy Security in the North Pacific*. Ulsan-si: Korea Energy Economics Institute, pp. 180–207.

Yoshimatsu, H. 2011. *Sino-Japanese Relations and Cooperative Institutions in Energy*. Kitakyushu: ICSEAD.

Zweig, D. 2010. *Resource Diplomacy Under Hegemony: Foreign Policy "Triangularism" and Sino-American Energy Competition in the 21st Century*. Los Angeles, CA: Pacific Council on International Policy.

Zweig, D. and Jianhai, B. 2005. China's Global Hunt for Energy. *Foreign Affairs* 84(5). Online: www.foreignaffairs.com/articles/61017/david-zweig-and-bi-jianhai/chinas-global-hunt-for-energy (accessed June 7, 2014).

3 Energy acquisition, usage, and China's engagement in Northeast Asian energy cooperation

Suyuan Sun

China has been increasingly engaging with other countries' energy producers and energy consumers—in Northeast Asia in order to enhance its energy security.[1] Progress has been made in energy acquisition and energy usage through both bilateral and multilateral channels. By and large, China puts its emphases on cooperation with energy-producing countries for energy acquisition and cooperation with other energy-consuming countries for energy usage.

Many questions, however, remain. How does China perceive the region of Northeast Asia as a whole in its strategic calculus of energy security? What concrete results has China achieved in its cooperation with energy-producing countries for energy acquisition and with energy-consuming countries for energy usage? What primary approach is China following to improve its energy security in this region? What role is China playing in building a regional energy regime?

This chapter will look into these questions and examine China's engagement in Northeast Asian energy cooperation. To facilitate this analysis, it's important to differentiate energy acquisition from energy usage. While energy acquisition is mainly about how a consuming country acquires fossil energy resources from a producing country, energy usage is about how a consuming country uses its fossil energy efficiently and in an environmentally friendly manner. Energy acquisition and usage are two main foci of China's engagement in Northeast Asian energy cooperation, which proceeds according to a different logic than an energy security focus.

Northeast Asia, as China's home region, is playing an increasingly larger role in China's strategic calculus for energy security. On the one hand, China has achieved remarkable progress in this region in bilateral energy cooperation with giant petroleum producer and exporter Russia. On the other, China's cooperation on energy usage with Japan, and to a lesser extent with South Korea, could help China improve its energy efficiency and reduce carbon emissions. China's energy diplomacy is guided by a self-help approach, featuring bilateral cooperation primarily with energy producers as a top priority and use of its state-owned national oil companies (NOCs) as strategic tools. China has played a very limited role in promoting the formation of a region-wide multilateral energy regime, as it is constrained by both an inability and a lack of will to do so. Thus, the prospects for bilateral cooperation on energy acquisition to be scaled up into one multilateral arrangement are dim, and the chance that cooperation on energy usage will be translated into cooperation on energy acquisition is quite slim.

This chapter consists of five sections. It begins with a discussion of China's strategic calculus about Northeast Asia with regard to its energy security, followed by two examinations: one of China's engagement with both energy producers and consumers on energy acquisition, and the other of its engagement on energy usage. Next comes an analysis of China's main approach to energy security, which discusses why China prefers a self-help approach, rather than a multilateral cooperative approach. The last section looks at the prospect for multilateral energy cooperation in Northeast Asia and the role that China plays in the process of regional energy regime-building.

Northeast Asia in China's strategic calculus

As China's home region, Northeast Asia figures more and more prominently in its strategic calculus for energy security. For China, Northeast Asia offers not only fossil energy resources, but also important technologies for energy saving. China has increasingly realized that, along with energy acquisition, energy usage—that is, energy conservation and environmental protection—is an indispensable aspect of energy security. Energy acquisition and energy usage have thus become two driving forces for China's energy engagement in Northeast Asia, as well as elsewhere in the world. Russia, as the biggest petroleum producer and exporter in Northeast Asia, stands out as one of China's major overseas fossil energy suppliers. With outstanding energy-saving technologies, Japan stands out as one of China's potential partners for energy usage.

China turns its attention to Northeast Asia

China became a net crude oil importer in 1996 and began to think about its energy security from a strategic perspective in the early years of the twenty-first century. For China, "energy security has become an issue of the 'high politics' of national security, not just the 'low politics' of domestic economic policy" (Lieberthal & Herberg, 2006). China has not only couched its energy policy more in strategic or geopolitical terms than in economic terms, but also expanded its concept of energy security to include both energy acquisition and energy usage. For China, energy security implies that its energy supply should be sufficient and reliable, that energy transportation should be safe and cheap, and, increasingly, that energy consumption should be efficient and environmentally responsible.

For China, energy security is mainly about acquisition of traditional fossil energy resources, even though new energy resources such as solar and wind energy have also caught Beijing's attention in recent years. Today, more than 40 percent of China's imported oil comes from the Middle East and North Africa, both politically unstable, and more than 85 percent of it is transported through the straits of Malacca, Hormuz, and Suez. Any serious disruption in either production or transportation could damage China's energy acquisition security.

Given long-lasting conflicts in the Middle East and North Africa, as well as more recent political turmoil since late 2010, a high degree of dependence on this single region for oil supply would make China's economy especially vulnerable to the disruption of energy supply (Sun, 2011). And since almost all of China's oil from the Middle East and North Africa has to be shipped home through sea lanes in the Indian Ocean, high reliance on the Strait of Hormuz and the Gulf of Aden at the source, and the Strait of Malacca in transit, represents a strategic vulnerability for China. Piracy off the coast of Somalia has been another serious threat to sea-lane transit. Security experts have warned that possible terrorist attacks against tankers transiting the Strait of Malacca may cut off or reduce the reliability of the busiest supply route in the world (Ziegler, 2006). Former President Hu Jintao once called this problem China's "Malacca dilemma" and considered it key to China's energy security (Zweig & Jianhai, 2005). Thus, China's concerns for energy supply and transportation make cooperation on energy acquisition with energy producers in Northeast Asia, in particular Russia, more attractive and even more cost-effective.

In addition to energy acquisition, Chinese attitudes on energy security have gradually expanded to include energy usage. With rapid economic growth in recent decades, China's primary energy consumption has increased greatly, and its carbon emissions have multiplied. China's energy intensity is higher than that of many industrialized countries. In 2011, for example, energy intensity in China was 26,130 Btu, almost six times higher than Japan's energy intensity at 4,553 Btu (U.S. Energy Information Administration, 2011). The dominant and increasing percentage of coal usage in China's energy mix has made carbon emissions a big problem. China emitted 8.7 billion tons of CO_2 in 2011, for example, compared with 1.2 billion tons in Japan (U.S. Energy Information Administration, 2011). The principle of shared but different responsibilities has granted China leeway in international climate change negotiations in Copenhagen, Bali, Durban, and elsewhere. But China understands that this principle does not exempt it from a real commitment to cut emissions. Therefore, developing a low-carbon economy by reducing its reliance on coal, improving its energy efficiency, and protecting the environment has gradually been integrated into China's concept of energy security. And China's concerns for energy conservation and environmental protection are prompting it to consider other big energy consumers in Northeast Asia, in particular Japan, for cooperation on energy usage.

Russia: key to China's demand for fossil fuels

As diversification has been a main approach of China's energy security strategy, Beijing has been conducting intense energy diplomacy to diversify its gas and oil imports. In this regard, Russia's rich reserve of gas and its high oil production have become factors in Beijing's calculus for energy acquisition security. Even though Mongolia also produces and exports coal and oil,[2] the limited amount it provides makes it less important than Russia in China's calculus; to a great extent, it is Russia that makes Northeast Asia a "strategic region" for China's energy security strategy. Russia and Central Asia have been confirmed as one of China's "strategic regions" (Dan, 2013). Russian and Central Asia have also been a focus of China's "going west" (*xijin*) strategy (*China Daily*, 2006; Blank, 2007; Wang, 2012). And China has increasingly attempted to approach Russia through Northeast Asia, as well as through Central Asia.

First, energy cooperation with Russia could help meet China's need for energy resource diversification and environmental protection. Natural gas is the main form of energy resource in Russia, in particular in the Russian Far East (RFE) and East Siberia, with 52.4 trillion cubic meters onshore and 14.9 trillion off-shore (Gazprom). Although the success of the American shale gas revolution has prompted the Chinese government to develop its large shale gas reserves, it is still a realistic choice at present for China to import natural gas because exploring indigenous shale gas reserves not only requires a huge sum of capital, as well as key technique, but can also have serious environmental consequences, which makes commercial production of shale gas unfeasible for the foreseeable future. In any case, importing natural gas from Russia supports China's efforts to transfer its energy consumption to some extent from oil or coal to gas, which is also more environmentally friendly.

Second, oil from RFE and East Siberia is a good option for China in its quest to diversify and shift from its too-heavy reliance on the Middle East and North Africa. Russian energy resources also help China reduce its vulnerability to transportation issues. Transporting oil overland from Russia to China is shorter than using the sea lane from the Middle East and Africa to China. More important, overland pipelines are generally a safer and more reliable form of transportation than are the sea lanes through the Malacca Strait.

Third, Russia's eastward-facing strategy meshes with China's demand. The great energy potential in RFE and East Siberia is helping drive Russia's eastward geopolitical shift. It is not surprising that the Kremlin decided to develop this energy-rich region in the post-Soviet era. In 1996, Russia moved the center of gravity in its general economic and political strategy toward the Asia-Pacific region. In 2002, the Kremlin announced a plan to develop its Far East oil and gas industry. Russia's federal 2020 energy strategy, issued in 2003, pointed out that the growing demand in the Asia-Pacific market would promote the eastward shift of the Russian energy industry. In 2007, the Kremlin authorized an outline for developing a unified gas drilling, transport, and supply system in the Far East and East Siberia, in order to export gas to China and other Asia-Pacific countries. In Russia's *2030 Natural Gas Industry Overall Development Outline*, drafted in 2008, Russia proposed constructing a gas pipeline system that would extend to China and South Korea (Han, 2009).

In recent years, certain other events have also promoted Russia's eastward shift in energy foreign policy. One is the American shale gas boom, thanks to which the United States has overtaken Russia as the largest gas producer in the world since 2009. The other is Russian disputes with the European Union over the crisis in Ukraine, which has pushed Russia to reduce its dependence on the European market and tap additional markets. Russia's eastward energy-exporting strategy definitely offers a new opportunity for China and other Northeast Asian counties to upgrade their regional cooperation on energy acquisition. It is clear that Russia is eager to export not only crude oil but also more refined oil products to both China and the rest of Asia. *The Energy Strategy of Russia for the Period up to 2030* projected that Russia's exports of liquid hydrocarbons (oil and oil products) to its eastern energy markets would grow from 8 percent in 2008 to 22 to 25 percent in 2030. Natural gas exports were projected to increase from 0 percent in the Asia-Pacific region in 2008 to about 20 percent in 2030 (Russian Ministry of Energy, 2010). Such a change in Russia's energy strategy warrants China's corresponding shift from working with Russia mainly through Central Asia to one of working through Northeast Asia, or at least giving them the same priority.

Japan: key to China's quest for energy-consuming technologies

Other consuming countries in the region, such as Japan and South Korea, are more problematic energy partners for China than is Russia. Since world petroleum reserves are relatively fixed and production of energy is relatively stable in the long run, energy consumers must compete intensely with other consumers for a larger market share, which effectively rules out Japan and South Korea as partners in energy acquisition. China's perception plays into similar perceptions by both Japan and South Korea. All three see the others as competitors for access to Russia's energy resources. The construction of the Eastern Siberia–Pacific Ocean (ESPO) pipeline is not a model of multilateral cooperation by both producing and consuming countries, but in fact a result of multilateral competition among them, which in turn serves as a new factor leading to further competition among consuming countries.

With energy usage becoming a recognized part of energy security strategy, however, the Chinese government has begun to seek coordination and cooperation with other consuming countries in Northeast Asia, especially Japan. In such areas as energy conservation and environmental protection, which can function independently of fossil energy acquisition, there is a high possibility that competing consumers may regard each other as potential partners, with complementary roles in both bilateral and multilateral cooperation envisaged. Japan has committed itself to improving energy efficiency since the first oil crisis in 1973 and has developed mature energy conservation technologies. Japan's efforts to reduce its dependence on oil have been so successful that the degree of energy efficiency in Japan is much higher than that in many other industrialized countries in the world. China's cooperation with Japan, and to a lesser extent with South Korea, could help China improve its energy efficiency, which in turn may ease competition among the three countries for fossil energy acquisition. Moreover, China's quest for better energy efficiency has become imperative because of environmental problems such as acid rain, greenhouse gases, and so on, which transcend national boundaries and cannot be solved within a nation's borders. In this regard, Japan and South Korea have become factors in Beijing's calculus for national energy security and have turned out to be China's potential partners in energy usage.

From China's perspective, Northeast Asian energy cooperation could help China not only improve overseas energy acquisition security, but also reduce pollution and other environmental harm. In the past ten years, the Chinese government has increasingly engaged in energy cooperation in Northeast Asia, both with producers and with consumers. On the one hand, China has been actively pushing substantial bilateral energy cooperation, mainly for energy acquisition, with the energy-producing countries in this region, Russia in particular. Bilateral energy cooperation has been an important component in Sino-Russo relations. On the other, China has attempted to coordinate and cooperate with other consuming countries to improve energy efficiency and to help protect the environment. In comparison with Sino-Russo cooperation on energy acquisition, China's cooperation with energy consumers mainly focuses on energy usage through various bilateral and multilateral forums, dialogues, and meetings.

Energy acquisition and China's engagement with energy producer Russia

China has made progress in energy cooperation with Northeast Asian countries. Among China's achievements, its bilateral energy deals with Russia are the most notable, while its bilateral agreements with other consuming countries, in particular on energy acquisition, have not been substantial and meaningful.

Russia has become a key energy supplier to China. Several milestones in the development of China–Russia cooperation on energy acquisition deserve a brief review here (Ivanov, 2006; Rosner, 2010). In October 2004, the China National Petroleum Corporation (CNPC) concluded a strategic partnership with Gazprom, the leading energy company in Russia. In July 2005, the China Petroleum and Chemical Corporation (Sinopec) signed a memorandum with Russian state-owned oil company Rosneft, seeking to establish a joint venture in exploration of the Venin mining field of Sakhalin-3. In October 2006, CNPC and Rosneft established a joint venture, Vostok Energy. They also signed a framework agreement on long-term cooperation. Two years later, CNPC and the Russian Oil Pipeline Transportation Company signed an agreement on constructing the branch line of ESPO, also called the Tanner line, from Taishet in East Siberia to the Pacific port city of Nakhodka. In February 2009, China and Russia signed the loans-for-oil agreement, in which, from 2011 to 2030, Russia would provide 15 million tons of oil to China annually, while China would provide $25 billion in loans to Rosneft and Russian state-owned oil pipeline company Transneft. In October 2009, CNPC and Gazprom signed a framework agreement on gas supplies and construction of a gas pipeline. In September 2010, the branch line of the ESPO pipeline to China was completed.

Even though it is hard to say that China has followed a coherent energy acquisition strategy toward Russia, its bilateral energy cooperation with Russia has seen breakthroughs, notwithstanding ups and downs. Compared to other energy importers such as Japan and South Korea, China has established a primary position as Russia's leading energy customer in Northeast Asia, which can be partially ascribed to Sino-Russo strategic cooperative partnership. Energy cooperation, in turn, functions as the spearhead of their overall relationship (Blank, 2006). Although China and Russia have engaged in some geopolitical and commercial rivalries (Danchenko *et al.*, 2010), China has closer and tighter political ties with Russia than with Japan and South Korea. China and Russia view each other as good neighbors and strategic partners. From 1992 till now, Sino-Russo relations have progressed smoothly, marked by a series of treaties signed by the leaders of the two nations (Yu, 2006). In 1996, the two countries signed a treaty of strategic cooperation partnership. In 2001, they signed the Sino-Russian Treaty of Friendship, which marked a new era in the development of bilateral relations. In June 2012, a joint statement announced a further deepening of trust in their comprehensive strategic partnership of coordination. As China's growth momentum is set to continue for coming decades, China and Russia will continue their close energy partnership in the near future; as Russian President Vladimir Putin wrote on June 5, 2012, in China's *People's Daily*, Sino-Russo energy cooperation has strategic implications: "For China, this means improving reliability and diversity of its energy sources. For Russia, it signifies a new exporting market in the rising Asia-Pacific region" (Putin, 2012). Moreover, China is the world's second-largest oil consumer, third-largest oil importer, and a small but growing consumer and importer of natural gas. China's huge foreign exchange reserve is also an important advantage; the reserve reached more than 3 trillion U.S. dollars in 2011, so that China is ready to invest in overseas energy sectors.

By contrast, China and other consuming countries have made few substantive agreements in the specific area of fossil energy acquisition. One exceptional case is with North Korea, the only consuming country in Northeast Asia with which China is cooperating on energy acquisition; China serves as almost the sole supplier of oil to North Korea (Lee, 2009). It is estimated that China is supplying North Korea with at least 70 percent of its energy in the form of crude oil. Some observers put the figure at 88 percent, with the rest coming in aid from the West (Tkacik, 2002). The Korean Peninsula Energy Development Organization (KEDO) was established in 1995, participated in by the United States, South Korea and Japan, against the background of the 1994 North Korean nuclear crisis. However, this multilateral arrangement failed to provide North Korea with needed energy, and North Korea failed to freeze its nuclear program as promised, so it is widely believed that North Korea's energy demand is mainly met by imports from China. Beijing has been providing critical energy aid for Pyongyang for more than 30 years. Besides aid, in 2005, the North Korean vice premier reportedly signed a joint investment agreement to develop its oil field in the Western Sea area with the support of the China National Offshore Oil Corporation (CNOOC).

In Northeast Asia, it is hard to find any meaningful agreements on energy acquisition that involve consuming countries in the region. By contrast, not only China but also other consuming countries in the region are actively engaging with Russia for its oil and gas. While China has made Russia one of its top ten oil suppliers in the world, Japan and South Korea are also enhancing their energy relations with Russia. Japan is involved in exploring oil and gas fields in RFE Sakhalin-1 and Sakhalin-2 projects, and cooperated with Russia in the ESPO pipeline project (Wang, 2004). In 2008, South Korea and Russia issued a memorandum of understanding on a deal for South Korea to import at least 7.5 million tons of natural gas annually (about 20 percent of its demand) from Russia through a pipeline beginning in 2015. Many bilateral arrangements have been set up between Russia and various Northeast Asian consumers, clearly signifying the prevalence of bilateral forms over multilateral ones in energy acquisition cooperation in Northeast Asia.

Energy usage and China's engagement with other energy consumers

While energy acquisition is the focus of China's bilateral cooperation with Russia, energy usage constitutes the main focus of China's agreements with Japan, and to a lesser extent with South Korea. In this chapter, energy usage is defined as how a consuming country uses its fossil energy resources efficiently and in an environmentally friendly manner. The most evident activity of China's engagement with other consuming countries in this region is over how to improve energy efficiency and how to manage the negative consequences of energy consumption in cooperation with other consuming countries. China has engaged in dialogues and practical projects with Japan and South Korea through both bilateral channels and multilateral opportunities.

China–Japan energy cooperation almost exclusively focuses on energy conservation and environmental protection, which has been featured in a few agreements. The initiative of Sino-Japanese energy cooperation has been sustained by commitments from the private sector (Yoshimatsu, 2010). Business firms usually act as initiators in Sino-Japanese cooperation on energy usage, and governments authorize the initiatives and arrange formal meetings and forums. Several industrial associations implemented projects to promote energy saving in China, a move that spurred Sino-Japanese official cooperation on energy conservation and environmental protection. In July 2005, the Japan Iron and Steel Federation (JISF), in collaboration with the China Iron and Steel Association (CISA), organized the Japan–China Advanced Technology Exchange Meeting for Environmental Protection and Energy Saving in Beijing. High-ranking business managers from the steel industry in both countries agreed to continue exchanges of information and expertise about environmental protection and energy conservation. In this context, the Chinese and Japanese governments organized the first Sino-Japanese Energy Conservation Forum in Tokyo in May 2006, where high-ranking officials could exchange perspectives, enhance mutual understanding, and promote further cooperation. In December 2006, top leaders of China's National Development and Reform Commission (NDRC) and Japan's Ministry of Economy, Trade and Industry (METI) signed a memorandum on implementing an energy conservation and environmental business model project to facilitate reciprocal cooperation (Itoh, 2008). Since then, the two countries have held energy conservation forums regularly and have launched several projects in the field of energy conservation and environmental protection.

China and South Korea have also begun bilateral cooperation on energy usage. In September 2009, CNPC signed a memorandum of understanding with the Korea National Oil Corporation (KNOC), enabling the two sides to cooperate in crude oil storage, trade, and marketing in the future.

Japan and South Korea are also involved in multilateral energy usage cooperation with China. The origin of multilateral energy cooperation among the three countries can be traced back to 1999, when the leaders of the three countries met informally for the first time. Since then, numbers of meeting mechanisms on different layers have been gradually established, including at the ministerial, senior official, and working-group levels. Although many of the initiatives launched by the three consuming countries have not yet translated into substantive results, mutual understanding, standard setting, and consensus-building have all been strengthened. Through multilateral forums and dialogues, the three countries have been able to understand each other's energy security concerns and reach consensus on environmental protection for sustainable development. In October 2003, leaders of the three countries published a joint declaration promoting trilateral cooperation, promising to work together to strengthen regional and world energy security (*People's Daily Online*, 2003). In 2011, leaders promised to cooperate on renewable energy and energy efficiency in order to realize sustainable development (*China News*, 2011), and in 2012 promised to cooperate on low-carbon economic growth (Xinhua News Agency, 2012). Since 1999, ministers of environment from China, Japan, and South Korea have met annually to promote their multilateral cooperation on environmental protection. This forum has become the major mechanism for environmental cooperation in Northeast Asia. In the latest dialogue in May 2012, each country's ministry of environment issued a joint statement and three agreements concerning the compatibility of their environmental standards (Xinhua News Agency, 2012). Cooperation on energy usage among China, Japan, and South Korea has also been launched on other multilateral cooperation occasions outside of the Northeast Asian region, such as ASEAN+3, the East Asia Summit (EAS), and Asia-Pacific Economic Cooperation (APEC). For example, the first ASEAN+3 energy ministerial meeting in June 2004 emphasized taking collective actions to strengthen the ASEAN+3 Energy Partnership for energy security and sustainability (ASEAN, 2004). At the eighth ASEAN+3 Ministers of Energy Meeting in September 2011 in Brunei, the ministers shared knowledge on oil stockpiling and exchanged opinions on oil and natural gas markets, renewable energy, and energy efficiency and conservation (ASEAN, 2011). Energy security and environmental protection has also become an important topic within the EAS. In January 2007, at the second summit, the participating countries signed the Cebu Declaration on East Asian Energy Security, considered a milestone for putting forward specific aims and measures for East Asian energy cooperation. Eight months later, the first EAS Energy Ministers Meeting (EMM) was held in Singapore and, in November, the 2007 Singapore Declaration on Climate Change, Energy, and the Environment was signed (ASEAN, 2007). From then on, the EAS EMM has been held every year. At the ninth APEC energy ministries meeting, ministers from China, Japan, South Korea, and other members of APEC announced a declaration on low-carbon paths to energy security (Ministry of Foreign Affairs, Japan, 2010). As far as energy usage is concerned, various summits and initiatives play an important role in exchanging information, sharing experiences, and promoting joint efforts among energy-consuming countries in the region. For China, it is necessary to collaborate with other consuming countries for energy usage. This will not change China's fundamental principle in energy security strategy and energy diplomacy with Northeast Asian countries, however. China's cooperation with Japan and South Korea is mainly limited to energy efficiency and environmental protection, rather than focusing on China's access to Russia's fossil energy. Moreover, China's interest in cooperation with other consuming countries on energy usage is not evidence of its interest in exploring Russia's fossil energy as a consortium with other consuming countries. Basically, China's stance on energy cooperation with Northeast Asian countries has been primarily shaped by its concerns for its own energy security in terms of energy acquisition and energy usage.

Self-help as China's primary approach to energy security

Regardless of its political and diplomatic rhetoric, China follows a self-help approach to ensure its energy security, as do many other energy consumers in the world. Self-help is an important concept in international politics. Structural realist Kenneth Waltz argues:

> To achieve their objectives and maintain their security, units in a condition of anarchy—be they people, corporations, states, or whatever—must rely on the means they can generate and the arrangements that they can make for themselves. Self-help is necessarily the principle of action in an anarchic order.
>
> (Waltz, 1979, p. 111)

The self-help approach is quite prominent not only in international politics in general, but in international energy politics in particular. In terms of energy security, a self-help approach signifies that a country relies on itself to secure its overseas energy acquisition mainly through bilateral governmental contracts with oil-producing countries. Obviously, multilateral energy cooperation for collective energy security, such as energy cooperation in the framework of the International Energy Agency (IEA), does not belong to the self-help category.

China's energy engagement in Northeast Asia follows varying strategic logic depending on whether the focus is energy acquisition or energy usage. As discussed above, China has mainly engaged with Russia on energy acquisition, as Russia is the most important energy producer in this region for energy acquisition; its bilateral link with North Korea on energy acquisition is a minor exception, with no implications for China's approach to energy security. By contrast, China has engaged with other energy consumers—Japan, and to a lesser extent South Korea—for energy usage in both bilateral and multilateral levels (see Table 3.1). The general guideline for China's energy acquisition is a self-help approach, whereas for energy usage it has taken a "mutual-help" approach. Because China's energy security strategy prioritizes acquisition over usage, self-help can be defined as China's primary approach to energy security.

Self-help as the general guideline for China's energy security has shaped China's stance in Northeast Asian energy cooperation. In this region China primarily relies on cooperation with energy producers for fossil energy acquisition and secondarily depends on cooperation with other energy consumers for energy conservation and environmental protection. China's approach to energy diplomacy in Northeast Asia is rooted in China's tradition of self-sufficiency, constrained by the international energy market and the international community in general, and shaped by fierce energy competition for Russia's oil and gas reserves with other consumers in Northeast Asia. Moreover, national oil companies, acting as main executors for exploring overseas oil and gas resources, reinforce China's self-help focus in acquiring fossil energy.

China uses a self-help approach as a general guideline in its energy diplomacy for energy acquisition, and Beijing is clear that China must rely on any means at its disposal to maintain its energy security. Beijing views its energy relations with both producers and consumers from relative realist perspectives. In terms of fossil energy acquisition, China thus perceives all producers as potential partners and all consumers as competitors. Taking China's energy policy in 2005 as an example, most of China's strategic partners were energy producers, countries with energy production potential, and transit nations, for example Russia, while other consuming states in Northeast Asia were not mentioned as energy security partners. China views bilateral cooperation with energy producers as its top priority for energy security, which has long been its principal approach to securing its access to overseas energy resources. China's arrangements with individual producers—Azerbaijan, Brazil, Indonesia, Iran, Kazakhstan, Russia, Saudi Arabia, Sudan, and Venezuela—all revolve around the promise of meeting China's demand for fossil energy. China also buys oil in international markets and has cooperated with India (an energy-consuming country) in exploiting oil in Kazakhstan and jointly entering into the Sudan oil exploitation project

Table 3.1 China's energy engagement in Northeast Asia

	With energy producers	*With energy consumers*
Energy acquisition	China–Russia China–Mongolia	China–North Korea
Energy usage		China–Japan China–South Korea China–Japan–South Korea Within ASEAN+3, EAS, and APEC, etc.

(Xu, 2007). Direct energy relations with oil-producing countries are of strategic importance for China's energy security, simply because such producers have what China needs. Northeast Asia is no exception. As Northeast Asian energy politics remain an anarchic arena, China has to rely on self-help to ensure its energy acquisition; in other words, China usually does not rely on collective actions or energy consumer alliances but on exclusive bilateral channels in seeking its fossil energy acquisition security in Northeast Asia. China's energy cooperation with Russia has increased its energy acquisition reliability and diversification (Diao, 2007). Cooperating directly with energy suppliers has been China's main method of securing energy acquisition. And this is equally applicable to Japan and South Korea as to other consumers in Northeast Asia. That is why bilateral arrangements prevail over multilateral ones in Northeast Asian countries' efforts at energy diplomacy for fossil energy resources in the region.

Historical experience has shaped China's energy policy and diplomacy, with self-help a prominent feature. This same approach to energy security strategy is consistent with its tradition of self-reliance and self-sufficiency, key traditional concepts that have dominated China's foreign policy. In the early years of the People's Republic, an economically and politically isolated China (partially the result of the U.S.-led embargo against China in 1950), aspired to economic self-sufficiency through a closed, planned economy that was not dependent on imported food or other raw materials. In the 1960s, due to political tensions, the Soviet Union suddenly terminated its oil supply to China and its technological assistance for developing China's oil industry, which left China with only one option in terms of energy, that is, self-sufficiency (Zha, 2006). This situation changed once China began to institute economic reforms and its "opening policy" in 1979, and especially when China became a net petroleum importing country in 1993.

The international petroleum market and the international community play a structural role in shaping China's self-help approach to pursuing energy security. In contrast to China's increasing integration into the world economy, China's approach to acquiring energy resources abroad is still one of self-reliance rather than depending on multilateral institutions. In the international petroleum market, China has no say in petroleum trading, pricing, and producing. Western countries and their major international oil companies (IOCs) play a dominant role in setting up the rules of game (Sun, 2010). The dollar became the currency of choice for international crude-oil transactions since the first oil crisis in 1973 (El-Gamal & Jaffe, 2010). As the newcomer in the international petroleum market, China was neither welcomed nor felt comfortable working with major Western oil companies. In 2003, both CNOOC and Sinopec were blocked from participating in the development of an oil field in the Caspian Sea, after the existing partners decided to increase their own stakes (*New York Times*, 2003). The obstacles the international community erected in response to China's pursuit of offshore oil and gas have put Beijing on the defensive (see Zha, 2006). China has to depend on its own national oil companies and assist them with close diplomatic ties with oil states such as Iran and Venezuela, which pursue foreign policies contrary to American and European interests or preferences.

In addition, China has not fully participated in most global international energy organizations. Before China became a net petroleum importing country in 1993, developed energy-consuming nations had already long participated in a relatively mature multilateral energy institution, the IEA, aiming to strengthen international energy security. (The IEA is an international organization attached to the Organisation for Economic Co-operation and Development (OECD), established in November 1974 in Paris.) China has been a special observer at the IEA committee meetings, but not a member of the IEA, because it is not a member of the OECD. Also, it is difficult for China to meet the 90-day emergency stock obligation recommended by the IEA, as well as some shared goals of commitments to collective international action to respond to energy emergencies, which require China to give up some sovereignty over use of its strategic petroleum reserve (SPR) (Kohl, 2010). At present China's SPR is about 30 days, far less than the standard recommended by the IEA. In fact, the relationship between China and the IEA is still limited to communication and dialogue. It is unlikely that China will join the IEA in the foreseeable future, notwithstanding some Chinese scholars who argue for China's membership in the IEA and other international energy institutions (Wang, 2009). The relationship between China and the Energy Charter Treaty (ECT) is similar. China is still a "junior partner," lacking sufficient bargaining power in global energy organizations, even though China is one of the biggest energy markets in the world (Guan & He, 2007). To some extent, China's self-help approach in energy diplomacy is not a choice, but a necessity.

Fierce energy competition among consumers for Russia's oil and gas led to China's self-help approach to energy diplomacy, especially prominent in Northeast Asia. As Kong points out, while Beijing's active petroleum diplomacy aims to enhance China's petroleum security, it risks pulling China into a strategic rivalry with other major oil-consuming nations over access to petroleum resources (Kong, 2010). As discussed above, China, Japan, and South Korea are peer energy competitors for fossil energy in the world in general and in Northeast Asia in particular. Their common weakness in terms of high dependence on energy imports simply does not lead to a desire for cooperation at either the global or regional level (Choo, 2006); it is an inherent barrier for Northeast Asian countries seeking to coordinate their competition on fossil energy consumption. Within the consuming countries, China, Japan, and South Korea see each other as rivals more than as partners, and their competition plays into a vicious circle. The competition for the oil pipeline from Angarsk in Russia's East Siberia to either Daqing (Angarsk–Daqing line) or Nakhodka (Angarsk–Nakhodka line) between China and Japan is a telling example (Yin, 2004). China, along with Japan and South Korea, prefers to individually, rather than collectively, manage energy relations with Russia. Therefore, self-help is a rational option for China, as it is for Japan and South Korea.

The Chinese government uses state-owned national oil companies as strategic tools to implement energy diplomacy and execute its "going-out" strategy, for which the NOCs receive diplomatic and economic support from the Chinese government. To achieve its petroleum security, China has been encouraging its three giant state-owned oil companies—PetroChina, Sinopec, and CNOOC—to seek overseas resources (Wu, 2009). With governmental support, the three NOCs have invested heavily in oil exploration ventures in Iran, Iraq, Kazakhstan, Kuwait, Nigeria, Peru, Russia, Syria, Sudan, Venezuela, and so on. In turn, Chinese NOCs, as important executors of China's energy diplomacy, also push for China's bilateral cooperation with energy-producing countries and reinforce China's self-help approach to energy security. China's NOCs are both commercial and political, with top company leaders also possessing official rank as high as the ministerial level. On the one hand, their political interests, in particular the potential for promotion for their top leaders to higher governmental posts (Lee & Shalmon, 2008), require China's NOCs to support the governmental self-help approach to energy diplomacy. On the other, their commercial interests drive China's NOCs to prefer bilateral energy cooperation with energy producers rather than multilateral agreements because they can easily secure the Chinese government's diplomatic and financial support (Downs, 2007).

In order to guarantee its energy security, especially access to overseas fossil energy resources, China has conducted intensive energy diplomacy, taking a self-help approach as the general guideline, with bilateral cooperation with fossil energy producers as the primary channel and NOCs as important agents. Although China's increasing proactive engagement with other consumers is contrary to a self-help approach, the cooperation is limited to the area of energy usage. The self-help approach definitely prevails in China's energy diplomacy for energy acquisition. In Northeast Asia, China has thus attempted to strengthen its relationship with the largest energy-producing country in this region, Russia, to increase its perceived sense of energy security, though its competition with other consuming countries casts doubt on this perception. China's self-help approach to energy security shapes not only its energy relations with other Northeast Asian countries, but also China's status and role in Northeast Asian energy regime-building.

China's role in multilateral energy regime-building in Northeast Asia

Some observers, including in China's academic circles, are pointing to a brighter future for energy cooperation in Northeast Asia. From this perspective, Northeast Asian energy cooperation is both possible and necessary for three reasons: First, the consuming countries face common energy security threats; second, they share common interests in importing foreign energy; and, third, all share a measure of energy dependence with Russia. Some Chinese scholars have advanced concepts such as a Northeast Asian energy community (Chen & Jin, 2005). Such concepts propose establishing an energy community in which both producing and consuming countries in the region participate, with an information sharing system, convenient investment system, and producing and transiting network, as well as common energy market. The true picture of Northeast Asian energy cooperation, however, is much less rosy. Generally speaking, Northeast Asian energy cooperation thus far has not been very promising, notwithstanding China's engagement with both energy producers and consumers, as discussed above. Scaling up from bilateral cooperation on energy acquisition to a multilateral institution is a difficult transition. It is also difficult for multilateral cooperation on energy usage to be translated into multilateral cooperation on energy acquisition. China thus far has not had much to contribute to the formation of a multilateral energy regime.

The outlook for Northeast Asian multilateral energy cooperation

As of this writing, no effective regional institution for regional energy security has been established in Northeast Asia. Members in the region lack both the ability and the willingness to set up a regional energy security framework. In terms of energy acquisition, bilateral energy cooperation on fossil fuels is the prime and initial pattern of China's, Japan's, and South Korea's engagement with energy producer Russia. But Russia's manipulating its energy tools and energy consumers' mutual competition and distrust have made it unlikely that those multiple bilateral arrangements can be integrated into a single multilateral agreement. In terms of energy usage, notwithstanding progress in multilateral cooperation among energy consumers, the distinct logic of energy usage cooperation has made it impossible to be upgraded into multilateral cooperation on energy acquisition.

Although energy interdependence exists between energy-consuming countries and energy-producing countries in Northeast Asia, it is not foreseeable for them to form a regional energy community in the future. Theoretically, the relationship between consuming and producing countries is interdependent, and energy cooperation between them should be easy. In fact, however, the cooperation does not proceed as smoothly as theory might indicate. The energy relations between the two sides (consuming and producing) are usually influenced by their competing concerns for energy security and a preference for each party's self-help approach. All Northeast Asian countries care about their own energy security, which means different things to different players. Despite the same apparent key concept of diversification, energy security strategies for consumers and producers are actually not congruent. And for Northeast Asian energy consumers and producers alike, their energy security strategies and stances on energy cooperation result from a self-help approach. For energy consumers, the concern is maintenance of sufficient energy supplies, prices commensurate with purchasing power, and guaranteed safe delivery of energy resources (Philip Andrews-Speed, quoted in Choo, 2006). For energy suppliers, the concern is maintenance of sufficient energy demand, prices conducive to national revenue growth, and guaranteed control over export of energy resources. This mismatch usually leads to mutual miscalculations and even mistrust between energy consumers and suppliers. The situation will become worse if energy suppliers, such as Russia, use their oil and gas resources as strategic leverage against energy consumers. Consequently, a zero-sum game between consuming and producing countries—that is, one country's gain is another country's loss—has impeded the realization of full potential for multinational cooperation on energy acquisition in Northeast Asia.

Russia, as the largest oil and gas producer and exporter in the region, is not willing to act as a public goods provider to help build a Northeast Asian energy community. On the contrary, Russia utilizes its energy resources from a strategic perspective and wields its advantage as an energy exporter over importers in Northeast Asia, as well as in Europe. For Russia as an energy empire, oil and gas are not only important sources of revenue, but also strategic tools for seeking to re-establish or further cement its position as a world power. In its relationship with consuming countries, Russia concerns itself with the maintenance of government's control over the production of oil and gas resources, transportation, and the market, etc. This has translated Russia's approach toward diversifying markets and pipeline routes into a much more vigorous one (Lo & Rothman, 2006).

Since the Russian government regards energy not only as an economic resource but also as strategic leverage useful in gaining advantage over other countries in the region, it tries to avoid a scenario of a buyer's monopoly market in its energy cooperation with Northeast Asian consuming countries. In other words, Russia focuses on developing its relationship with the three major energy consumers individually, instead of working with all three together. The Putin administration clearly sought to use its power to interpret Northeast Asian geopolitics as a tool to maximize its own benefit by playing off China and Japan against each other (Itoh, 2008). As China and Japan scrambled for access to Russia's East Siberia oil pipeline, the Russian government abandoned both the Angarsk–Daqing line with China and Angarsk–Nakhodka line with Japan, and replaced them with the ESPO, which enhanced Russia's strategic presence in Northeast Asia. The major gas deal concluded by Russia and China in May 2014 is another case in point (Miller, 2014). After one decade of negotiation with China on the gas pipeline, the deal does not indicate in any way that Russia has changed its stance on its energy cooperation with consuming countries. The gas price in this contract still has not been made public, a reminder of the difficulties of energy cooperation with Russia, which is reluctant to make concessions in energy trading. Moreover, the gas deal with China implies that Russia will be able to extend its gas market to other Asian countries and will play a dominant role as a gas supplier to the Asian market in the future.

As energy consumers, China, Japan, and South Korea see each other as rivals more than as partners in competing for direct energy supply from producing countries. Although they share common interests in importing fossil energy from overseas, it is very difficult for Northeast Asian consuming countries to translate their common weakness in energy dependence into an impetus for energy cooperation. Concern for relative gains leads these three major energy consumers to perceive their access to Russia's energy resources as a zero-sum game. Fundamentally speaking, China's energy security policy is still the outcome of the self-help approach; the same logic is applicable to Japan and South Korea. From the perspective of energy demand in Northeast Asia, China is facing great challenges from Japan and South Korea, and vice versa. Competition on energy acquisition is the dominant logic underlying their energy relations.

In addition, mutual distrust remains a serious impediment to the development of Northeast Asian energy cooperation, in particular at the multilateral level. To a large extent, historical maritime and island disputes impede the cultivation of mutual trust. Besides China's disputes with Japan over the Diaoyu/Senkaku Islands in the East China Sea (Pan, 2007), similar maritime disputes, to a lesser extent, exist between China and the two Koreas over China's Yellow Sea/Korea's West Sea, between South Korea and Japan over the Dokdo/Takeshima islands, and between Japan and Russia over the Kurile Islands. It is most likely that energy competition and geopolitical confrontation in this area may fall into a vicious downward spiral, which would severely hamper multilateral energy cooperation in Northeast Asia. Now and then these maritime disputes re-emerge, souring relationships among Northeast Asian countries. An energy expert once defined a "'Northeast Asian Arc of Crisis,' stretching from energy-rich Sakhalin in the Northeast, across Korea and around Japan to the energy-deficient Fujian and Guangdong provinces of China in the southwest" (Calder, 1996, p. 5). Even though the Chinese government has proposed a general principle of "shelving the disputes and working for joint development" with regard to its energy relations with Japan in the disputed East China Sea, mistrust between China and Japan remains. Distrust among consuming countries has prevented them from coordinating their competition for Russia's oil and gas, not to mention forming an energy consumers' organization so that they can take collective action in doing business with energy-producing countries in Northeast Asia and beyond. The 2013 dispute between China and Japan over the East China Sea undoubtedly furthered political distrust, another obstacle for China and Japan's cultivation of a shared need for energy security, therefore constraining the two consuming countries from taking collective action to secure their energy security.

As a result, two or more bilateral arrangements on energy acquisition could not simply be combined to create a multilateral regime. The construction of ESPO might have been the most fruitful energy cooperation in Northeast Asia so far, but it is, in fact, just a consequence of multilateral competition, not one of cooperation. Russia hopes that more than one country will join in the development of oil and gas in its Far East and East Siberia.

A multilateral cooperation mechanism does not exist at all in the oil pipeline bargaining process. It was only after Beijing accepted Rosneft's demand to raise oil prices and granted the latter a $25 billion loan that construction of the last 110 kilometers of RFE oil pipeline extending to China finally began, which ensured construction of China's Daqing branch and a steady oil supply according to the long-term oil contract between China and Russia (Xu & Huang, 2010). In the competition with Japan for Russia's East Siberia oil, China had to abandon the original Angarsk–Daqing line planned in 1994, and instead gained a branch line from Angarsk in Russia to Daqing, China, at the cost of more than ten years of delay, a higher oil price, and higher construction expenses. Therefore, what the ESPO shows is not a multilateral cooperation among China, Japan, and

Russia, but Russia's divide-and-rule strategy against China and Japan. Though the ESPO is by a certain definition a multilateral venture, it holds little promise of becoming a region-wide multilateral institution. The gas deal between Russia and China mentioned above also was not a harbinger of multilateral energy cooperation in the region, since it was concluded in the traditional bilateral manner, that is, a long-term commercial contract on energy trading supported and promoted by bilateral governments.

While barriers to energy usage cooperation among energy-consuming countries do not seem as formidable, such cooperation cannot be translated into multilateral cooperation on energy acquisition. Concern for relative gains dominates consuming countries' calculus for energy security on acquisition. Access to fossil energy is usually regarded as a zero-sum game. This explains, to some extent, why there is no joint effort being made by the three major consuming countries in Northeast Asia in dealing with Russia. Facing scarce energy resources, it is predictable that they scramble for favorable deals with the same energy producer in this region. As far as energy usage is concerned, however, consuming countries do not see each other as peer competitors: Technologies and facilities for energy efficiency and environmental protection could be shared, and one country's gain does not necessarily mean another country's loss. Consuming countries' concerns for relative gains in energy usage are not as important as gains in energy acquisition, so consuming countries could pay more attention to absolute gains in energy usage. Even sharing energy reserves with other consumers in emergency situations, which falls into the category of energy usage, does not pose a threat to the energy security of any participant. Since cooperation on energy acquisition and cooperation on energy usage follow very different logics, there is no channel linking them together. Concerns for energy acquisition cannot be eased by progress in energy usage cooperation between consuming counties, so it is impossible for consuming countries to upgrade their cooperation on energy usage to cooperation on energy acquisition at either the bilateral or multilateral level.

Future regime-building for Northeast Asian energy cooperation, in particular on energy acquisition, depends mainly on the contributions of major regional players. Without the proactive participation of Russia and China, for example, no substantial improvement in Northeast Asian energy cooperation can be achieved (Han, 2009). In this effort, the largest energy producing country, Russia, and the largest energy consumer, China, should play more constructive roles. However, China is not taking a constructive role because it cannot afford to implement a multilateral institution that includes the other two energy competitors in Northeast Asia.

China's limited role in Northeast Asian energy regime-building

China's engagement in Northeast Asian energy cooperation can be divided into two types. One is bilateral cooperation with Russia on energy acquisition, as evinced by China's energy strategy, policies, and some specific energy cooperation projects with Russia. The other one is China's involvement in energy usage cooperation with Japan and South Korea, the other main consuming countries in this region. Besides respective bilateral agreements with Japan and South Korea, China has also been quite proactive in working with them jointly, participating in various multilateral forums, meetings, and dialogues. Nonetheless, China sees no imperative to build a regional regime in either energy acquisition or energy usage. This is not only because of China's unwillingness, but also because of its inability.

On energy acquisition, China is not willing to promote regime-building mainly because self-help is its primary approach to energy security, as previously discussed. In the last two decades, constrained by the rules of the international petroleum market and international community, China feels compelled to take a self-sufficient route to secure overseas energy access, and prefers to rely on bilateral relations and long-term contracts with oil-producing countries rather than on multilateral mechanisms. Chinese national oil companies have had to turn to some problematic regimes such as Sudan, Iran, and Myanmar, which are shunned by many international oil companies but enjoy a relatively good relationship with China (Kong, 2010). Since the early 1990s, by investing in and deepening political relations with energy-producing countries around the world, China has steadily developed its petroleum business, including upstream exploration, pipelines, and refinery facilities in a number of countries. More recently, Beijing secured several long-term purchasing agreements in sub-Saharan Africa, the Middle East, Southeast Asia, and South America. For China, individual bilateral cooperation with energy producers is preferable to engagement with them as part of a multilateral energy regime.

On energy acquisition, China's inability to build an energy regime lies in its weakness as a seeker of fossil resources. In Northeast Asia, although China enjoys more fruitful energy cooperation with Russia than do its peer competitors such as Japan and South Korea, its energy relationship with Russia is ambivalent, complex, and asymmetrical in Russia's favor. China's achievements in energy cooperation so far are not sufficient to be scaled up into a region-wide multilateral institution. China–Russia bilateral cooperation on energy acquisition can hardly serve as a building block in this regard. The underachieving energy relationship between Russia and China is partially due to Russia's deep-rooted geopolitical concerns about China and Beijing's mistrust of, and frustration with, Moscow. Russia fears that fueling China's rise would enhance China's threat to the RFE. A dramatic expansion of Russian energy exports to China would undoubtedly heighten Russian fears about becoming a "resource appendage" to China—an unwelcome development that, in the minds of some Russians, would cement Russia's status as the junior partner in the bilateral relationship (Itoh, 2011). Despite the 2009 groundbreaking loans-for-oil deal, the development of Sino-Russo energy relations is likely to continue along a slow and bumpy road. They also have disputes over natural gas issues, such as the gas pricing formula, delaying the construction of a cross-border natural gas pipeline. In the future, Sino-Russo energy cooperation will probably follow a "one step forward, two steps back" pattern (Danchenko *et al.*, 2010).

China is also unwilling and unable to contribute to building a regime for energy usage. Its unwillingness lies in the fact that China does not want to shoulder any unexpected burdens that may come with transfer of energy-saving technologies. Beijing believes that it can improve its energy efficiency and reduce its emissions mainly at its own pace, while it enjoys those technologies without benefit of such regimes. Its inability results from the fact that China is not a provider but a seeker of energy-saving technologies. In Northeast Asia and elsewhere in the world, China is at the receiving end of cooperation with Japan on energy conservation and environment protection. And, to some extent, the Chinese government does not want Japan to take a leadership role in a possible energy-saving regime because of its difficult relationship with Japan in other areas. Even though it has made some progress in energy usage by cooperating with Japan and South Korea through many bilateral and existing open multilateral channels, China does not see a regional regime on energy usage as a desirable option. Moreover, although the Chinese government has already taken part in some multilateral energy proposals or signed some joint agreements with Japan, South Korea, and other countries in the area of energy conservation and environment protection, multilateral energy cooperation in fossil energy involving Northeast Asian producing and consuming states has simply not been considered an option.

China has attempted to make international cooperation a pillar of its energy diplomacy. In 2006, the working report of then the National Energy Leading Small Group (*guojia nengyuan lingdao xiaozu*) asked for a further enlargement of international energy cooperation. It stated that China should proactively engage in international bilateral and multilateral energy cooperation and strengthen dialogues with international energy organizations and cooperation with multinational energy companies. In the *China's Energy Policy 2012* white paper, China further emphasizes "strengthening international cooperation" at both bilateral and multilateral levels in its energy policy (Information Office of the State Council of China, 2012). But China is still a long way from becoming a regime builder for multilateral energy cooperation on either energy acquisition or energy usage in Northeast Asia.

Conclusion

To understand and then promote regional energy cooperation in Northeast Asia and China's role in such cooperation, it is important to differentiate not only the bilateral level from multilateral one, but also energy acquisition from energy usage. Energy-consuming countries usually follow different approaches to their energy security in terms of acquisition and usage. This differentiation has implications for both policy studies and theoretical research that deserve more systematic exploration.

Northeast Asia as China's home region is becoming more and more important in China's strategic calculus for energy security. China's energy diplomacy follows the logic of self-help. While it puts emphasis on bilateral cooperation primarily with energy producer Russia, China's respective bilateral cooperation with

Japan and South Korea as consumers is limited to areas of energy usage other than fossil energy acquisition. China also coordinates with other consuming countries in energy usage both within the region and through other existing multilateral channels beyond the region.

China's role in Northeast Asian energy cooperation is limited, with little contribution to a region-wide multilateral energy institution. Beijing mainly relies on its own resources to secure overseas energy, not on collective action, such as cooperation with other consumers in exploring oil and gas in RFE and East Siberia. In the foreseeable future it is not very likely that Northeast Asian countries will establish multilateral energy cooperation or a so-called Northeast Asian energy community. It is very difficult for these countries to prevent themselves from struggling with each other for energy resource acquisition. It is also very difficult for them to abandon relative interests in competing for overseas energy access with other consumers. For China, it is a realistic option to strengthen its energy relationship with Russia for energy acquisition and coordinate with other consuming countries on energy usage.

A region-wide multilateral institution for energy cooperation is a definite hope for the future, but it is still a long and difficult road for Northeast Asian countries. Only by overcoming the zero-sum competition for energy resources and geopolitical concern can Northeast Asian countries achieve multilateral energy cooperation. To fulfill this goal, effective management of competitive pressures, as well as major obstacles, is a prerequisite for Northeast Asian countries to explore the great potential for their energy cooperation at the regional level. Whether this effort may finally lead to a Northeast Asian energy community remains to be seen.

Notes

1 Northeast Asia in this chapter mainly refers to six countries: China, Japan, North Korea, South Korea, Russia, and Mongolia.
2 Mongolia is analyzed in a separate chapter.

References

ASEAN. 2004. *Singapore Declaration on Climate Change, Energy, and the Environment*. Jakarta: ASEAN.
ASEAN. 2007. *Joint Ministerial Statement of the 8th ASEAN+3 (China, Japan and Korea) Ministers on Energy Meeting*. Jakarta: ASEAN.
ASEAN. 2011. *Forging Closer ASEAN+3 Energy Partnership*. Jakarta: ASEAN.
Blank, S. 2006. *Russo-Chinese Energy Relations: Politics in Command*. London: GMB Publishing.
Blank, S. 2007. China's Emerging Energy Nexus with Central Asia. *China Brief* 6(15), May.
Calder, K.E. 1996. *Pacific Defense: Arms Energy and America's Future in Asia*. New York: William Morrow.
Chen, Z. and Jin, J. 2005. Dongbeiya nengyuan anquan yu dongbeiya nengyuan gongtongti tantao (in Chinese) [On Energy Security and Energy Community in Northeast Asia]. *Dongbeiya Luntan* [*Northeast Asia Forum*] 6: 9–12.

China Daily. 2006. "Go West" Policies Bolster Ties With Central Asia. *China Daily*. Online: www.china.org.cn/english/BAT/184271.htm (accessed March 25, 2013).

China News. 2011. Di sici zhong ri han lingdaoren huiyi xuanyan [Statement of the 4th China–Japan–South Korea Summit]. *China News*, May.

Choo, J. 2006. Energy Cooperation Problems in Northeast Asia: Unfolding the Reality. *East Asia: An International Quarterly* 23(3): 91–106.

Danchenko, I., Downs, E., and Hill, F. 2010. *One Step Forward, Two Steps Back? The Relations of a Rising China and Implications for Russia's Energy Ambitions*. Washington DC: Brookings Institution.

Dan, S. (ed.) 2013. *Zhongguo nengyuan anquan de guoji huanjing* (in Chinese) [*International Environment of China's Energy Security*]. Beijing: Sheke wenxian chubanshe [Social Sciences Academic Press].

Diao, X. 2007. Zhong'e liangguo de nengyuan anquan yu hezuo (in Chinese) [The Energy Security and Cooperation between China and Russia]. *Dongbeiya Luntan* [*Northeast Asia Forum*] 6: 47–52.

Downs, E. 2007. The Fact and Fiction of Sino-African Energy Relations. *China Security* 3(3): 42–68.

El-Gamal, M.A. and Jaffe, A.M. 2010. *Oil, Dollars, Debts, and Crisis: The Global Curse of Black Gold*. New York: Cambridge University Press.

Guan, Q. and He, F. 2007. Zhongguo de nengyuan anquan yu guoji nengyuan hezuo (in Chinese) [China's Energy Security and International Energy Cooperation]. *Shijie Jingji yu Zhengzhi* [*World Economics and Politics*] 11: 45–53.

Han, L. 2009. Eluosi nengyuan chukou zhanlue dongyi yu dongbeiya nengyuan hezuo (in Chinese) [The Eastward Shift of Russia's Energy Export Strategy and Energy Cooperation in Northeast Asia]. *Yafei Zongheng* [*Asia and Africa Review*] 5: 11–16.

Information Office of the State Council of China. 2012. *China's Energy Policy 2012*. Beijing: Information Office of the State Council of China.

Itoh, S. 2008. China's Surging Energy Demand: Trigger for Conflict or Cooperation with Japan? *East Asia: An International Quarterly* 25(1): 79–98.

Itoh, S. 2011. *Russia Looks East: Energy Markets and Geopolitics in Northeast Asia*. Washington, DC: CSIS.

Ivanov, V.I. 2006. Russia's Energy Future and Northeast Asia. *Asia-Pacific Review* 13(2): 46–59.

Kohl, W.L. 2010. Consumer Country Energy Cooperation: The International Energy Agency and the Global Energy Order. In A. Goldthau and J.M. Witte (eds) *Global Energy Governance: The New Rules of the Game*. Berlin: Global Public Policy Institute, pp. 217–19.

Kong, B. 2010. *China's International Petroleum Policy*. Santa Barbara, CA: Praeger Security International.

Lee, H. and Shalmon, D. 2008. China's Oil Strategies in Africa. In R.I. Rotberg (ed.) *China into Africa*. Washington, DC: Brookings Institution, pp. 109–36.

Lee, J.-A. 2009. To Fuel or Not to Fuel: China's Energy Assistance to North Korea. *Asian Security* 5(1): 45–72.

Lieberthal, K. and Herberg, M. 2006. China's Search for Energy Security: Implications for U.S. Policy. *NBR Analysis* 17(1): 10–15.

Lo, B. and Rothman, A. 2006. *China and Russia: Common Interests, Contrasting Perceptions*. Asian Geopolitics Special Report, May.

Miller, A. 2014. Russia and China Signed the Biggest Contract in the Entire History of Gazprom. *Gazprom News*, May 21. Online: www.gazprom.com/press/news/2014/may/article191451/ (accessed June 5, 2014).

Ministry of Foreign Affairs, Japan. 2010. Fukui Declaration on Low Carbon Paths to Energy Security: Cooperative Energy Solutions for a Sustainable APEC. Online: www.mofa.go.jp/policy/economy/energy/pdfs/emm_declaration201006.pdf (accessed January 9, 2012).

New York Times. 2003. China Oil Giant Dealt a Setback. *New York Times,* May 13, p. C9.

Pan, Z. 2007. Sino-Japanese Dispute over the Diaoyu/Senkaku Islands: The Pending Controversy from the Chinese Perspective. *Journal of Chinese Political Science* 12(1): 71–92.

People's Daily Online. 2003. Zhong ri han tuijin sanfang hezuo lianhe xuanyan (in Chinese) [Joint Statement of Promoting Trilateral Cooperation Among China, Japan and South Korea]. Online: en.people.cn (accessed March 12, 2004).

Putin, V. 2012. Eluosi yu Zhongguo: hezuo xintianti (in Chinese) [Russia and China: New Cooperation]. *People's Daily,* June 5.

Rosner, K. 2010. China Scores Again in Energy: Russia and Central Asia. *Journal of Energy Policy,* January 12.

Russian Ministry of Energy. 2010. *Energy Strategy of Russia for the Period up to 2030.* Moscow: Ministry of Energy of the Russian Federation.

Sun, S. 2010. Guoji shiyou gongsi yanjiu (in Chinese) [*A Study on International Oil Companies*]. Shanghai: Shanghai renmin chubanshe [Shanghai People's Publishing House].

Sun, S. 2011. Zhongdong beifei bianju yu xifang shiyou anquan de beilun: jianlun zhongguo de shiyou anquan (in Chinese) [The Middle East and North African Turmoil and Oil Security Dilemma of the West: Reflecting on China's Oil Security]. *Waijiao Pinglun* [*Foreign Affairs Review*] 2: 26–37.

Tkacik, J. 2002. China's Korean Conundrum. *The Asian Wall Street Journal,* December 2.

U.S. Energy Information Administration (EIA). 2011. *International Energy Statistics.* Washington, DC: EIA.

Waltz, K.N. 1979. *Theory of International Politics.* New York: McGraw-Hill.

Wang, J. 2012. "Xijin": zhongguo diyuan zhanlue de zaipingheng (in Chinese) ["Going West": Rebalancing of China's Geopolitical Strategy]. *Global Times,* October 17.

Wang, L. 2009. Zhongguo yu guoji nengyuan jigou: yixiang guifan yanjiu (in Chinese) [China and International Energy Institutions: A Perspective of Norm]. *Guoji Guancha* [*International Review*] 4: 11–17.

Wang, S. 2004. E'ri youqi guanxi de sange cengmian (in Chinese) [The Three Levels of Oil and Gas Relations Between Russia and Japan]. *Dongbeiya Luntan* [*Northeast Asia Forum*] 5: 62–6.

Wu, F. 2009. Zhongshang zhuyi haishi ziyou zhuyi? Shixi xifang xuejie dui zhongguo nengyuan waijiao de zhenglun (in Chinese) [Mercantilism or Liberalism? An Initial Analysis of the Debate Among Western Academic Circles on China's Energy Diplomacy]. *Guoji Luntan* [*International Forum*] 2: 38–43.

Xinhua News Agency. 2012. *Di wuci zhong ri han lingdaoren huiyi guanyu tisheng quanmian zhanlue huoban guanxi de lianhe xuanyan* (in Chinese) [*Joint Statement of the 5th China–Japan–South Korea Summit on Promoting Their Comprehensive Strategic Partnership*]. Online: http://news.xinhuanet.com/world/2012-05/14/c_111944937_2.htm (accessed June 6, 2012).

Xu, B. and Huang, S. 2010. Cong shuangbian boyi dao duobian hezuo: zhongri'r shiyou guanxian zhengduan de anli yanjiu (in Chinese) [From Bilateralism to Multilateralism: The Petroleum Pipeline Dilemma among Russia, China, and Japan]. *Shijie Jingji yu Zhengzhi* [*World Economics and Politics*] 3: 141–54.

Xu, Q. 2007. *China's Energy Diplomacy and Its Implications for Global Energy Security*. *Dialogue on Globalization*, FES Briefing Paper, 13. Beijing: FES.

Yin, X. 2004. Dongbeiya nengyuan hezuo zhong de zhongguo yu riben (in Chinese) [China and Japan in Northeast Asian Energy Cooperation]. *Riben Yanjiu [Japan Studies]* 3: 84–90.

Yoshimatsu, H. 2010. Regional Cooperation in Northeast Asia: Searching for the Mode of Governance. *International Relations of the Asian-Pacific* 10(2): 247–74.

Yu, B. 2006. Hou lengzhan shiqi de zhong'e guanxi (in Chinese) [Sino-Russian Relationship in the Post-Cold War Era]. *Guoji Zhengzhi Yanjiu [International Politics Quarterly]* 2: 116–36.

Zha, D. 2006. China's Energy Security: Domestic and International Issues. *Survival* 4(1), Spring: 179–90.

Ziegler, C.E. 2006. Energy Factor in China's Foreign Policy. *Journal of Chinese Political Science* 11(1): 1–23.

Zweig, D. and Jianhai, B. 2005. China's Global Hunt for Energy. *Foreign Affairs* 84(5). Online: www.foreignaffairs.com/articles/61017/david-zweig-and-bi-jianhai/chinas-global-hunt-for-energy (accessed June 7, 2014).

4 Japan's public–private approach to energy security cooperation in Northeast Asia

Llewelyn Hughes

In this chapter I review the Japanese government's strategy for managing security of energy supplies and the implications of this strategy for regional cooperation and competition. I focus in particular on how the government's approach to Northeast Asian energy security is influenced by the weak commercial position of Japanese firms in international markets, and by the structure of the fuel markets within which they compete.

I make two arguments. First, the supply-side approach taken by the Japanese government toward risk management in the energy sector focuses on diversifying the fuels and the locations from which fuels are imported, and on strengthening the competitive position of domestic firms in international fuel markets. Second, the implications of its approach for the likelihood of regional cooperation and competition are conditioned by the structure of the private markets for fuels. In particular, while often overlooked, *the private regime governing trade and investment in oil and gas enables a significant degree of cooperation between Japan, China, South Korea, Russia, and other countries,* even as the Japanese government maintains parochial elements in its strategy for managing perceived risks associated with fuel imports.

The first part of this chapter describes the strategies pursued by the Japanese government and by Japanese firms as they seek to manage the perceived risks associated with fuel imports. It begins by outlining the capabilities of the government in the energy sector and the most prevalent forms of industrial organization across different fuels. I also discuss how this affects the structure of supply and demand for fuels within the Japanese economy.

In the second section I argue that substantial cooperation occurs between Japan and its neighbors, although this is mediated by private markets rather than by intergovernmental agreements. I also delineate areas in which the Japanese government has actively promoted international cooperation at the intergovernmental level. The third and final section of the chapter considers the effect of the March 11, 2011 Fukushima earthquake and nuclear crisis on the makeup of Japan's energy mix, and how forms of private and public governance are changing as a result of the disaster.

Government interests and firm capabilities

Japan as a country consumes more energy than is produced domestically. This makes it reliant on imports to meet a substantial share of this demand. Japanese firms also control a small share of resources internationally relative to the volumes consumed at home. These enduring facts of Japanese energy supply and demand place the perceived national security risks associated with energy imports at the center of Japanese energy policy.

Japan has few domestic reserves of fossil fuels that are exploitable at competitive prices. Even for coal, which is the most abundant fuel domestically, production is low relative to demand. In 1981, for example, Japan produced 18 percent of total coal consumed domestically, yet this fell to less than 1 percent by 2012. In volume terms, consumption stood at 124.4 million tonnes of oil equivalent (MTOE) of anthracite, bituminous, sub-bituminous and lignite coal in 2012, while firms produced just 700,000 tonnes of oil equivalent domestically.

Japan has even fewer reserves of crude oil and natural gas available. Crude oil consumption domestically stood at 24 million tonnes in 1981 and 204 million tonnes in 2010, yet there is almost no crude oil produced domestically. This is also the case for natural gas, where consumption increased from 22 MTOE in 1981 to 85 MTOE in 2010, and increased once again to 105.1 MTOE in 2012, as Japan's electricity firms substituted nuclear power generation with natural gas following the 2011 disaster (BP, 2012).

The deficit in domestic energy production positions energy security, along with environmental stewardship, at the core of the Japanese government's public policy goals in the energy sector. The Basic Law on Energy, which was passed in 2001 and codified the government's long-standing approach to governance in the energy sector, identifies energy security and environmental stewardship as the most important goals of public policy, with the use of market principles relegated to a third principle. Nuclear energy has been central to this strategy, although its share of the fuel mix has plummeted as a result of the Fukushima disaster of 2011, and its future remains uncertain.

One policy response to the lack of domestic reserves focuses on lowering energy demand per unit of output. The government applies a variety of subsidies, taxes, and regulations to improve the efficiency with which energy is used. Excise taxes are levied on a wide range of energy sources, including crude oil, oil products such as gasoline and diesel, liquid petroleum gas, coal, Organisation for Economic Co-operation and Development (OECD), and electricity.[1] The energy intensity of the Japanese economy is one of the lowest in the OECD, although it has remained static since the 1990s, and the result is not wholly attributable to the incentives put in place by the government.[2] Japan has high population density, for example, relative to many of its peers, reducing demand for transport-related fuels. Energy prices are higher than other OECD countries for reasons unrelated to attempts by the government to lower energy use per unit of output.

The share of manufacturing, which tends to be more energy intensive than the services sector, has fallen as a ratio of total economic output. In addition, there is evidence that Japan's energy efficiency policies are influenced by electoral politics and other considerations that are unrelated to the public policy goal of reducing the amount of energy per unit of economic output (see, for example, Lipscy & Schipper, 2013).

On the supply side, which is the focus of this chapter, the government uses fiscal instruments, in the form of incentives to firms, to diversify the fuels used within the economy to meet energy demand, and the location from which these fuels are sourced.

Geographic diversification aims to reduce political risk by broadening the countries from which fuel is drawn to supply the domestic market, and by lowering producer market power. On the revenue side, public investment since 1972 has been supported by an expansion in the use of special taxes as the revenue base for oil (1972), nuclear power siting (1973), natural gas (1980), and energy efficiency (1993) (Hughes, 2012). In terms of spending, the Japan Oil, Gas and Metals National Corporation (JOGMEC) and the Japan Bank for International Cooperation (JBIC), two state finance corporations, subsidize firms operating in oil and gas, and include geographic diversification as a core criterion for determining which energy-related projects receive state subsidies.

The most important vehicles used to promote fuel diversification through public financing are private sector firms. The government retains an 18.9 percent equity stake in INPEX, along with a preferred share with veto rights that gives it veto power over important managerial decisions.[3] In addition, the government holds a 34 percent share of Japan Petroleum Exploration (JAPEX), with a further 5 percent held indirectly through INPEX.

Given its deep involvement in shaping incentives in the energy sector, the Japanese government unsurprisingly has a well-developed set of institutions through which it integrates industry and other interests as it seeks to shape patterns of energy supply and demand in its favor (Hughes, 2012). The most important entity with responsibility over Japan's energy security policy is the Ministry of Economy, Trade and Industry (METI). Data show that energy and environmental policy, including energy security, has increased within the portfolio of areas that the government is charged with managing: In budgetary terms, energy plays a larger role than other sectors within the METI budget; the number of employees working on energy-related issues has increased in relative terms; and the number of energy-related laws passed by the ministry has increased over time.[4]

The foundations of Japan's energy policy are codified in the Basic Law on Energy. Article Three of the law requires the government to submit a Basic Energy Plan (BEP) to the cabinet every three years, outlining how Japan will achieve energy policy-related goals. This provides industry and the government an opportunity to renegotiate how Japan's energy security, environmental, and other energy-related public policy goals are pursued, both domestically and internationally. As with the standing committees, the BEP is developed through negotiations among the government, industry, and academic and other specialists.

The plan is then submitted to the cabinet for approval and forms the basis for the provision of subsidies and other incentives provided to firms.

Policy in energy security is managed through a series of advisory councils that incorporate the interests of organizations, including those with an interest in energy policy, such as consumer representatives and firms. They also have substantial representation from technical experts. In 2010, for example, of 244 members within these committees, 41 percent were industry representatives, 43 percent were academics, think-tank members, and other researchers, 6 percent were from local and central governments, and 10 percent were from consumer associations and other civil society bodies.

These committees have an important influence on the strategy the Japanese government uses to support exploration and production efforts internationally, as well as the industrial organization of the Japanese energy sector. In response to the poor performance of international investments subsidized by the government, for example, the terms under which project financing is provided to firms was reorganized in the 2000s to reduce the share of risk money provided by the government, on the recommendation of a review committee within the ministry (Hughes, 2014). Project companies invested in by the government were also reorganized in order to increase scale, with one result the completion of a merger between INPEX and Teikoku Oil in 2008. Although small in international terms and not vertically integrated into refining or marketing like its international peers, the firm is positioned as a Japanese "mini-major," and produced 246,000 barrels per day (bpd) of crude and 162,000 barrels of oil-equivalent a day of natural gas in 2013 (INPEX, 2013).

The largely private organization of Japan's energy sector means the Japanese government's energy security strategy unfolds through the provision of subsidies to change the incentives for private sector entities. It also gives firms a substantial role in determining which projects receive support from the state. Two public finance organizations—JOGMEC and JIBC—are particularly important.

The Japan Oil, Gas and Metals National Corporation

The Japan Oil, Gas and Metals National Corporation (JOGMEC) is a public corporation created in 2004 by the Law Concerning the Japan Oil, Gas and Metals National Corporation. It replaced the Japan National Oil Company (JNOC), which was abolished following the poor performance of its investments. JOGMEC is responsible for maintaining the strategic stockpile held by the Japanese government. (Firms with storage capacity in Japan are also required to maintain and make available to the government stocks of oil and oil products for use during supply disruptions.) JOGMEC is also responsible for providing financing to Japanese firms operating in the upstream in oil, natural gas, metals and minerals, coal, and geothermal energy.

Formally, JOGMEC's mission is defined as "making contributions in a wide range of fields, from surveys of oil and gas resources, through exploration, development, production, to stockpiling, as its mission to ensure a stable supply of oil and gas, under Japan's energy policy" (JOGMEC, 2012a, p. 2). It carries out this mission by providing project financing to companies engaged in exploration, development, and production, and by supporting energy-related infrastructure projects such as the development of liquefaction facilities. JOGMEC also finances firms seeking to purchase assets in the upstream. In the exploration phase, where financial risks are greater, JOGMEC provides a substantial share of the exploration costs, up to 75 percent of required capital. For the acquisition of assets, JOG-MEC provides up to 50 percent of the capital needed to move to the production phase, up to a limit of 50 percent of the total investment of the project company.

Financing provided by JOGMEC to project companies requires participation by firms with headquarters in Japan. Firms can, however, engage in joint exploration and development opportunities with non-Japanese firms. Japanese firms are also not required to participate in projects as the operator. JOGMEC also provides financing for the development of natural gas projects and the infrastructure needed to liquefy the gas for maritime transport. JOGMEC's support for firms extends beyond early exploratory work into guaranteeing the liabilities associated with the development of projects, including project financing provided by JBIC. JOGMEC can guarantee up to 75 percent of the debt for financing provided by JBIC or private banks to the Japanese project company participating in the project. Total equity finance provided for oil and gas exploration and production and gas liquefaction facilities to the end of fiscal year 2011 stood at 104.3 billion yen ($1.043 billion at 100 yen to the dollar), with guarantees standing at 250.9 billion yen ($2.509 billion) (JOGMEC, 2012b, p. 27).

In terms of geographic location, projects in the Asia-Pacific region make up the largest number of projects invested in by JOGMEC, with 166 projects (excluding Japan) receiving financing, against 53 projects in the Americas, 33 in Africa, 26 in the Middle East, 21 in Europe, and ten in the former-Soviet Union. In terms of volumes of crude oil lifted, the Asia-Pacific region lies behind the Middle East as the second most important region (JOGMEC, 2012a, pp. 4–6).

Japan Bank for International Cooperation

The second public body with a role in supporting private firms in managing the energy security in oil and gas is the Japan Bank for International Cooperation (JBIC). JBIC has a broader remit than that of JOGMEC, focusing on the provision of public financing to support not only upstream resources acquisition, but also climate change-related activities, as well as providing industry and infrastructure finance, and supporting financial sector stability (JBIC, 2012).[5] In the energy sector, JBIC, like JOGMEC, has the mission of "supporting development/acquisition of resources in the upstream sector and a stable supply of resources." It does so by providing project financing and loan guarantees, focused on the development phase of upstream energy projects. Overseas investment loans made up 60 percent of the total commitments from JBIC in fiscal year 2011.

JBIC's activities are explicitly linked to Japan's international position in energy markets. JBIC notes that lending from within its Energy, Natural Resources and

Environmental Finance Group is driven by increased competition for acquiring and developing upstream resources in order to increase stability of energy supplies into Japan. It further notes that supply risks are increasing because of growing demand in developing states in the Asia-Pacific region. Consistent with the energy strategy developed by the government, JBIC sees geographic and fuel diversification at the core of Japan's strategy to manage security of supply risks. JBIC also identifies overseas financing as an important instrument for improving relations between it and the governments of resource-producing countries. This includes offering financing for packaged infrastructure projects in those countries.

The Asia-Pacific region is an important focus of JBIC investments in the energy sector. In 2011, JBIC signed a memorandum of understanding (MoU) to establish a fund designed to increase energy efficiency in China, with the goal of promoting joint projects between Chinese and Japanese firms using the latter's more advanced environmental technologies. JBIC also signed an MoU with Mongolia's Ministry of Finance, with the goal of increasing economic cooperation between the two countries, including in upstream resources development.

The Asia-Pacific region received the second largest of total JBIC commitments in fiscal year 2011, at 17 percent of total investments, compared with 26 percent for Latin America and the Caribbean, 15 percent in the Middle East, and 14 percent in Europe. Of the 458 billion yen of loans disbursed by JBIC in the natural resources sector in fiscal year 2011, energy-related resources made up 59 percent, with 40 percent of that in natural gas, 12 percent in coal and 7 percent in crude oil (JBIC, 2012, pp. 84–6). In fiscal year 2011, on the one hand, export loans were provided at between 1.1 percent and 1.39 percent, depending on the length of the repayment period, with an upper limit of 60 percent of the total project financing able to be covered by JBIC. For overseas investment loans, import loans, and untied loans, on the other hand, the rate stood at 0.875 percent, with an upper limit of 60 percent applied once again (JBIC, 2012, p. 97).

To summarize, the government has significant institutional capacity in the energy sector, in terms of both policy development and the deployment of state resources. The government's interest in developing these capabilities is to promote security of energy supplies through the geographic diversification of supply across the markets for different fuels, and by diversifying fuel types themselves, in order to reduce the risks associated with the over-reliance on any given fuel type. It has also sought to enhance the competitiveness of domestic firms in the energy sector. The next section discusses how this has helped affect the structure of energy supply and demand within the Japanese economy, and the competitiveness of Japanese firms.

Japanese firm capabilities

The government has had some success in diversifying fuels, particularly increasing its use of nuclear power. It has been less successful, however, in promoting domestic firms' competitiveness. Japan does not have an integrated and diversified energy firm operating across multiple fuels and stages of production. Instead, it has multiple firms that tend to operate within discrete fuel markets in terms of the final delivery of energy. The exceptions to this are the Japanese trading companies. These firms operate in the upstream segment across multiple fuels, but are not integrated across the supply chain, preferring instead to supply fuels to other firms for processing, distribution, and marketing to the final consumer. In the case of oil and gas, they also typically participate financially in return for a share of production, rather than acting as operators.

Across each of the most important fuels there are thus a number of firms that focus on that sector, generating a variety of forms of corporate organization across different fuels and at different stages of the supply chain. This is also the case in electricity, where the most important electric power companies (EPCOs) manage generation across different fuels and have traditionally been vertically integrated, but have not transformed into a general energy firm model with operations encompassing upstream fuel production in addition to electricity generation, transmission, and sales.

Japanese firms in oil and natural gas are thus weak compared with those based in other major industrialized economies. Only one Japanese firm is ranked in Platts' index of the top 50 energy firms, with only five firms in the top 100. The highest-ranked firm is JX Holdings, which stands at number 45, followed by INPEX Corporation (59), Tokyo Gas (68), Tonen General (82), and Idemitsu Kosan (94). Returns on investment are also relatively poor. JX Holdings, for example, ranks 177th in terms of its return on capital invested (ROIC), while INPEX stands at 97th, Tokyo Gas 83rd, Tonen General 47th, and Idemitsu Kosan 184th (see Table 4.1).

Table 4.1 Global ranking of Japanese energy firms

Firm	Industry	Global rank	Assets (U.S.$ million)	Rank	ROIC (%)	Rank
JX Holdings	Refining	45	73,332	32	3	177
INPEX Corp.	E&P	59	36,451	78	6	97
Tokyo Gas	Gas utility	68	20,084	128	6	83
Tonen General	Refining	82	13,961	175	9	47
Idemitsu Kosan	Refining	94	27,503	104	3	184
Osaka Gas	Gas utility	120	15,795	156	4	148
Tokyo Electric	Electric utility	162	151,092	15	−8	315
Chubu Electric	Electric utility	168	59,299	45	−1	292
Kansai Electric	Electric utility	174	76,963	28	−4	307
EPDC	IPP*	175	21,873	120	2	243
Tohoku Electric	Electric utility	199	43,187	69	−3	298
Kyushi Electric	Electric utility	209	45,628	59	−10	320
Showa Shell	Refining	214	12,431	188	0	281
Chugoku Electric	Electric utility	215	29,226	101	−1	293

Source: Based on data taken from Platts' *Top 250 Energy Companies 2013* (http://top250.platts.com/).

Note: *Independent power producer.

In addition, Japan's group companies within the diversified trading houses of Mitsubishi, Mitsui, Sumitomo, Itochu, and Marubeni take physical positions upstream, and have also benefited from the government's willingness to underwrite project risk through financing and loan provision. They typically do not act as operators, however, instead taking a financial position in return for a share of production. Mitsubishi Exploration, for example, invests in oil and liquefied natural gas (LNG) projects in West Africa, the Asia-Pacific region, the Gulf of Mexico, and the North Sea, and is invested in the Sakhalin-2 project. Mitsui Oil Exploration also has positions globally, although it seldom functions as an operator, preferring instead to hold rights to gas and oil produced from fields in which it is invested. Group companies within the trading firms also take physical positions in upstream coal development and production, including investments in Australia.

Japanese energy firms remain weak on a global basis despite long-standing attempts by the government to improve their competitiveness. A particular focus has been on creating a vertically integrated oil and gas major that can function as an operator and can compete with major integrated firms. As Table 4.1 shows, however, Japanese firms operating in oil remain largely vertically and horizontally fragmented. In the case of refining, the government erected barriers to trade in order to protect the domestic refining industry; this, however, has tended to encourage industry fragmentation rather than increase scale. The negative effect of import barriers on refining firms' performance can be seen in the effects of the liberalization of importation of refined products, which began in 1986 and was driven both by a recognition of the failure of protectionism to promote scale among Japan's refiners and by demands from industry and consumers for lower costs. Import liberalization led to substantial reorganization of the industry, including mergers and acquisitions, although returns in the refining segment of the industry remain low.

Beginning in 1995, the Japanese government also implemented limited liberalization of the regional monopoly model that historically provided supply in both the gas and power sectors. Demand in the power sector has been met by ten regional monopolies (including Okinawa), and while liberalization of the power sector saw limited decreases in electricity prices, there have been few new market entrants. The regional power monopolies have also largely avoided competing in each other's service areas.[6] Similarly, in the case of gas, Japan has a limited domestic pipeline infrastructure centered on the major population hubs of Kansai and Tokyo, with supply met by Osaka Gas and Tokyo Gas, but little direct competition between them.[7] Both Japanese gas and power firms remain overwhelmingly domestic in orientation, and have not diversified beyond their traditional business areas. This stands in contrast to the diversified, multinational energy business models chosen by ENI (Italy), Centrica (United Kingdom), Iberdrola (Spain), E.ON (Germany), and RWE (Germany).

The result—Japan's energy landscape

Oil continues to dominate primary energy supply to the Japanese economy, largely because substitutes for oil products used in transportation are unavailable at competitive prices.[8] The Japanese government intervened heavily in the energy sector in its attempt to reduce the role of oil, and this has affected the types of fuels used by final consumers.[9] Prior to the 2011 disaster, which has had a profound effect on the fuel mix in Japanese electricity generation, crude oil made up approximately 41 percent of the country's Total Primary Energy Supply (TPES), due to the continued dominance of gasoline and diesel in the transportation sector.

Within the electricity sector, the diversification of fuels has focused on nuclear power, which constituted approximately 20 percent of the installed power generation and 26 percent of total generated electricity prior to the 2011 disaster. Natural gas stood at approximately 24 percent of generation capacity and 28 percent of generated electricity. Coal was 16 percent of generation capacity and 25 percent of generated electricity; oil was 19 percent of generation capacity and 13 percent of generated electricity. Finally, renewable energy sources, including hydropower, stood at 21 percent of generation capacity and 9 percent of generated electricity (METI, 2010).[10]

Incentives to shift the balance of fuels away from substitutes for oil (and coal) have thus demonstrated some success. This has also led to greater diversification of suppliers across all fuels, although within single fuel segments, suppliers remain geographically concentrated.

Crude supplies remain focused in the Middle East, with Saudi Arabia supplying almost a third of total crude imports in 2011 (31.1 percent), the United Arab Emirates 22.5 percent, Qatar 10.2 percent, Iran 7.8 percent, and Kuwait 7 percent. Russia is the largest producer outside the Middle East, supplying 4.1 percent of total imports in 2011, with the Middle East standing at 85.1 percent of total imports.[11] Natural gas suppliers are more diversified geographically. Total imports from the Middle East stood at 29.5 percent in 2011. Major exporters outside the Middle East were Malaysia (18.2 percent), Australia (16.3), Indonesia (9.5), Russia (9.3), and Brunei (7.4). Finally, coal supplies are less diversified, but are focused on areas with less geopolitical risk. Most notably, Australia represents 61.5 percent of total imports, followed by Indonesia (19.4 percent), Russia (6.5), and Canada (5.1).

Japan's energy security regime thus extends across a range of different fuels, each of which presents the government and firms with different challenges in terms of securing energy supplies. Firms tend to be vertically specialized and operate within particular fuel markets; Japan does not have the kind of diversified energy group found in Italy with ENI, or in France with Total. While the government has significant institutional capabilities in developing and implementing energy policy, its ability to shape energy markets in order to improve Japanese energy supply security is constrained both by the capabilities of private sector firms and by the structure of the fuel markets these firms operate in. The complexity of managing energy security within these markets has increased as a result of the 2011 disaster, and the consequent drop of nuclear power within Japan's energy mix.

Implications for energy cooperation and competition

What are the implications of the Japanese government's strategy for managing the energy security risks described above, and for cooperation and competition in Northeast Asia? The Japanese government identifies the rise of demand in the Asia-Pacific region as a factor increasing energy security risks, thus requiring greater effort to improve the competitive position of domestic firms in international markets. The 2010 BEP noted the rise of demand in the region as justification for reinvigorating public financing of upstream subsidy development, for example, as well as identifying increased competition for securing the rights to exploit upstream resources.[12] This leads some analysts to raise concerns about the risks associated with state-backed competition among firms based in the Northeast Asian states and the governments that support them.

This section posits that focusing on the prospects for interstate cooperation or competition between states alone misses the crucial role that *the private regime governing trade and investment in oil, gas, coal, and other natural resource markets plays in promoting cooperation between firms based in the Northeast Asian states.* This means that parochial efforts to promote the interests of firms headquartered in Japan are leading to cooperation, although this is mediated by private markets rather than intergovernmental agreements.

The private regime governing trade and investment in natural resources has two characteristics. First, the central participants are private actors rather than states.[13] Second, the regime is focused on voluntary contracting between these private actors (Abbott & Snidal, 2010). This does not mean that states are irrelevant, but rather that they play a secondary role by influencing the incentives of private actors through subsidizing the businesses' activities, controlling managerial appointments, and other policy instruments. Governments in resource-producing countries are also able to determine the distribution of wealth associated with the exploitation of those resources.

In the case of fossil fuels, this private, voluntary contracting enables multiple firms to bid for, and participate in, the financing and development of energy-related projects. As described below, this makes it possible for China, South Korea, and Japan to cooperate in the joint development of energy resources, and meet the perceived risks associated with energy imports, even as governments subsidize domestic firms in order to promote energy security.

Cooperation in the private regime governing resource markets

Access to the rights to exploit upstream resources is often portrayed as a zero-sum game that generates important security concerns. There is little doubt that competition can be intense, as firms, backed by home governments, seek to secure the rights to develop oil and gas fields and to increase the share of production they receive from them. Competition for upstream resources has also been used by governments, including in Japan, to justify the reinvigoration of support for firms developing resources in oil and natural gas upstream.

Yet, despite this framing of upstream resource competition, evidence shows substantial cooperation in oil and natural gas between Japanese companies, backed by the Japanese government, with firms based elsewhere in Northeast Asia. This cooperation is mediated through private contracts, however, rather than through intergovernmental agreements at the bilateral or regional level.

Proven reserves of crude oil in the Asia-Pacific region, and in Northeast Asia in particular, are limited. Data show that the Asia-Pacific holds just 2.5 percent of global proven crude oil reserves. Other than in China, which has 0.9 percent of global proven reserves, countries in Northeast Asia have negligible reserves of crude available to be exploited domestically (BP, 2012). Proven reserves of natural gas in the Asia-Pacific and Russia are a larger share of global reserves than is the case for crude oil. Proven reserves of natural gas in the Asia-Pacific were 8 percent of the global total in 2011, with Russia holding 21.4 percent. The Middle East, however, held 38.4 percent of the global total, against 48.1 percent of proven reserves of crude oil in the Middle East, 5.3 percent for Russia, and just 2.5 percent for the Asia-Pacific.

The Asia-Pacific was responsible for 14.6 percent of total gas produced globally in 2011, with China at 3.1 percent, Indonesia at 2.3 percent, Malaysia at 1.9 percent, and Australia at 1.4 percent of this total. The Middle East, however, represented 16 percent of global gas production, while Europe and Eurasia were at 31.6 percent, with Russia responsible for 18.5 percent of that. This contrasts with oil, where in 2011 the Asia-Pacific made up 9.7 percent of global production, 5.1 percent of which is China, while the Middle East made up 32.6 percent, and Europe and Eurasia were responsible for 21 percent of global production in 2011, of which 12.8 percent was Russia.

The goals of fuel and geographic diversification, coupled with the less carbon-intensive nature of natural gas, make it an increasingly important share of the energy mix throughout Northeast Asia, including in Japan. Japan dominated the consumption of natural gas in the Asia-Pacific region before the rise in Chinese demand. In 1990, Japanese consumers made up 31.1 percent of total demand, while China stood at 9.9 percent. This shifted in 2011, with Japan responsible for 17.9 percent of total regional demand, compared with 22.1 percent in China (BP, 2012).[14] The absence of regional pipeline infrastructure means gas reaches the Japanese market as liquefied natural gas, before being regasified to allow distribution through the domestic pipeline network.

In the 1990s, Japan and South Korea were responsible for approximately 70 percent of total LNG demand in the Pacific (Ebinger *et al.*, 2012). China has substantial domestic reserves of natural gas, in contrast to Japan. While infrastructure constraints remain, investments in pipelines also enable natural gas to play an increasingly important role in the energy mix on China's east coast. In addition, Chinese firms the China National Offshore Oil Corporation (CNOOC) and the China National Petroleum Corporation (CNPC) signed a series of long-term contracts through the 2000s, and are constructing new LNG terminal capacity to land the new supplies (Higashi, 2009). This is likely to lead to a shift in the relative market share of Japan regionally.

Most important, the flexible structure of private contracting means that, while access to both oil and gas reserves upstream is often portrayed in zero-sum terms, efforts by the Japanese government to improve the position of domestic firms in the international oil market have not precluded cooperation with other states in Northeast Asia. On a bilateral basis, in 1978 Japan and China inked a long-term trade agreement for the period 1978–85. In return for Japan exporting machinery and materials to China, the latter agreed to export crude oil to Japan from the Daqing field, as well as coking and steam coal for use in steel fabrication and power generation. Beginning in 1978, Japanese firms explored for and developed offshore reserves in the Bohai Sea, and in December 1979 the two countries signed the Agreement on the Joint Exploration and Exploitation of Petroleum and Natural Gas. The agreement covered more than 25,000 square kilometers in the Bohai Sea. Exploratory drilling commenced in December 1980 (Lee, 1984, p. 22).

More importantly, recent cases from the oil industry demonstrate the ability of the private regime governing natural resource markets to bring about bilateral cooperation between Chinese and Japanese firms. The Japanese refinery market has struggled with overcapacity since the 1980s and 1990s. One response has been to orient domestic refineries to meet rising demand in other markets. Given this, in 2004 JX Nippon Oil and Energy (formerly Nippon Oil) signed an agreement with PetroChina to export a share of its oil products refined in Japan into the Chinese market, thus facilitating the integration of trade flows between the two economies. Cooperation was deepened in 2010 when PetroChina then bought a 49 percent stake in JX Nippon Oil's Takaishi refinery, located in Osaka, with the two firms forming a joint venture structure to use the refinery for supplying oil products to the Asian market using PetroChina's regional marketing capabilities.

Regional energy security cooperation occurs through the market-based activities of Northeast Asian firms, even absent formal cooperation between firms in the form of cross-border acquisitions or joint marketing agreements such as those described above. Exports of oil products to Japan from South Korea, for example, grew significantly in the wake of the 2011 disaster, which harmed Japan's refinery capacity, reaching $7.39 billion in 2011, and making Japan the second-largest market for South Korean product exports after China (Yonhap News Agency, n.d.). Over 2013, Japanese consumers imported an average of over 160,000 kiloliters of gasoline monthly from South Korea, over 380,000 kiloliters of naphtha, and almost 140,000 kiloliters of heavy oil. They also imported products from China, although more intermittently.[15]

Cooperation through the private regime governing energy markets also occurs in natural gas. The market structure of gas differs substantially from that of crude oil both because it is more regionalized and because the political risks associated with producer countries differ. There is nevertheless also evidence of cooperation between firms. In Indonesia, the largest oil and gas upstream developer in Japan— INPEX—participates in the Tangguh gas field, along with a number of other

Japanese firms, including the Mitsubishi Corporation, Nippon Oil Exploration, Mitsui and Company, and the Sumitomo Corporation. Production began in 2009, with BP as the main operator of the project. CNOOC also participates through a 13.9 percent stake. Similarly, in the Prelude Floating LNG project in Western Australia, Shell acts as operator of Permit Area WA-44-L, controlling 72.5 percent of the rights to the project, INPEX controlling 17.5 percent, and the South Korean KOGAS (Korea Gas Corporation) controlling 10 percent of the project. In addition, KOGAS agreed to purchase 3.64 million tonnes a year from Shell's LNG global supply portfolio. Taiwan's CPC controls a 5 percent stake in the project, and signed an agreement to buy 2 million tonnes per year for 20 years from Shell, beginning in 2016 (Wilkinson, 2012).

Another case of cooperation is Nexen, which is based in Canada and owns a portfolio of oil and gas projects in the North Sea, West Africa, the United States, and Canada. The firm became a wholly owned subsidiary of China's CNOOC after the latter acquired it in 2013. Nexen is also a partner with INPEX and JGC Corporation, both Japanese firms, in the development of shale gas projects in the Cordova, Horn River, and Liard basins in Alberta, Canada, with the gas expected to be converted to LNG for shipping to Asian markets. The acquisition of Nexen has not altered the commercial terms agreed to by the Japanese firms, meaning the latter are cooperating in joint project development, rather than simply being financial investors in which a third firm acts as operator.

In addition, Shell has proposed constructing an LNG facility on the coast of British Columbia in Canada with South Korea's KOGAS, the CNPC, and Japan's Mitsubishi Corporation. The project includes a natural gas receiving and LNG production facility, and a marine terminal capable of accommodating two LNG carriers, with the goal of transporting gas across the Pacific to Northeast Asia. The facility is designed to be able to process up to 24 million tonnes per annum of LNG, and is expected to operate for 25 years (McCarthy, 2012; LNG Canada, 2013).

Governments are not irrelevant to this cooperation. In many cases Japanese firms are supported financially by the government through subsidies and other forms of support as they engage in projects internationally in order to increase their share of exploration and production activities. While headlines often focus on competition between Japan and China over resource access, Japanese firms, with the support of public financing from the government, are nevertheless involved in a number of cooperative ventures with Chinese and South Korean firms.

Japanese consortia are also involved in projects in Russia, most notably the Sakhalin-1 project, which is operated by Exxon-Neftegas, a subsidiary of ExxonMobil. A Japanese consortium, Sakhalin Oil & Gas Development Company (SODECO), owns 30 percent of the project, with an investment of $3.6 billion in the $12 billion project. JOGMEC agreed in 2010 to provide liability guarantees covering 50 percent of the loan to SODECO in developing the first stage of the Odoptu field. The Japanese government also participates directly in the project through its stake in JAPEX, which is a member of the SODECO consortium. In 2013, Rosneft and SODECO, which are partners in Sahkalin-1, signed a long-term contract for Rosneft to supply 1 million tons of LNG annually, with delivery to begin in 2019 (Rosneft, 2013a). Rosneft also has an agreement to sell LNG from the Russian Far East to Marubeni Corporation, beginning in 2019 (Rosneft, 2013b). Japanese firms Mitsui (12.5 percent) and Mitsubishi (10 percent) are also invested in Sakhalin-2. Once again project financing is provided by the Japanese government, through JBIC, which provided $3.7 billion in financing. Sakhalin-2 is expected to meet about 8 percent of Japan's total LNG imports. More limited volumes of crude are also produced (JBIC, 2008).

Hard cases: pipelines and territorial disputes

Efforts by the Japanese government to diversify suppliers and promote the competitiveness of domestic firms have thus not precluded cooperation among firms and governments in China, South Korea, and Russia, though this is most commonly mediated by commercial arrangements rather than interstate agreements. There are nevertheless cases in which attempts to promote the diversification of suppliers have seen governments replace firms as the central actors in managing competition and negotiating cooperation. An important case is the financing of the construction of a pipeline to enable the transportation of East and West Siberian oil to markets in the Asia-Pacific, and competition between China and Japan over the development of gas fields in the East China Sea. The pipeline matters because it unlocks stranded oil and gas reserves in East and West Siberia.[16] For consumers in Northeast Asia, access to Russian oil reserves enables the diversification of supply from the Middle East. This is also the case in Japan, where analysts argue that oil and gas resources in Siberia are attractive because of their proximity to Japan and their potential to contribute to the improvement of energy-related infrastructure in the Asia-Pacific. There are also commercial benefits of securing access to Russian oil: A tanker journey from Nakhodka to Japan takes approximately three days. This compares to an average of 20 days from the Middle East, thus enabling refiners to reduce inventory costs.

The Japanese government supported the development of infrastructure enabling the transportation of East Siberian oil to markets in the Asia-Pacific. The first Basic Energy Plan released by the Agency for Natural Resources and Energy (ANRE) in 2003 noted the usefulness of an Eastern Siberia–Pacific Ocean (ESPO) oil pipeline for diversifying supply from the Middle East (ANRE, 2002, pp. 23–4). Japanese Prime Minister Junichiro Koizumi noted Japan's interest in supporting the construction of a pipeline to Nadhodka during a state visit to Moscow in January 2003. The head of ANRE visited Russia five times in the same year, and reports suggest the Japanese government proposed $7 billion in financing through JBIC, with $5 billion earmarked for the pipeline (*Chunichi Shimbun*, 2003; Buszynski, 2006; Minoura, 2011, pp. 39–40).

In November 2005 the two governments announced a program for energy cooperation, noting both countries' desire to develop a "long-term strategic partnership" in the energy sector, encompassing oil, gas, and coal project development and processing, as well as cooperation in energy efficiency and renewable energy technologies. The agreement specifically noted the interest of both governments in promoting cooperation in the ESPO, and in the development of oil and gas reserves in Sakhalin.

After protracted negotiations between the Japanese, Chinese, and Russian governments, the ESPO is being completed in two phases, with the latter stage connecting East Siberian oil to the Pacific coast. The pipeline already supplies Russian oil to East Asian markets, including both China and Japan, representing an important shift in the balance of supply. Previously, Russian oil flowed almost exclusively west to European markets. From 2010, crude began to flow to East Asia through the ESPO, with an average of 300,000 barrels a day exported through 2010 (Motomura, 2012). Construction of stage one of the pipeline (ESPO-1) began in April 2006 and was completed in October 2009, with oil shipped by rail to the Kozmino terminal on the Pacific coast for export. Shipments to Japan began in February 2010, with Japan supplied with 30 percent of total ESPO crude in 2010, with South Korea taking 29 percent, the United States 16 percent, Thailand 11 percent, China 8 percent, the Philippines 3 percent, Singapore 2 percent, and Taiwan 1 percent.[17] The second stage of the ESPO (ESPO-2) connects directly to the Kozmino port, although questions remain regarding the volumes of crude that will be available.

The East China Sea

The most intractable energy dispute in Northeast Asia concerns the right to exploit gas reserves in and near a disputed area of the East China Sea. Bilateral attempts to jointly develop gas and oil reserves that are located in the disputed Exclusive Economic Zone (EEZ) claimed by both countries have stalled.

Differences in the geological claims that form the basis of the dispute are summarized elsewhere.[18] The resource potential of the East China Sea was first noted by a survey by the Economic Commission for Asia and the Far East in 1969. Following basic seismic testing, the survey team noted that "sediments beneath the continental shelf and in the Yellow Sea are believed to have great potential as oil and gas reservoirs," and that "a high probability exists that the continental shelf between Taiwan and Japan may be one of the most prolific oil reservoirs in the world." It also noted that detailed seismic testing, as well as exploratory drilling, was required to determine the size of the resource base (Emery et al., 1969, pp. 4, 41).[19]

Today, estimates of the total amount of oil and gas reserves exploitable in the East China Sea vary. The U.S. Energy Information Administration (EIA) estimates between 60 million and 100 million barrels of proven and provable oil reserves, far short of the optimistic assessment of the 1969 UN survey. Estimates for natural gas stand at between 1 trillion and 2 trillion cubic feet, although assessments produced by CNOOC are more optimistic (U.S. Energy Information Administration, n.d.).

The commercial value of the reserves remains an open question. Since 1992, CNOOC has contracted with 16 non-Chinese firms to conduct exploratory drilling around the area of Chunxiao; all, however, were dry.[20] In 2003, the China Petroleum and Chemical Corporation (Sinopec), with a 30 percent share, signed an agreement with CNOOC (30 percent), Shell (20 percent), and Unocal (20 percent) to jointly explore for, develop, and market gas and oil resources in the East China Sea, with CNOOC functioning as operator. CNOOC booked 21 million barrels of oil and 402 billion cubic feet of gas in net reserves in 2005 (China.org, n.d.).[21] Shell and Unocal, the foreign partners of CNOOC and Sinopec, withdrew from the joint agreement to develop gas reserves after the appraisal stage, however, citing uncertainty about reserves and development costs.[22] Sinopec downgraded its proven oil and gas reserves in 2004, citing a reclassification of reserves booked from the Xihu trough in the East China Sea (China Petroleum and Chemical Corporation, 2003, p. 18).

Regardless, the development of oil and gas resources in the East China Sea remains a source of tension between the Japanese and Chinese governments. An important reason is that, unlike the other cases described in this chapter, the energy problem in the East China Sea overlays a sovereignty dispute. Both governments have thus been careful to ensure that the behavior of the other does not compromise their territorial claims. In a press conference on June 22, 2004, the press secretary of the Ministry of Foreign Affairs noted the Japanese government's concern over the right to exploit resources within sovereign territory, and the possibility that the commercialization of the gas field at Chunxiao may contravene this right: "As Foreign Minister Kawaguchi pointed out, even if the exploration takes place on the part, even from our understanding, of China's sovereign rights, it may lead to the exploitation of natural resources which actually lie under Japan's sovereign rights" (Ministry of Foreign Affairs, Japan, 2004).

The center of negotiations between the two governments is the Chunxiao oil and gas field (referred to as Shirakaba in Japanese). In August 2003, China began to construct a production platform at the field, located approximately 5 kilometers from the median line proposed by Japan as a potential settlement for the maritime territorial dispute in the East China Sea between the two countries. The Japanese government expressed its concern about the development of the field, requesting that information on the structure of the field be provided to Japan so that it could determine whether the gas reserves in the field could be located across the proposed median line. After conducting seismic testing on Japan's side of the proposed median line between 2004 and 2005, it announced that both the Chunxiao and Duanqiao (Kusunoki) fields breached the median line, and that there was a possibility that the Tianwaitien (Kashi) field is also connected (METI, 2005).

The two governments began consultations over the East China Sea in 2004. In 2008, they reached a Principled Consensus on the East China Sea Issue, which included an agreement to carry out joint exploration activities within an area overlapping the median line, thus attempting to use state resources to facilitate private sector cooperation. It also allowed for equity participation by Japanese firms in the development of the Chunxiao field, and the joint development of gas fields over the median line, without prejudicing the maritime claims made by the two countries (Ministry of Foreign Affairs, Japan, n.d.). In March 2011, however, a representative of CNOOC announced the firm had begun to produce at the Chunxiao field. The Japanese government interpreted the shift to the production phase as breaking the agreement reached between the two governments. In July 2013, news media reported that CNOOC had submitted plans to develop seven further fields on the Chinese side of the median line to the Chinese government. In Japan, Secretary General Suga of the Liberal Democratic Party stated the government had noted its "grave concern" to China regarding this change. Prime Minister Abe Shinzo also referred to this as "clearly in contravention to the agreement" reached between the two countries (*Asahi Shinbun*, 2013a, 2013b).

March 11, 2011 and the prospects for Northeast Asian energy cooperation

The Japanese government's energy security strategy has thus focused on two goals: diversifying the fuels and the geographic location of imports, and promoting the competitiveness of domestic firms. This has met with mixed success. While the range of fuels used by Japanese consumers is more diverse than would have been the case absent government intervention, Japanese firms operating in oil and gas remain weak in international terms.

The parochial attempt to improve the competitive position of Japanese firms in international resource markets has nevertheless not precluded cooperation between Japanese firms and firms based in other countries in the region. There are numerous examples, detailed above, of firms from Japan, China, and South Korea jointly participating in oil and gas projects, as well as in marketing and sales in refining, even when sponsored explicitly or implicitly by their home governments. The private regime governing oil and gas thus functions to ameliorate any security implications associated with the approaches adopted by these countries.

An important exception noted above lies in the dispute between Japan and China over the development of gas and oil reserves located in a region of the East China Sea. The dispute has thus far proven impossible for the two governments to mediate, in part because it is complicated by a disagreement over maritime sovereignty. A second reason may lie in the poor competitive position of Japanese oil firms relative to their Chinese counterparts. While the Japanese and Chinese governments initially negotiated equity participation for Japanese firms in the Chunxiao field and joint development of fields in the northern area within disputed maritime boundaries in the East China Sea, INPEX has little technology to offer CNOOC or other Chinese firms, compared with Shell and Unocal, CNOOC's original partners in the East China Sea development. CNOOC management has also noted that it has little need for Japanese financing in the project. It is thus plausible that the difficulty in negotiating a resolution in the East China Sea reflects the commercial interests of Chinese firms, in addition to the zero-sum structure of the maritime dispute.[23]

This final section examines how the March 11, 2011 tsunami and nuclear disaster have affected Japanese energy planning, and what the implications of this change are likely to be for regional cooperation in energy security.

For decades, nuclear power was central to the Japanese government's strategy for managing energy security and environmental problems. Nuclear power was positioned by the government as low cost relative to fossil fuels on a per kilowatt-hour basis. It was also positioned as less risky in geopolitical terms than other fuels, and useful for meeting the government's climate change commitments. Echoing this, the 2010 BEP established a target of constructing nine additional nuclear units by 2020, and more than 14 by 2030, while also increasing the capacity utilization rate, with the goal of increasing the share of nuclear power to 50 percent of total electricity generated. In contrast, coal-fired generation was targeted to fall in terms of installed capacity and generated electricity by 2030, as was natural gas.

It is unsurprising, given this, that the disaster is fundamentally reorganizing the structure of supply and demand for electricity. The revised BEP, released publicly in February 2014, signals a smaller role for nuclear power in Japan's energy mix than had been envisioned in the previous plan. Indeed, the establishment of an independent safety regulator—housed separately from the industry regulator in the Ministry of Environment—institutionalizes a new constraint on the development of nuclear generation. The law establishing the regulatory agency also enshrined in law a limit to the operation of nuclear units of 40 years, extendable by 20 years if the regulator finds the plant meets safety requirements. Given that the first-generation units became operational in Japan beginning in 1970, this increases the institutional constraint on the further use of nuclear energy.

The revised BEP continues to emphasize nuclear power as an important source of energy that meets Japan's energy security, environment, and economic goals. Its future share in Japan's electricity generation mix remains uncertain, however, and depends on public opinion, the commercial health of Japan's electricity utilities, how the government chooses to manage the spent-fuel reprocessing program, and other factors. A further influence on the development of nuclear power within Japan's generation mix is the reform of the electricity market and how this will affect the willingness and ability of the private-sector electricity utilities to finance the costs of additional nuclear capacity.

The implications of this change in the relative importance of fuels within Japan has mixed implications for the prospects of cooperation between Northeast Asian states. Regardless of the future status of nuclear power, the 2011 disaster promises to increase state support for Japanese firms' attempts to procure resources internationally. The 2014 BEP notes that the fundamental weakness of Japan's energy system is its reliance on non-domestic resources and the 2011 disaster has increased the reliance on imported fossil fuels, particularly from the Middle East (METI, 2014). Data bear out this conclusion. The loss of nuclear power led utilities to increase the amount of oil-fired power generation, for example, rising in 2011 from 2.2 percent to 12.8 percent of electricity generated. Japan's electricity utilities also planned on adding 5.2 gigawatts of natural gas capacity to the

66.3 gigawatts (7.8 percent) already in operation in 2014.[24] To manage the loss of nuclear power, the government shortened the environmental assessment period for coal-fired thermal capacity, easing the replacement of nuclear power with coal following negotiations between the Ministry of the Environment and METI (*Nikkei Asian Review*, n.d.). In the new energy plan, coal was also repositioned as an important baseload fuel in Japan's electricity generation mix (METI, 2014, p. 20).

The response of the Japanese government to this shift, unsurprisingly, is to re-emphasize the importance of strengthening the competitiveness of Japanese firms in fuel procurement internationally:

> Taking into consideration our country's energy supply structure, which has a high degree of reliance on overseas resources, and weakening domestic energy demand, domestic firms must positively promote internationalization, strengthen overseas operations, and actively work to develop overseas demand as their own market, if the energy sector is to contribute to stability of energy supplies, and further strengthen its competitiveness.
>
> (METI, 2014, p. 15)

This may serve to increase the importance of the private regime governing natural resources, by enhancing Japan's energy security, and, by extension, increase opportunities for cooperation among firms based in Japan and elsewhere. Nevertheless, Japanese firms face daunting challenges in improving their competitive position internationally. Nine of every ten barrels of global oil reserves are controlled by national oil companies, limiting the ability of firms to increase scale. This problem is exacerbated by ongoing political risk in countries such as Iraq and Libya, where new opportunities exist that could potentially be exploited by firms other than the national oil companies. Stagnant demand for oil products and the poor performance of refiners in Japan reduce the merits of vertical integration for upstream operators. In addition, Japanese firms lack the technical expertise of their competitors, which might give them a commercial advantage in bidding for positions in areas where it is more difficult to operate. Given this, JOGMEC is identified as crucial in supporting state efforts to strengthen the international position of domestic firms in the upstream through the provision of risk money.

In addition, the Japanese government has identified the possibility of greater formal intergovernmental cooperation in order to improve the negotiating power of consumer states through initiatives such as the Japan–South Korea Gas Dialogue, and the LNG Producer–Consumer Dialogue. The second Dialogue conference was held in Tokyo in September 2013 and included representatives from South Korea, Taiwan, and India, in addition to private sector and government representatives from Qatar, Indonesia, and other producer countries, with the third Dialogue held in 2014. Thus, other than special cases in which resource extraction is overlaid with sovereignty disputes, the structure of private contracting upstream is likely to invigorate state support for domestic firms internationally within a cooperative framework of private contracting. The 2011 disaster is thus likely to have a positive effect on the prospects for cooperation in energy security in Northeast Asia.

Implications

There are three implications that emerge from this chapter. First, the evidence presented above shows that the Japanese government continues to place improving the competitive position of domestic firms at the center of its strategy for managing energy security risks. It also suggests that any assessment of the implications of this strategy for the prospects of international cooperation in Northeast Asia must take into account not only how governments and firms have sought to shape resource markets to their benefit, but also how the private regimes governing trade and investment in these markets condition the implications of this intervention for cooperation and competition. Although often overlooked, this chapter shows there is substantial cooperation among firms based in South Korea, China, Japan, and Russia, although this is mediated through private contracting, rather than formal intergovernmental cooperation.

Second, the strategy developed by the government following the 2011 earthquake and nuclear disaster remains a work in progress, but is unlikely to have negative implications for the prospects of cooperation between states in Northeast Asia. In the short term, the disaster increased demand for heavy oil, which was used as a substitute for nuclear generating capacity. While the commercial position of Japan's electricity utilities has been undermined by the disaster, the different demand functions for oil products and for nuclear power imply it is unlikely to have a long-term effect on the demand for oil. Further, although the government has announced its intention to reinvigorate efforts to promote the commercial interests of domestic firms in both oil and natural gas, it has continued to emphasize the provision of risk money to private actors, rather than seeking to use bilateral contracting between governments to ensure security of energy supplies, as was done in the wake of the energy crises of the 1970s.

Third, although it is not a focus of this chapter, at the Climate Change Conference, COP 19, held in November 2013 in Warsaw, the governing Liberal Democratic Party announced it was abandoning the extremely aggressive climate change goals announced by the former government at COP 15. Instead, it committed to reducing greenhouse gas emissions by 3.8 percent from 2005, equivalent to a 3.1 percent increase from 1990. Mechanisms promoting regional and multilateral cooperation in climate change already play a role in the new climate strategy, and these are also likely to play a larger role in response to the 2011 disaster. In the 2010 Bill of the Basic Act on Global Warming Countermeasures, the government linked bilateral cooperation with developing countries to its own efforts to reduce CO_2 emissions through the Clean Development Mechanism/Joint Implementation instruments enshrined in the Kyoto Protocol, as well as through a Bilateral Offset Credit Mechanism (BOCM) it began to pilot in 2010, and for which it has signed agreements with Thailand, Vietnam, Indonesia, India, and the Mekong Region.[25] The loss of domestic nuclear power generation thus has profound implications for the role of regional cooperation in Japan's climate change strategy.

Notes

1 For a summary of Japanese energy-related taxes in English, see Ministry of Finance, Japan (2010).
2 Energy intensity is a measure of how much energy is used in order to produce a unit of economic output.
3 Article 108 of Japan's 2006 revised company law establishes a share class enabling special voting rights.
4 See Hughes (2012, p. 98) for calculations. The management of energy policy is complicated by the March 11, 2011, nuclear disaster, described below.
5 Project financing has undergone a number of reorganizations, with JBIC emerging from a combination of the Export-Import Bank of Japan and the Overseas Economic Cooperation Fund in 1999, before the latter was spun off into the Japan International Cooperation Agency (JICA) in 2006.
6 As discussed below, the power sector is now undergoing fundamental reorganization as a result of the nuclear accident following the March 11, 2011 earthquake and tsunami in the Tohoku region.
7 There is competition between the power and gas firms over final consumers in the residential sector, as noted by Hattori (2011).
8 Oil-fired generation (heavy and crude) constituted 41.4 percent of installed capacity, and 57.6 percent of total electricity generated in 1970, falling to 17.8 percent of the installed base and 2.2 percent of electricity generated in 2010.
9 For a historical overview, see Samuels (1987).
10 The difference between generation capacity and electricity generated emerges because of the fuel costs and differences in the stability of different fuel types supplying electricity to the grid. The higher fuel costs for heavy oil relative to nuclear power and coal, for example, mean it tends to be used for power generation only when demand is high.
11 Reliance on Middle Eastern suppliers fell to a low of 67.9 percent in 1987. METI identifies the reduction of the exports as a share of total production in China, Indonesia, Malaysia, and Vietnam as an important reason for the reorientation of supply back toward the Middle East (METI, 2013, pp. 115–17).
12 "Ajia wo chushin ni sekai no enerugii juyo ha kyuzo wo tutzuketeori, shigen keneki kakuho wo meguri kokusai kyoso ha shiretsuka shiteiru." [International competition for securing resource rights is heating up as world energy demand continues to rapidly increase, centered on Asia.] See Agency for Natural Resources and Energy (ANRE, 2010, p. 2).
13 For the purposes of this chapter I conceive of National Oil Companies (NOCs) as private actors, for two reasons. First, they operate within private markets, which have different incentives to those facing governments. Second, there is substantial variation in the degree to which governments are able to align the incentives of NOC management with those of the firms; however, in most cases their ability to do so is limited. See Victor *et al.* (2012).
14 The totals for natural gas are likely to change significantly in the future given the ongoing shale gas and tight oil revolutions.
15 Data drawn from monthly import statistics compiled by the Petroleum Association of Japan.
16 See the Stulberg chapter in this volume for more details.
17 The terminal is capable of managing 13–14 tankers per month of the 10,000 ton Aframax class, for a total of 1,300,000–1,400,000 tons per month of export potential (Motomura, 2012, pp. 13–15).

18 See Valencia (2007). On Japan's position see Smith (2012).
19 A description of the methods used in the seismic testing are available in Emery *et al.* (1969, p. 12). The report notes that positions described "are considered accurate within 3 km, except in the northern part of the Yellow Sea and in Taiwan Strait where some of them may be as much as 6 km in error."
20 The first successful drill was conducted by Primeline Petroleum in October 1997 (Endo, 2012, p. 101).
21 CNOOC net reserves recorded in CNOOC (2005, p. 21).
22 This statement is not inconsistent with the possibility that the firms made this decision because of the possibility of political risk, which is a component of any decision over the commercial exploitability of resources. There is also some evidence that the Japanese government engaged the firms regarding the disputed sovereignty of the reserve base. See *Mainichi Shinbun* (2010).
23 This possibility is alluded to by Motomura (2012, pp. 105–6).
24 Data from a Reuters survey of utilities. See Tsukimori and Kebede (2013).
25 Japan will not participate in the second commitment period of the Kyoto Protocol, but it has not withdrawn from the Protocol, and continues to use the Kyoto Mechanisms.

References

Abbott, K.W. and Snidal, D. 2010. Strengthening International Regulation Through Transnational New Governance: Overcoming the Orchestration Deficit. *Vanderbilt Journal of Transnational Law* 42: 501–78.

Agency for Natural Resources and Energy (ANRE). 2002. *Enerugii Kihon Keikaku 2003* [Basic Energy Plan 2003]. Tokyo: METI.

Agency for Natural Resources and Energy (ANRE). 2010. *Enerugii Kihon Keikaku* [Basic Energy Plan]. Tokyo: METI.

Asahi Shinbun. 2013a. Chugoku, higashi shina kai ni gasu shisetsu kensetsu ka—seifu "judai na kenen" [Is China Constructing Gas Infrastructure in the East China Sea? Government—"Grace Concern."]. *Asahi Shinbun*, July 3.

Asahi Shinbun. 2013b. Abe shusho "chugoku ha goi ihan"—higashi shinakai no gasu den tandoku kaihatsu [PM Abe States "China is Contravening the Agreement"—Unilateral Development of Gas Fields in East China Sea]. *Asahi Shinbun*, July 6.

BP. 2012. *BP Statistical Review of World Energy 2012*. London: BP.

Buszynski, L. 2006. Oil and Territory in Putin's Relations with China and Japan. *Pacific Review*, 19(3): 287–303.

China National Offshore Oil Corporation (CNOOC). 2005. *Annual Report*. Hong Kong: CNOOC.

China.org. 2004. Oil Giants Depart Xihu Trough Gas Project. *China Through a Lens*. Online: www.china.org.cn/english/2004/Sep/108515.htm (accessed November 4, 2013).

China Petroleum and Chemical Corporation. 2003. *Annual Report and Accounts*. Beijing: Sinopec.

Chunichi Shimbun. 2003. Nihon ga 70 oku doru yushi teian sekiyu paipurain kensetsu roshia tantosho akasu [Japan Proposed a $7 Billion Loan for Oil Pipeline Construction: Russia's Minister Reveals]. *Chunichi Shimbun*, October 14.

Ebinger, C., Massy, K., and Avasarala, G. 2012. *Liquid Markets: Assessing the Case for US Exports of Liquefied Natural Gas*. Washington, DC: Brookings Institution.

Emery, K.O., Hayashi, Y., Hilde, T.W.C., Kobayashi, K., Koo, J.H., Meng, C.Y., Niino, H., Osterhagen, J.H., Reynolds, L.M., Wageman, J.M., Wang, C.S., and Yang, S.J. 1969.

Geological Structure and Some Water Characteristics of the East China Sea and the Yellow Sea. In *Technical Bulletin, Committee for Co-ordination of Joint Prospecting for Mineral Resources in Asian Offshore Areas (CCOP), Economic Commission for Asia and the Far East, Volume 2*, pp. 3–43.

Endo, A. 2012. Higashi shinakai ni okeru yugasuden kaihatsu to sono haikei [The Background and Development of Gas Fields in the East China Sea]. *Kaikanko Senryaku Kenkyu* 2(1).

Hattori, T. 2011. *Gas-to-Electric Substitution and Competition in Residential Energy Market in Japan*. Paper presented at Fourth Annual Conference on Competition and Regulation in Network Industries, November 25.

Higashi, N. 2009. *Natural Gas in China: Market Evolution and Strategy*. International Energy Agency Working Paper Series, June. Paris: IEA/OECD.

Hughes, L. 2012. Climate Converts: Institutional Redeployment, Industrial Policy, and Public Investment in Energy in Japan. *Journal of East Asian Studies* 12(1): 100–1.

Hughes, L. 2014. *Globalizing Oil: Firms and Oil Market Governance in France, Japan, and the United States*. London: Cambridge University Press.

INPEX. 2013. *Annual Report 2013*. Tokyo: INPEX.

JBIC. 2008. *About JBIC*. Online: www.jbic.go.jp/en/about/press/2008/0616-01 (accessed February 2, 2010).

JBIC. 2012. *JIBC Profile: Role and Function*. Tokyo: JBIC.

JOGMEC. 2012a. *JOGMEC's Activities: Oil and Natural Gas Resources Field*. Tokyo: JOGMEC.

JOGMEC. 2012b. *Annual Report*. Tokyo: JOGMEC.

Lee, C.-J. 1984. *China and Japan: New Economic Diplomacy*. Stanford, CA: Hoover Institution Press.

Lipscy, P. and Schipper, L. 2013. Energy Efficiency in the Japanese Transport Sector. *Energy Policy* 56: 248–58.

LNG Canada. 2013. *LNG Canada Project: Summary of the Project Description*. Vancouver, BC: LNG Canada.

Mainichi Shinbun. 2010. Chugoku gasuden kaihatsu: meja tettai—nihon seifu ga hatarakikake [Chinese Gas Field Development: Majors Withdraw—Japanese Government Engaged Them]. *Mainichi Shinbun*, October 1.

McCarthy, S. 2012. Nexen Forms Shale Gas Venture with Japan's Inpex. *The Globe and Mail*, September 6.

Ministry of Economy, Trade and Industry (METI), Japan. 2005. *Annual Report*. Tokyo: METI.

Ministry of Economy, Trade and Industry (METI), Japan. 2010. *The Strategic Energy Plan 2010: Meeting Global Challenges and Securing Energy Futures*. Tokyo: METI.

Ministry of Economy, Trade and Industry (METI), Japan. 2013. *Enerugii Hakusho 2013* [*Energy White Paper 2013*]. Tokyo: METI.

Ministry of Economy, Trade and Industry (METI), Japan. 2014. *Basic Energy Plan 2014 (Proposed)*. Tokyo: METI.

Ministry of Finance, Japan. 2010. *Comprehensive Handbook of Japanese Taxes*. Tokyo: Ministry of Finance.

Ministry of Foreign Affairs, Japan. 2004. Press Conference. Online: www.mofa.go.jp/announce/press/2004/6/0622.html#3 (accessed November 4, 2013).

Ministry of Foreign Affairs, Japan. n.d. Ministry of Foreign Affairs. Online: www.mofa.go.jp/mofaj/area/china/higashi_shina/press.html (accessed November 5, 2013).

Minoura, H. 2011. Energy Security and Japan–China Relations: Competition or Cooperation? Unpublished manuscript, George Washington University, January 31, 2011.

Motomura, M. 2012. Kakudai suru Hokuto Ajia no Enerugii Furo [Expanding Energy Flows from North East Asia]. *Sekiyu Tennen Gasu Rebyu* 46(2): 13–34.

Nikkei Asian Review. n.d. Online: www.nikkei.com/article/DGXNASGG02002_S3A400C1EB2000/(accessed November 7, 2014).

Rosneft. 2013a. Rosneft Press Release, June 21. Online: www.rosneft.com/news/pressrelease/2106201313.html (accessed October 29, 2013).

Rosneft. 2013b. Rosneft Press Release, June 21. Online: www.rosneft.com/news/pressrelease/2106201315.html (accessed October 29, 2013).

Samuels, R.J. 1987. *The Business of the Japanese State: Energy Markets in Comparative and Historical Perspective.* Ithaca, NY: Cornell University Press.

Smith, S.A. 2012. Japan and the East China Sea Dispute. *Orbis,* Summer: 370–90.

Tsukimori, O. and Kebede, R. 2013. Japan on Gas, Coal Power Building Spree to Fill Nuclear Void. Reuters, October 16. Online: http://uk.reuters.com/article/2013/10/16/uk-japan-power-outlook-idUKBRE99F02120131016 (accessed November 7, 2014).

U.S. Energy Information Administration (EIA). n.d. *East China Sea.* Online: www.eia.gov/countries/regions-topics.cfm?fips=ECS (accessed November 4, 2013).

Valencia, M.J. 2007. The East China Sea Dispute: Context, Claims, Issues, and Possible Solutions. *Asian Perspective* 31(1): 127–67.

Victor, D.G., Hults, D.R., and Thurber, M.C. 2012. *Oil and Governance: State-owned Enterprises and the World Energy Supply.* New York: Cambridge University Press.

Wilkinson, R. 2012. Shell Sells More of Prelude Floating LNG Project. *Oil & Gas Journal,* May 10.

Yonhap News Agency. n.d. *Yonhap News Agency.* Online: http://english.yonhapnews.co.kr/business/2012/02/02/30/0501000000AEN20120202001000320F.html (accessed July 22, 2013).

5 South Korean perspectives on Northeast Asian energy security cooperation

Jae-Seung Lee

Introduction

A stable energy supply has long been a major concern for energy security in South Korea. Due to the scarcity of natural resources within its borders, South Korea has had to rely on imported energy resources to sustain rapid economic growth and support high energy consumption, especially in the energy-intensive industrial sector.[1] Dependence on overseas energy supply was 97.3 percent in 2001 and has changed little in more than a decade, at 96 percent in 2012 (Korea Energy Statistics Information System (KESIS), n.d.). In spite of efforts to diversify import sources, South Korea depends heavily on oil and gas imports from the Middle East.[2]

In order to enhance its energy security, South Korea has tried to diversify the sources of energy imports on the one hand and to develop alternative energies on the other. Russia has emerged as a key alternative source to replace oil and gas imported from the Middle East. Since the early 2000s, South Korea has been increasingly interested in energy cooperation in its home region of Northeast Asia, with a special emphasis on Russian energy projects. A number of oil and gas development projects in East Siberia and the Russian Far East have become a major focus of South Korea's energy diplomacy.

In pursuing Northeast Asian energy cooperation, South Korea has had an additional factor to consider in its energy security calculations: North Korea. The energy shortage in North Korea itself has become not only a serious economic problem, but also a security threat.[3, 4] Nuclear energy as a power supply has been North Korea's rationale for its nuclear program, but a series of nuclear weapons tests has undercut that assertion. Currently, North Korea does not seem to have the capability to overcome its energy shortage and related economic downturn (Lee, 2010a, pp. 222–4). An oil pipeline and energy aid from China have long provided an indispensable umbilical cord for North Korea to maintain a minimal level of economic activity; these, in turn, have deepened its economic and political dependence on China. By running a gas pipeline from Russia through its territory, North Korea could derive transit revenue and gas supply, which would resolve its energy problems. A trans-North Korea gas pipeline from Russia was also considered as an option to persuade North Korea to abandon its nuclear program and was seen as a stepping-stone to the unification of the two Koreas by enhancing energy interdependence (Lee, 2010a, p. 225).

In fact, South Korea's perception of energy security has had two dimensions: First, energy security could be pursued as an objective to guarantee a stable energy supply. Second, energy cooperation could be used also as a means to achieve a higher security goal, especially peace-building on the Korean Peninsula, by enhancing various forms of regional political and economic cooperation (Lee, 2010a, p. 218). It has not been surprising, in this context, that the "North Korean factor" has appeared whenever regional energy interconnection is discussed.[5] Based on these dual perceptual dimensions, the issue of regional energy cooperation reflects both economic and political interests in South Korea.

However, the objective of energy security cannot be managed sufficiently by South Korea alone. South Korea's energy security could better be enhanced by close cooperation with both energy-producing and energy-consuming countries in the Northeast Asian region. In fact, the challenges of energy security are not unique to South Korea. China and Japan have faced similar problems of energy supply. The three countries are all major energy consumers and importers. The Middle East has also remained the largest source of Japanese and Chinese oil imports. As a consequence, the three Northeast Asian countries' energy security has been exposed to similar supply risks in the Middle East, which has a high level of geopolitical uncertainty. These three countries have tried to reduce their dependency on Middle Eastern oil and have been looking toward Russia, Central Asia, and Africa to diversify their oil import sources and to promote energy security.

It has been assumed that cooperation between producing and consuming countries, as well as alliances among consuming countries, would be beneficial in Northeast Asia because China, Japan, and South Korea can diversify their energy supply while Russia can effectively realize investments in East Siberian energy development. Northeast Asian energy cooperation has been expected to increase economic and political interdependence, which would further enhance regional economic integration.[6]

However, this alleged common necessity has not always led to the successful implementation of energy cooperation, due to a number of political and economic obstacles. China has adopted an aggressive external energy policy to increase its energy supply, and this policy stance has often intensified its competition with other major energy consumers in the region.[7] Japan and South Korea have also joined in the mercantilist competition to secure their own energy procurement, both within and beyond Northeast Asia. South Korea's pursuit of energy cooperation in Northeast Asia has reflected the multidimensional nature of both high politics and low politics elements (Lee, 2005, 2010a).

This chapter examines the South Korean perspective on major issues of Northeast Asian energy cooperation and discusses its role in these activities. The second section surveys major bilateral and multilateral initiatives for regional energy cooperation in which South Korea has participated. The third section discusses the constraints of the existing energy cooperation scheme in Northeast

Asia; this section also explores the North Korean factor in considering South Korea's strategy for regional energy security cooperation. The fourth section examines South Korea's new momentum and growth in green energy and its implications for Northeast Asian energy cooperation. The final section concludes with the prospects and tasks for South Korea's pursuit of Northeast Asian energy cooperation.

South Korea and regional energy cooperation

South Korea's initiatives for energy cooperation in Northeast Asia

South Korean initiatives on Northeast Asian energy cooperation first targeted the linkage with Russian gas and oil production.[8] The Asia-Pacific energy market has expanded and Russia has a strong intention to integrate more closely in this region. The big energy markets in Northeast Asian countries have naturally become a major consideration of Russia's Far Eastern strategy. Russia has been looking for a new import market beyond Europe. The South Korean gas market has grown particularly fast in past decades and its market size is substantial. A pipeline for natural gas has become a major item on the cooperation agenda for South Korea and Russia.

While importing liquefied natural gas (LNG) has been generally preferred by major Korean importers, a trans-Korean Peninsula pipeline has often been considered as an option in the Six Party Talks and to increase interdependence among Russia, North Korea, and South Korea. For South Korea, the pipeline promises a stable long-term gas supply, while North Korea seeks a chance for a significant inflow of hard currency in annual transit fees. Theoretically, Russia's new market in Northeast Asia, South Korea's stable gas supply, and North Korea's transit revenue would lead to a potential win-win situation for all three countries.

The Roh Moo Hyun administration (2003–17) picked up the issue of Northeast Asian energy cooperation under the slogan "Building the era of Northeast Asia." The Presidential Committee on Northeast Asian Cooperation (PCNAC), together with the Ministry of Commerce, Industry and Energy (MOCIE), the Ministry of Foreign Affairs and Trade (MOFAT), and the Korea Energy Economics Institute (KEEI), elaborated the plan and conducted a feasibility study of energy linkage with Russia and China. The South Korean national oil and gas company also increased its involvement in Northeast Asian energy projects.

Two projects have received special attention. The Kovykta gas project aimed to construct a pipeline from Irkutsk in Russia to China and South Korea. The South Korean consortium led by Korea Gas Corporation (KOGAS) finished the feasibility study and discussed possible pipeline routes. However, South Korean participation in the Kovykta project lost momentum when the Russian government announced a plan to use Kovykta gasfields for domestic supply under the

United Gas Supply System (UGSS) plan in 2005. The Sakhalin-1 project (ExxonMobil consortium) was discussed internally as an option to link Russian gas sources and the two Koreas via pipeline. However, South Korea did not have the influence to strongly advocate for the supply route, which instead was routed to China. South Korea instead has imported LNG from the Sakhalin-2 gas field since 2009.

The Lee Myung Bak administration (2008–12) placed major emphasis on overseas energy development, especially in its first two years. The geographical focus was expanded to other parts of the world, including Africa, Central Asia, and Latin America. South Korea and Russia agreed to import natural gas from Yakutsk starting in 2017. This alternative plan was considered a way to partly replace Russian gas imports South Korea would have seen from the earlier Kovykta project. However, the final transportation route is still being discussed. While Russia strongly prefers the trans-North Korea pipeline, the South Korean government has been more cautious because of political risks. Discussion on the Kovykta project has not entirely disappeared and resurfaces in the policy community from time to time.

The Eurasian Initiative, announced by the Park Geun Hye administration in 2013, brought more momentum to the effort to promote energy connections with Russia and China. The initiative seeks to connect the Far East, starting in South Korea, and traveling through Siberia and Central Asia to Europe. Inspired by the idea of "the resurrection of Silk Road," this initiative seeks to provide an environment to enhance economic ties with Russia and China (National Unification Advisory Council, n.d.). Actual implementation of related energy cooperation, however, remains to be seen.

Besides the gas pipeline project, a number of research and feasibility studies have been conducted on a trilateral power grid network linking Russia, North Korea, and South Korea. An Asia super-grid has been suggested that would link China, Mongolia, Russia, Japan, North Korea, and South Korea. The Korea Electric Power Corporation (KEPCO) has recently advanced the idea of connecting Busan, South Korea's second-largest city, to Japan's Tsushima Island and Kyushu with a 200-kilometer underwater cable (*Korea Joongang Daily*, 2014). Masayoshi Son, chairperson of the Japanese company SoftBank, is said to support the idea of these projects.

As a multilateral mechanism for energy cooperation in Northeast Asia, South Korea and United Nations Economic and Social Commission for Asia and the Pacific (UNESCAP) jointly proposed the Intergovernmental Collaborative Mechanism on Energy Cooperation in North-East Asia (ECNEA), which was officially established in Ulaanbaatar in November 2005.[9] The ECNEA originally focused on six Northeast Asian countries: Russia, Mongolia, China, Japan, South Korea, and North Korea. Since 2005, the ECNEA has held annual senior officers' meetings (SOMs) together with two working groups—the Working Group on Energy Policy and Planning, and the Working Group on Coal. However, China and Japan did not officially participate in the process. These countries' political commitment to the ECNEA has not been strong, and Japan has insisted that the abductees issue should be settled as a precondition for the diplomatic discussion with North Korea. Without a strong incentive for membership, China and Japan have participated as observers.

The South Korean government proposed the Korea–China–Japan Trilateral Energy Dialogue in July 2007. This dialogue is designed to strengthen ties among Northeast Asian energy-consuming countries and enhance their bargaining power in global energy meetings. However, this institution was based on even weaker political commitments from the participating countries and did not function well as a major regional energy institution.

South Korea's participation in regional multilateral energy cooperation

At the East Asian and Asia-Pacific level, there has been a series of cooperation initiatives in which South Korea has participated, together with other Northeast Asian countries. The Asia-Pacific Economic Cooperation (APEC) organization has discussed energy issues in its biannual Energy Ministers Meetings (EMMs) and semiannual Energy Working Group Meetings. ASEAN+3 began to hold its EMMs and added the Energy Policy Management Group and annual forums. The East Asia Summit (EAS) held its EMM back-to-back with the ASEAN+3 EMM and instituted the Energy Cooperation Task Force and various working groups. In addition to these intergovernmental initiatives, a number of nongovernmental discussions such as academic and research forums and private sector dialogues have been initiated to address the region's diverse energy agenda. South Korea has tried to enhance its visibility in these multilateral energy cooperation initiatives. However, the level of discussions in most of these cooperative initiatives is low, and the initiatives have often lacked effective implementation mechanisms. The overall development of Northeast Asian energy cooperation is still in its infancy (Lee, 2010a, pp. 225–6). Table 5.1 summarizes major multilateral initiatives on energy cooperation in East and Northeast Asia.

The challenges of Northeast Asian energy cooperation for South Korea[10]

Geopolitical constraints

South Korea's energy cooperation in Northeast Asia has been affected by a series of geopolitical constraints. The pursuit of national energy security to guarantee stable energy procurement has resulted in consequences that have brought into conflict the interests of the respective countries. The potential sources of conflicts stemming from energy competition include the territorial, the diplomatic, and the political. Despite the alleged necessity of energy cooperation, the actual implementation of energy projects in Northeast Asia has reflected strong competition among the major energy-consuming countries in the region, and numerous initiatives for cooperation have made little progress.

Table 5.1 Energy initiatives in East and Northeast Asia

Initiative	Abbreviation	Type	Energy subsector
ASEAN+3 through ACE	ASEAN+3	Intergovernmental	
Asia-Pacific Economic Cooperation	APEC	Intergovernmental	
Asia Pacific Partnership on Clean Development and Climate	APP-CDC	Partnership	
Central Asia Regional Economic Cooperation	CAREC	Program	Electric power, energy efficiency
Energy Charter Treaty	ECT	Intergovernmental	Electric power, energy efficiency
Intergovernmental Collaborative Mechanism on Energy Cooperation in North-East Asia	ECNEA	Intergovernmental	
Eurasian Economic Cooperation	EurAsEC	Intergovernmental	Electric power, fossil fuels
Greater Mekong Subregion Program	GMS Program	Program	
Greater Tumen Initiative	GTI	Program	Electric power
Mekong Program	Mekong Program	Intergovernmental	Electric power
Partnership for Equitable Growth	PEG	Partnership	Fossil fuels
Renewable Development Initiative	RDI	Program	Renewable energy
Shanghai Cooperation Organization	SCO	Intergovernmental	

Source: UNESCAP (2008); *Energy Security and Sustainable Development in Asia and the Pacific* (2008); from Lee and Yu (2012).

As energy supply is limited within the region, energy rivalries among Northeast Asian consumers have intensified (Lahn & Paik, 2005). For example, Japan and China have been competing for years over the Eastern Siberia–Pacific Ocean (ESPO) oil pipeline project. Amid this competitive environment, Russia, the major supplier in the region, has recognized the advantage of using its energy resources to maximize its strategic and political leverage (IEA, 2003). Furthermore, energy development projects have often prompted sensitive territorial disputes. There remains a potential risk for a maritime dispute among Japan, China, and the two Koreas in terms of offshore oil and gas field development (Murphy & Fackler, 2003; Calder, 2006a, 2006b). The dispute in the South and East China seas indicates that similar disputes could recur among the Northeast Asian countries in the Yellow Sea or in the East China Sea. The pursuit of strategic energy security, therefore, has often led to conflicts rather than cooperation among the stakeholders.

In short, Northeast Asian energy cooperation is likely to be influenced by the political and security environments in which the remnants of the Cold War still hinder full-scale cooperation. Political trust is still uncertain, and historical antipathy still lingers in this region. From this geopolitical perspective, energy cooperation in Northeast Asia is necessary not only for the facilitation of energy supply projects but also for the prevention of these potential conflicts stemming from attempts to strengthen national energy security.

Institutional constraints

The limited progress of energy cooperation has been due to a lack of political will and insufficient institutional momentum to achieve active regional economic and political cooperation. Many obstacles to energy security cooperation have originated from both the lack of a strong political will of the governments involved and the uncertainties of potential benefits of cooperation. For example, China has tried to address the energy supply problem by strengthening its relationships with energy-producing nations on its own, not through collaborations with its rivals in the region (Downs, 2004; Choo, 2006; Lieberthal & Herberg, 2006; Xu, 2006; Zha, 2006). Japan also has pursued active energy cooperation with producing countries and tried to increase its overseas natural resources development.[11] Regarding the scope of regional energy cooperation, Japan has been proactive in promoting energy cooperation in Southeast Asia and the Asia-Pacific region instead of in Northeast Asia. South Korea's focus has been more on stable energy cooperation with Russia.

Furthermore, potential mutual benefits that could be derived from energy cooperation have not been clearly conceived or spelled out, and the sense of urgency has not been strong enough. Without a clear vision of tangible gain, it has been hard to build institutional consensus on regional energy cooperation among these countries.

Domestic constraints

Since the latter half of the 2000s, a number of energy development projects with Russia have made little progress compared with similar projects in the Middle East, Central Asia, or Africa. This slow progress of Russian energy development in the upstream sector has left policymakers and entrepreneurs in South Korea discouraged. Their trust in Russian legal and political transparency was already weak, and the Russian upstream sectors have been perceived as risky for pursuit of long-term projects, which in turn has increased business uncertainties. In fact, Russia has not been a prioritized target country since the Roh Moo Hyun administration.

For South Korea, both commercial and political risks of the Northeast Asian pipeline projects have been huge and remain unresolved. The pipeline would typically require a long-term contract between Russia, as the energy producer, and South Korea, as the importer. However, the global gas market has been extremely volatile in the past few years and doubts have been raised about the price index linking gas prices to oil prices, which has been commonly used for long-term contracts. Without proper pricing mechanisms, a larger-scale pipeline project cannot gather sufficient commercial momentum; financing for pipeline construction has also been a major commercial issue.

There are also concerns about whether North Korea can be trusted not to use the pipeline to gain leverage over South Korea's energy supply. Russia stressed its guarantee of alternative gas supply if North Korea should block supply, but, so far, South Korean market participants have not expressed much confidence in this contingency plan. It is doubtful to what extent Moscow and Gazprom can actually influence the North Korean regime. In the worst-case scenario, both Russia and South Korea might have to rely on North Korea's goodwill to safely run the pipeline. Another concern is that North Korea could divert the revenue from the pipeline transit fees to its nuclear and missile program, which has raised the political cost of pursuing trans-North Korea pipeline. Furthermore, North Korea may be reluctant to open the construction sites, which could be militarily sensitive. The construction of the pipeline itself could be regarded as a security challenge to North Korea.[12]

Momentum for regional green energy cooperation: a new breakthrough?[13]

The introduction of a green-energy paradigm has brought renewed momentum and opportunity to energy cooperation in Northeast Asia. Momentum for green cooperation has recently begun to build in South Korea. The Low Carbon Green Growth Strategy (hereafter called the green growth strategy) was initiated during the Lee administration, and was adopted as the nation's new development paradigm to maximize the potential of green technology and clean energy. Based on strong political support, South Korea began to promote its green energy initiatives in the arena of international and regional energy cooperation. As a major policy objective, the green growth strategy aimed to make Korea a green growth leader, as well as a bridge between developed and developing countries (Presidential Commission on Green Growth, 2009; Lee, 2013). The establishment of the Global Green Growth Institute (GGGI) is an attempt to pursue international collaboration for low-carbon, green energy initiatives.

In fact, the emphasis on an alternative energy strategy has been envisioned in China, Japan, and South Korea since the mid-2000s. The alternative energy strategies in these countries share some similarities, among them a strong state-led initiative to boost renewable energy resources such as wind, solar, and hydrogen and low-carbon development efforts (Lee, 2013). Alternative energy initiatives in the three countries have also included nuclear energy as a crucial pillar of the strategy. Compared to fossil fuels, these alternative resources, especially the renewable energy sources, are seen as more conducive to cooperation, as they have a supply structure that does not lend itself as much to a zero-sum outlook (i.e., one country's advantage is by definition another country's loss). These alternative sources share more common benefits. Green energy sources are not as embedded in the existing supply structure of fossil fuels and are free from the geopolitical uncertainties of the Middle East and North Africa. For example, the Gobitec Project, which was suggested by the Hanns Seidel Foundation of South Korea, plans to transmit Mongolian wind energy to South Korea and Japan through a proposed "super-grid network" (Seliger, 2010; requoted in Lee, 2013).

However, the 2011 earthquake and Fukushima nuclear accident in Japan changed the landscape of the green development paradigm in the region. On the one hand, nuclear power as a major energy transition from carbon-based fuel sources was either delayed or modified. Japan still seems undecided whether to keep nuclear power generation as a major pillar in its energy mix. The scale of nuclear power generation in China and Korea has also been affected. On the other hand, the Fukushima accident brought up two issues for energy cooperation in Northeast Asia: nuclear safety and increased use of gas and renewable energy. The issue of nuclear safety had already begun to be discussed among a number of countries in the region and had potential for more multilateral cooperation. The post-Fukushima energy paradigm could also lead a faster phase-in of clean and renewable energies in the region, which could galvanize new forms, agendas, and dialogues for energy cooperation.

However, this "green momentum" is facing both internal and external challenges. The global renewable energy market is undergoing a recession, and a number of earlier green growth projects have been delayed or cancelled in South Korea. Political momentum for green growth has waned, despite its acknowledged importance. At the regional level, green energy cooperation also faces obstacles (as is the case of fossil fuel cooperation). A low level of institutionalization among the Northeast Asian countries, poor infrastructure for renewable energy, and low to marginal production using renewable energy sources are among the barriers to full-scale green energy cooperation. Furthermore, green energy and low-carbon strategies are being implemented in the context of a strong industrial policy, which could lead to another round of neo-mercantilist energy competition in the region (Lee, 2013). The recent development of shale gas in North America is a potential game-changer for the green energy paradigm in Northeast Asia: It will certainly enable a diversified gas-supply structure and contribute to energy security in China, Japan, and Korea with the stabilization of global gas market. The concern, however, is that a more reliable supply and increased use of gas could delay implementation of renewable energy sources and related investment.

Conclusion

With the dual objectives of energy supply and peace-building on the Korean Peninsula, South Korea has been actively pursuing further energy cooperation in this region over the past decade. It has been widely accepted that Russian energy resources would be and should be an important option for South Korea's future energy supply. Besides the previous attempts to build a linkage with Russian energy resources, South Korea has also looked for new opportunities to engage proactively in regional energy cooperation. There has also been an expectation that energy cooperation in Northeast Asia that includes North Korea could mitigate its energy-supply shortage and economic vulnerability. Energy cooperation could help pave the way for a smooth peace-building effort on the Korean Peninsula.

However, Russia has pursued energy development in the Far East very slowly, which has left the policy and business community cool toward further efforts. Even though Russian gas and oil imports remain important, the uncertainties involved in regional energy development projects have often intimidated the participants. The emergence of alternative options from other parts of the world has further raised questions about the importance of Russian energy resources. In fact, the recent shale gas boom in North America has changed the global gas market, increasing the prospects of a stable supply of natural gas at moderate prices. While the actual amount of North American shale gas to be imported by Northeast Asian countries might be limited, its impact on the global market would certainly curb gas prices. However, traditional gas producers such as Russia and major importers in Northeast Asia do not necessarily see eye-to-eye on a scenario of cheap gas supply stemming from the shale gas boom. Differing price expectations of major Northeast Asian gas importers and of the major exporter— Russia—could complicate negotiations to set up a long-term supply contract. South Korea may have less incentive to close the deal quickly and to fix rates for Russian gas under a long-term contract, at least in the near future.

As discussed earlier, energy cooperation in Northeast Asia faces a huge task: to overcome the spiral of competition among the consuming countries and to move to a common response to their energy security agendas. Geopolitical tension in the Northeast and East Asian regions has seriously escalated in recent years because of territorial and political disputes among Japan, China, and Korea. Meanwhile, resolution of the North Korean factor remains a precondition for South Korea's regional energy cooperation.

Northeast Asian energy cooperation is, inevitably, a difficult challenge for South Korea and requires much stronger political and economic will throughout the entire region in the future. As the internal pressures for energy cooperation in Northeast Asia remain weak, and the institutional framework remains undeveloped, South Korea alone may not be able to make a breakthrough in building a multilateral scheme for regional energy cooperation. Energy relations among Northeast Asian countries have been mainly bilateral thus far, and the basis of multilateral cooperation remains tentative. Moreover, China, Japan, and

South Korea do not really agree on the urgency of energy cooperation among themselves. Lack of strong political will and weak institutions mean that a firm framework on which actual energy cooperation measures could be implemented remains to be developed, and the lack thereof has discouraged a number of initiatives for regional energy cooperation.

South Korea's energy security strategy toward the Northeast Asia region should deal with the double-edged diplomatic tasks of securing domestic energy supply while enhancing multilateral ties with neighboring countries. To make South Korea's initiatives of energy cooperation more effective, creative agenda-setting to maximize the regional public goods is necessary. A series of soft-energy and low-carbon initiatives, such as focusing on renewable energy and energy efficiency, could function as a good supplement to upstream development and infrastructure interconnection in Northeast Asia.

Notes

1 Korea's high energy consumption is largely due to the country's energy-intensive industrial structure, which includes petrochemical, steel, and other heavy industries.
2 Oil imports depended largely on the Middle East, which accounted for more than 80 percent of South Korea's total oil imports.
3 The energy crisis in North Korea was triggered mainly by the cutoff of its petroleum supply, which had been supplied by China and Russia, after the breakdown of the Communist bloc in 1990. North Korea at that time could not afford to import oil even at a subsidized price.
4 Regarding the energy situation in North Korea, see Von Hippel and Hayes (2007) and Von Hippel et al. (2008).
5 For North Korea-related energy projects, see Von Hippel and Hayes (2003).
6 Previous studies addressing Northeast Asian energy cooperation include the following: Harrison (2002, 2002–3), Swanström (2005), Fallon (2006), Chang (2007), Ryu (2007), Choi (2009), and Lee (2010b).
7 For the impact of the China factor on the Asian energy market, see Manning (2000), Dannreuther (2003), Paik (2004), and Bustelo (2005).
8 Besides the gas pipeline project, a number of researches and feasibility studies have been done on the trilateral power grid network linking Russia–North Korea–South Korea. At the South Korea–Russia summit in 2010, the Korean government also agreed to increase the import of Russian oil to 7.5 million tons.
9 In September 2001, the senior officers' meeting (SOM) in UNESCAP adopted the Khabarovsk Communiqué, and the Energy SOM and the Working Group were installed. In April 2003, the Vladivostok SOM agreed to hold regularly the Inter-Governmental Steering Committee of Senior Officials (Lee, 2010a, p. 225).
10 Discussion in this section is drawn from Lee (2010a, pp. 217–19, 226–7).
11 Japan's New Energy Strategy, announced in 2006, highlights the following measures: improving energy efficiency by 30 percent by 2030; reducing its dependence on petroleum to lower than 40 percent by 2030; reducing its dependence on petroleum in the transport industry to approximately 80 percent by 2030; and maintaining nuclear power as a proportion of the total power production at 30–40 percent (Choo, 2006; METI, 2006).

12 Brad Babson also pointed out North Korea's weak legal infrastructure and argued that "there must also be meaningful economic reform in North Korea that includes both a rational energy development strategy, and improvement in economic contract management practices that are internationally acceptable" (Babson, 2012, p. 2).
13 The discussion in this section is partly drawn from Lee (2013).

Bibliography

Babson, B. 2012. A "Pipe Dream?" Russia, North and South Korea's Gas Pipeline Quest. *The Diplomat*, October 31. Online: http://thediplomat.com/2012/10/russias-pipeline-dreams-in-korea/ (accessed June 4, 2014).

Bustelo, P. 2005. *China and the Geopolitics of Oil in the Asian Pacific Region*. Elcano Royal Institute Working Paper, No. 38. Madrid: Elcano Royal Institute.

Calder, K.E. 2006a. China and Japan's Simmering Rivalry. *Foreign Affairs* 85(2), March/April. Online: www.foreignaffairs.com/articles/61515/kent-e-calder/china-and-japans-simmering-rivalry (accessed March 4, 2014).

Calder, K.E. 2006b. *Korea's Energy Insecurities: Comparative and Regional Perspectives*. Seoul: KEI.

Chang, D. 2007. Energy and Regional Cooperation in Northeast Asia. *Journal of East Asian Affairs* 21(2), Fall/Winter: 167–95.

Choi, H.J. 2009. Fueling Crisis or Cooperation? The Geopolitics of Energy Security in Northeast Asia. *Asian Affairs: An American Review* 36(1), Spring: 3–28.

Choo, J. 2006. Energy Cooperation Problems in Northeast Asia: Unfolding the Reality. *East Asia: An International Quarterly* 23(3), Fall: 91–106.

Dannreuther, R. 2003. Asian Security and China's Energy Needs. *International Relations of the Asia Pacific* 3(2): 197–219.

Downs, E.S. 2004. The Chinese Energy Security Debate. *The China Quarterly* 177, March: 21–41.

Fallon, K.S. 2006. Promoting an Energy Partnership in Northeast Asia. *Pacific Focus* 21(1), Spring: 175–200.

Fetters, J. 2003. *KoRus Pipeline: Sakhalin to Seoul*. KEI-KIEP Policy Forum on Northeast Asian Energy Cooperation, January 7.

Harrison, S.S. 2002. *Toward Oil and Gas Cooperation in Northeast Asia*. Asia Program Special Report. Washington, DC: Woodrow Wilson International Center for Scholars.

Harrison, S.S. 2002–3. Gas and Geopolitics in Northeast Asia: Pipelines, Regional Stability, and the Korean Nuclear Crisis. *World Policy Journal* 19(4), Winter: 23–36.

International Energy Agency (IEA). 2003. *Russia's Energy Strategy to 2020*. Online: www.iea.org/textbase/papers/2003/strategy2020.pdf (accessed July 28, 2009).

International Energy Agency (IEA). 2006. *World Energy Outlook*. Paris: OECD/IEA.

Jaffe, A.M. 2001. The Potential of Energy as a Geopolitical Binding Factor in Asia. *Post-Soviet Geography and Economics* 42(7), October–November.

Kim, K-R. 2005. *Energy Cooperation with North Korea: Issues and Suggestions*. Seoul: Korea Institute for National Unification.

Korea Energy Statistics Information System (KESIS). n.d. Online: www.kesis.net/es/graph/graph_05.swf. (accessed September 17, 2009).

Korea Joongang Daily (2014) Kepco Wants Grid Linked to Japan. *Korea Joongang Daily*, August 23. Online: http://koreajoongangdaily.joins.com/news/article/Article.aspx?aid=2993919 (accessed April 25, 2014).

Lahn, G. and Paik, K.-W. 2005. *Russia's Oil and Gas Exports to North-East Asia.* Chatham House Paper, April. Online: www.chathamhouse.org/sites/files/chathamhouse/public/Research/Energy,%20Environment%20and%20Development/roilgas.pdf (accessed February 21, 2010).

Lee, J.-S. 2005. Energy Security and Northeast Asian Cooperation: High-Politics Approach Toward Low-Politics Agenda [in Korean]. *International and Area Review* 14(1), March: 21–49.

Lee, J.-S. 2010a. Energy Security and Cooperation in Northeast Asia. *The Korean Journal of Defense Analysis* 22(2), June: 217–33.

Lee, J.-S. 2010b. Political Economy of Energy Cooperation in Northeast Asia. In V. Gupta and G.K. Chong (eds) *Energy Security: Asia Pacific Perspectives.* New Delhi: Manas Publications.

Lee, J.-S. 2013. Towards Green Energy Cooperation in Northeast Asia: Implications from European Experiences. *Asia Europe Journal* 11(3), August: 231–45.

Lee, J.-S. and Yu, J. 2012. *North-East Asian Perspectives on the Challenges to Energy Security and the Sustainable Use of Energy.* North-East Asia Sub-regional Consultation Meeting for the Asia-Pacific Energy Forum 2013, November 12–13, Incheon, Republic of Korea, UNESCAP Consultant Report.

Lieberthal, K. and Herberg, M. 2006. China's Search for Energy Security: Implications for US Policy. *NBR Analysis* 17(1), April: 5–42.

Manning, R.A. 2000. *The Asian Energy Factor: Myths and Dilemmas of Energy, Security, and the Pacific Future.* New York: Palgrave.

Ministry of Economy, Trade and Industry, Japan (METI). 2006. *New National Energy Strategy.* Online: www.enecho.meti.go.jp/english/data/newnationalenergystrategy2006.pdf (accessed September 16, 2009).

Murphy, D. and Fackler, M. 2003. Asia's Pipeline Politics. *Far Eastern Economic Review* 166: 12–16.

National Energy Policy Development Group. 2001. *National Energy Policy.* Online: www.wtrg.com/EnergyReport/National-Energy-Policy.pdf (accessed May 11, 2009).

National Unification Advisory Council. n.d. President Park Geun-hye's "Eurasia Initiative." Online: www.nuac.go.kr/english/sub04/view01.jsp?numm=36 (accessed April 25, 2014).

Paik, K-W. 2004. *The Implications of China's Gas Expansion Towards Natural Gas Market in Asia.* Chatham House Paper, February. Online: www.chathamhouse.org/sites/files/chathamhouse/public/Research/Energy,%20Environment%20and%20Development/rchinagas.pdf (accessed June 9, 2010).

Paik, K-W. 2005. *Pipeline Gas Introduction to the Korean Peninsula.* Chatham House Paper, January. Online: http://chathamhouse.org/sites/files/chathamhouse/public/Research/Energy,%20Environment%20and%20Development/kpjan05.pdf (accessed June 9, 2010).

Presidential Commission on Green Growth (PCGG). 2009. *Road to Our Future: Green Growth, National Strategy and the Five-Year Plan (2009–2013).* Seoul: PCGG.

Ryu, Ji-C. 2007. Energy Cooperation in Northeast Asia: Perspectives from Korea. In P. Drysdale, K. Jiang, and D. Meagher (eds) *China and East Asian Energy: Prospects and Issues*, Asia Pacific Economic Papers, No. 369. Canberra: Australia–Japan Research Centre, pp. 123–36.

Seliger, B. 2010. *Renewable Energy Cooperation between Japan, Korea and China—Tackling Climate Change, Increasing Energy Security, Engaging North Korea and Moving Forward Northeast Asian Integration with the "Gobitec" Project.* Korea and the World Economy,

IX: New Economic Order after the Global Financial Crisis, June 25–26, 2010. Incheon, Korea: Hanns Seidel Foundation.

Stern, J. 2005. Gas Pipeline Co-operation Between Political Adversaries: Examples from Europe. Chatham House Paper, January. Online: www.chathamhouse.org/sites/files/ chathamhouse/public/Research/Energy,%20Environment%20and%20Development/ jsjan05.pdf (accessed June 6, 2011).

Swanström, N. 2005. An Asian Oil and Gas Union: Prospects and Problems. *The China and Eurasia Forum Quarterly* 3(4), November: 81–97.

Takeda, Y. 2005. KEDO Adrift. *Georgetown Journal of International Affairs* 6(2), Summer.

UNESCAP. 2007. *Trans-Asian Energy System: A UNESCAP Initiative.* Bangkok: UNESCAP.

UNESCAP. 2008. *Energy Security and Sustainable Development in Asia and the Pacific.* Bangkok: UNESCAP.

UNESCAP. 2010. *Five Year Strategy (2010–2014) to Implement the Intergovernmental Collaborative Mechanism on Energy Cooperation in North-East Asia.* Bangkok: UNESCAP.

Varadarajan, S. 2006. *Energy Key in the New Asian Architecture.* Online: www.globalresearch. ca/index.php?context=viewArticle&code=VAR20060125&articleId=1802 (accessed July 28, 2009).

Von Hippel, D.F. and Hayes, P. 2003. *Regional Energy Infrastructure Proposals and the DPRK Energy Sector: Opportunities and Constraints.* Paper presented at the KEI-KIEP Policy Forum, Washington, DC, January 9.

Von Hippel, D.F. and Hayes, P. 2007. *Fueling DPRK Energy Futures and Energy Security: 2005 Energy Balance, Engagement Options, and Future Paths.* Nautilus Institute Special Report, 07-042. Berkeley, CA: Nautilus Institute.

Von Hippel, D.F., Hayes, P., Williams, J., Greacen, C., Sagrillo, M., and Savage, T. 2008. International Energy Assistance Needs and Options for the Democratic People's Republic of Korea (DPRK). *Energy Policy* 36(2), February: 541–52.

Xu, Y.-C. 2006. China's Energy Security. *Australian Journal of International Affairs* 60(2), June: 265–86.

Zha, D. 2006. China's Energy Security: Domestic and International Issues. *Survival* 48(1), Spring: 179–90.

6 Mongolian perspectives on Northeast Asian energy security cooperation

Charles Krusekopf

Introduction

Overshadowed by its much more populous, powerful, and wealthy neighbors, Mongolia is often overlooked in regional energy discussions. However, the country has the potential to play a more important role as a supplier of energy for the region and a potential corridor for Russian energy exports to China. Mongolia has substantial deposits of coking and thermal coal, uranium, and oil, and vast potential for renewable energy development of both wind and solar power. It provides the most direct route for the transmission of Siberia's energy, including hydropower and natural gas, to major Chinese cities including Beijing, and has the potential to supply renewable energy and coal to Korea and Japan. Mongolia's geographic position and resource endowment are of interest to all countries in Northeast Asia, and Mongolia is an active participant in regional energy discussions. However, Mongolia has struggled to emerge as a significant player in these discussions due to internal and external challenges, including a lack of direct access to international markets, poorly developed domestic infrastructure, a lack of domestic capital and skills, a cautious attitude toward foreign investment, and the interests, suspicions, and rivalries of China, Russia, and other regional powers.

Mongolia is both advantaged and disadvantaged through its geographic position, sandwiched between the two regional giants, China and Russia. On the positive side, these two countries are Mongolia's main energy partners and cooperation has been growing. China is willing to buy all of Mongolia's energy exports, and Russia is able to supply Mongolia with the energy products it lacks, including refined petroleum products, electricity, and natural gas. Mongolia has actively courted its neighbors in an effort to increase domestic energy production and export capacity. Mongolia's location, however, puts the country at a disadvantage with regard to pricing of energy imports and exports, and makes it vulnerable to political and economic manipulation and pressure. Mongolia has expanded its energy relationships, with a focus on regional partners including Japan, South Korea, and North Korea. These countries offer Mongolia potential new markets or export channels, and sources of much-needed capital and technology to develop Mongolia's domestic energy resources and infrastructure. However, Mongolia's geographic position and the lack of a regional energy infrastructure have slowed its emergence as an energy supplier and participant in the region.

Mongolia has much to gain from regional cooperation on energy, as a regional approach would help Mongolia develop markets beyond China for its energy exports and reduce Russia's influence over Mongolia's energy supply. The country is an active supporter of regional energy initiatives promoted by the United Nations (UN) and other agencies. However, while Mongolia supports such initiatives on a diplomatic level, pragmatically it has pursued a policy of energy development that has focused on bilateral arrangements. As a small, poorly developed country surrounded by superpowers, Mongolia is not well positioned to lead a regional energy effort. It is generally a price taker whose inclusion in regional initiatives is at the discretion of the larger powers in the region. For example, Mongolia would benefit greatly from inclusion in the growing energy trade between Russia and China, but to date those powers have not allowed Mongolia to participate. Mongolia's primary source of negotiating power comes from its ability to play one regional country off against another, yielding an energy policy that supports regional energy integration while primarily pursuing bilateral arrangements with its neighbors.

Mongolia's profile on energy issues has been raised in recent years through its emergence as a coal exporter and through proposals for a number of large energy projects in the country, including major expansions of coal production, coal-fired electricity exports, coal gasification and coal to liquids, uranium mining, renewable energy schemes, and cross-Mongolia oil and natural gas pipelines and electricity transmission lines. While all of these ideas are built on some logic and have potential, they all remain unconstructed proposals that face numerous hurdles in their development. Mongolia has a poor track record of bringing major projects to fruition due to ineffective government policies, a lack of capital and resources, and challenging economic and geographic conditions. The country is likely to develop and play a larger role in a regional energy regime in the future, but its emergence will take significant time and depends on the willingness of its neighbors to finance and support development of the necessary infrastructure, facilities, and cooperative arrangements. Mongolia's dependence will to some degree support its regional integration, but also prevents the country from playing a leading role in shaping that integration.

The sections below provide a more detailed view of Mongolia's perceptions and objectives with regard to regional energy cooperation, its level of interest in cooperation, and its ability to contribute as a resource supplier and regional energy network hub. Finally, the chapter highlights areas of greatest potential for Mongolia for energy cooperation, both bilaterally and regionally, with other Northeast Asian states.

Mongolia's perceptions of and objectives for Northeast Asian energy cooperation

In order to understand Mongolia's objectives in its energy engagements in Northeast Asia, it is important to understand its main policies on energy and its foreign policy framework. In the energy field, Mongolia has two overriding concerns.

First, the country seeks to increase its domestic energy capabilities to provide the energy needed to fuel economic growth and to reduce its reliance on imported Russian petroleum products and electricity. Mongolia has an overall goal to be energy independent in supply. Second, the country is seeking to expand energy exports and partnerships to diversify export markets beyond China and enhance value-added processing and industrial production within Mongolia. These goals have been adopted by the Mongolian government, and are generally considered to be win-win propositions that enhance national security and also promote economic development. Mongolia faces a number of challenges in reaching its energy goals, but its concerns over the security of its imports and exports shape its approach to Northeast Asian energy matters.

Mongolia's foreign policy framework also shapes the country's approaches to energy issues. Mongolia has developed a balanced foreign policy approach, which recognizes as its first priority its close, special relations with its two neighbors, China and Russia, while at the same time emphasizing the need to build strong ties to third-neighbor countries and international organizations. This approach was formulated after the fall of the Soviet Union, and has been successfully implemented for almost 25 years. During this time Mongolia has steadily developed its ties with Russia and China, while also building close ties with Western countries, international organizations, and its regional neighbors.

Mongolia's "third neighbors," including the United States, the European Union (EU), Japan, and South Korea, see the country both as a strategic partner in a crucial region of the world, and as a potential market and economic partner that offers trade and business development opportunities. They have provided Mongolia with hundreds of millions of dollars in economic assistance, and offer access to advanced technology and capital to speed its development. Mongolia has also developed a role as a non-threatening middle player between East and West, most prominently displayed through its relationship with North Korea. Mongolia has maintained close ties to its old friend from Communist days, with Mongolian President Elbegdorj invited in 2013 as the first foreign leader to visit North Korea after the rise to power of Kim Jong-un. Mongolia has assisted both Japan and the United States on issues related to North Korea, earning goodwill and highlighting its role as a neutral, non-threatening state with no serious current or historical grievances against any other country.

Mongolia plays an oversized role on the international stage, taking leading posts in international organizations and among developing countries, and receiving an oversized share of international aid and development funds. As a leading democracy among developing nations, Mongolia recently served as the chair of the Community of Democracies, an intergovernmental body that supports democratic principles worldwide, and in 2014 the Mongolian Minister of the Environment, Sanjaasuren Oyun, was elected as the first head of the United Nations Environment Assembly (UNEA). Mongolia has been able to balance its ties both with Western powers and organizations and with newly emerging regional groupings. For example, Mongolia is an observer at both ASEAN and the Shanghai Cooperation Organization (SCO), and participates in annual military drills with a wide range of countries including the United States, China, and Russia. Mongolia was invited to be a founding nation in the new Chinese-promoted Asian Infrastructure Development Bank, while also continuing to receive assistance from the World Bank, Asian Development Bank, European Bank for Reconstruction and Development, and other Western-dominated institutions.

While Mongolia's efforts to develop third-neighbor relations have achieved some success, on a practical level China and Russia remain the dominant players Mongolia must consider with regard to energy issues, as it remains hostage to geography. In 2013 and 2014, Mongolia placed a special emphasis on strengthening its relations with both Russia and China, a push that coincided with growing Russian and Chinese interest in the region. The interest of all sides is evidenced by a string of high-level meetings and agreements between the countries. The Mongolian President and Prime Minister met with their Russian and Chinese counterparts at several regional meetings, and Mongolia hosted back-to-back state visits by Chinese President Xi Jinping and Russian President Vladimir Putin in late August and early September 2014 (Xinhua, 2014). These meetings resulted in a range of agreements and proposals for cooperation, including efforts in the energy field to expand energy production and develop infrastructure such as railroads and roads to connect to regional transportation networks.

Mongolia's growing ties with its neighbors are spurred in part by a string of internal and external pressures that have created economic difficulties in Mongolia. In 2011, the Mongolian economy grew by a world-leading 17.5 percent, spurred by high commodity prices and a rapid inflow of foreign investment from Western countries. Since that time, growth has slowed, and in the first half of 2014 Mongolia encountered significant economic issues as foreign investment fell by 70 percent from the year before, inflation jumped to 14.9 percent, and the value of the Mongolian currency, the tugrik, fell by 17 percent (Kohn & Humber, 2014). Mongolia's woes were caused by weakening prices and slowing demand for key exports such as coal, restrictive foreign investment laws passed during better times, and ongoing disputes with foreign investors including Rio Tinto, the global mining giant that is the largest foreign investor in Mongolia to date.

The loss of Western investment has encouraged Mongolia to seek new investments from its neighbors, despite misgivings about their interests and control over the Mongolian economy. During President Xi's visit, Mongolia and China signed a number of accords, including the upgrading of political and security ties to the level of a "comprehensive strategic partnership," new agreements giving Mongolia access to several seaports in northeast China, and pledges to support new initiatives in transportation and resource processing, including a feasibility study for a coal gasification facility (Shi, 2014). Russia and Mongolia have been negotiating a Midterm Strategic Partnership Development Program to guide Russian and Mongolian economic cooperation over the next five years. During his visit in September 2014, President Putin was expected to sign the accord that will promote the joint development of the Mongolian railway infrastructure and the promotion of trade and investment between the two countries (News.mn, 2014b).

Despite these growing ties between Mongolia and its neighbors, significant tensions and limitations in the bilateral and trilateral relationships between Mongolia, Russia, and China remain. Mongolia benefits from the traditional rivalry between Russia and China as the two giants jockey for influence in the country. For example, on the one hand, Mongolia turned to China for help in breaking Russia's monopoly over refined petroleum sales in Mongolia by reaching agreements to import refined fuels from China. On the other hand, Mongolia has actively courted Russia to help end China's monopsony on Mongolian energy exports, through proposals to develop new rail infrastructure and agreements that would facilitate the export of Mongolian coal through ports in the Russian Far East (RFE). While its efforts have yet to materialize on a large scale, it is likely that Mongolia will continue to encourage competition between its superpower neighbors in an effort to improve its position in negotiations over price and delivery terms for its energy imports and exports.

Another issue that limits Mongolia's interest and ability to participate in regional arrangements is that, while the country recognizes the need to cooperate with its neighbors on energy and infrastructure development projects, it remains deeply fearful of both the intentions of foreign countries and investors, and the potential to be dominated by one or the other of its neighbors. Mongolia has been careful to develop its relations with each of its neighbors on a relatively equal footing, and relations with both countries have advanced at a similar pace. However, Mongolia's greatest domestic concern is the growing power and influence of China. For nearly 70 years, from 1921 to 1990, Mongolia was closely aligned with the Soviet Union, and for those seven decades almost all of Mongolia's infrastructure and trade was oriented toward Russia. The fall of the Soviet Union and the rise of China as an economic power and market have shifted the dynamic in the region, and Mongolia's economic focus has shifted south. China has emerged as Mongolia's largest foreign investor and the market for almost all of Mongolia's exports of minerals and other natural resource products (World Bank, 2012).

While Mongolia maintains close and equal official ties with both Russia and China, in practice many people in Mongolia mistrust China and the intent of Chinese companies, while holding positive views of Russia. Public opinion polls in Mongolia highlight that Russia is by far the most preferred foreign partner country for Mongolia, with the United States a distant second and China third (Sant Maral Foundation, 2012). Public perceptions of China have improved in recent years, especially at the elite level, due to expanded business, cultural, and educational ties. However, many Mongolians continue to hold anti-Chinese views, as demonstrated by protests against Chinese workers and companies, concerns about the low quality of Chinese products, and everyday discrimination against Chinese residents and visitors in Mongolia (Mendee, 2011). Mongolians continue to hold a lingering suspicion that China still sees Mongolia as part of its territory, and that China has a long-range goal of taking over Mongolia through economic domination and settlement. Mongolians do not feel that Russia has the same intentions, pointing out that Russia has a smaller population, ample supplies of resources, and the vast expanses of Siberia to settle.

Mongolia is fearful of Chinese control over the production and transport of Mongolian natural resources, and the Chinese monopsony over the purchase of Mongolian natural resources. China's interests are seen to be procuring raw materials at minimum costs for the benefit of Chinese industry. Mongolia is concerned that Chinese companies would sell Mongolian products to Chinese buyers at artificially low prices, and would impede efforts for value-added processing in Mongolia. To date Mongolia has allowed small-scale Chinese investment and accepted Chinese loans for infrastructure projects, but has blocked Chinese firms from ownership stakes in major Mongolian mines and infrastructure projects. Mongolia has passed several pieces of legislation aimed at limiting foreign control over natural resource deposits, infrastructure, and other assets it deems strategic. These limitations are generally aimed at China, but the rules apply to all foreign investors and affect both the ability and interest of foreign firms looking to participate in resource projects in Mongolia.

While Mongolia's main concerns have been focused on Chinese domination of its economy and assets, it also harbors suspicions about Russian intentions. Mongolia has closely watched the situation in Ukraine, and is concerned that Russia will use its control over Mongolia's energy supplies to exert pressure on Mongolia. Mongolia has grown increasingly anxious about the security of its fuel supplies, highlighted by an incident in 2011 when Russia hiked export taxes and restricted export of petroleum products, resulting in severe fuel shortages in Mongolia that raised prices and halted work on several mining projects. Mongolia feared that Russia was using its power over Mongolia's oil supplies to force Mongolia to include Russian companies in plans to develop Mongolia's natural resources (Jacob, 2011). Supplies soon returned to normal after pleas from the Mongolian president, but the incident intensified Mongolia's search for ways to reduce dependence on imported Russian fuel.

Mongolia and Russia have also clashed at times over Russian ownership of key assets in Mongolia. Based on Soviet-era investments, Russia owns 50 percent of Mongolia's current rail network and 50 percent of several large mines in the country, including a major copper mine and other facilities. In 2009, Russian blocked a $188 million aid package from the United States to upgrade the Mongolian railway system, asserting its 50 percent ownership share in the railway (Jones, 2009). Russia has also pressed Mongolia to maintain its use of the wider Russian railway gauge rather than adopting the narrower gauge railway used by China and other countries, and sought to block efforts by Mongolia to build direct rail links from its mines in the South Gobi to Russia.

Mongolia is interested in partnering with Russia on transportation infrastructure to offer it an alternative path to the sea that avoids China, but little progress has been made due to the high costs of the infrastructure and the limited interest of Russia in shipping Mongolian coal through the RFE to Pacific ports. Russia is a significant and growing source of coking and thermal coal in the Asian market, and Russian railways and ports are at maximum capacity handling Russian-produced coal for export (Gambrel, 2014). Russia has no inherent interest in facilitating Mongolian production and export of competing energy resources, unless it has a direct interest in the trade, such as through ownership stakes in mines or railways.

While Mongolia harbors suspicions about its neighbors, it also recognizes the need to develop close relations and a working partnership. Mongolia has achieved some success in maintaining balanced relations with both of its neighbors by opening opportunities for them to engage in the development of energy resources within the country, while still blocking efforts that Mongolia feels would threaten its sovereignty and independence, or tip interests too far to one side or the other. On the one hand, examples of cooperation include signing a long-term coal supply contract with China, improvements in railway infrastructure and cross-border transit stations, and the engagement of Russian firms in development of uranium deposits. On the other hand, Mongolia has blocked efforts by Chinese state-owned enterprises to buy major coal deposits, been reluctant to develop rail infrastructure that would lock Mongolia into exports of natural resources to China, and blocked proposals that it felt gave Russia too much control over Mongolia's rail network.

Mongolia is able to maintain and exercise its national sovereignty because neither of its neighbors has felt that its core interests were threatened by Mongolian actions or the influence of the other superpower. Russia and China have both been willing to play by Mongolia's rules and tolerate its foreign and energy policy approaches, generally attempting to use positive approaches to build relations with Mongolia rather than power approaches. China appears assured that, no matter who owns or develops natural resources in Mongolia, those resources will be sold primarily to China. Russia resents its loss of status in Mongolia, but as long as Mongolia does not emerge as a major competitor to Russia in energy and other fields, and Chinese influence in Mongolia is limited, its interests remain intact. The status quo balance of power might shift at some point in the future, and Mongolia alone would be powerless to stop aggression or heavy pressure from either of its neighbors. However, the balancing presence of two great powers as neighbors does offer Mongolia some assurance of its continued independence and national sovereignty.

Mongolia's level of interest in cooperating with other Northeast Asian countries

On a broad level, greater energy cooperation within Northeast Asia offers Mongolia the opportunity to achieve multiple national goals, including energy policy goals to reduce reliance on Russia and China for imports and exports of energy, development policy goals to enhance processing of natural resources within the country, and foreign policy goals of deepening ties with both of its neighbors and a range of third-neighbor states. Mongolia actively supports the full range of formal, regional discussions on energy, as these efforts allow it to participate on an equal footing with its larger neighbors. However, on a more practical basis these discussions have yielded few tangible results, and Mongolia has focused on building bilateral relations and pursuing individual projects with specific nations.

As part of its multilateral foreign policy and an interest in participating on an equal footing with its larger neighbors, Mongolia has been an active participant in a wide range of efforts aimed at promoting regional energy security and cooperation. Mongolia is currently engaged in ten organizations discussing Northeast Asian energy issues (Working Group on Energy Planning and Policy, 2010). The most important and active of these include the Energy Charter Treaty (ECT) and the Intergovernmental Collaborative Mechanism on Energy Cooperation in North-East Asia (ECNEA). Mongolia ratified the ECT in 1999, and has been active in the organization, hosting meetings and carrying out required reviews and studies. In 2010, Mongolia hosted the sixth meeting of the Regional Task Force on Electricity Cooperation in Central and South Asia. At the meeting, the Ulaanbaatar Declaration on Promoting Regional Energy Cooperation was adopted, which recommended continued work to create legal, technical, and regulatory frameworks for cross-border energy transit and trade, and the development of model investment agreements for the energy sector (Task Force on Promoting Regional Electricity Cooperation between Central and South Asia, 2010). While these agreements remain at a theoretical level, Mongolia has a strong interest in pushing forward among Northeast Asian countries to diversify supply sources and facilitate potential exports of electricity.

Mongolia was a founding member and active participant of ECNEA, an organization created by senior officials from Mongolia, the Russian Federation, the Republic of Korea (South Korea), and the Democratic People's Republic of Korea (North Korea) under the auspices of the UN Economic and Social Commission for Asia and the Pacific (UNESCAP). The organizational meeting for this group was held in Ulaanbaatar in November 2005, and Mongolia has participated in both annual meetings of senior officials and working groups on energy planning and policy and coal (Working Group on Energy Planning and Policy, 2010). Mongolia has also been an active participant in the Greater Tumen Initiative (GTI) and hosted the inaugural meeting of the GTI Energy Board in 2009. The Energy Board is working to develop concrete projects related to energy cooperation in the Tumen River region, which includes eastern Mongolia, northeast China, the RFE and the Koreas (UNDP China, 2009). The GTI has made little headway since its founding in 1995, but has recently been revived due to new discussions about regional infrastructure development. Mongolia's eagerness to host these regional meetings emphasizes both the priority Mongolia places on enhancing its energy security and energy development, and its search for ways to engage its neighbors on a more equal basis. Mongolia is keen to explore the use of the GTI to open the door for potential exports through North Korean ports.

Despite its interests and active involvement in the formal regional energy discussions, a number of factors limit Mongolia's ability to play a larger role in the development of multinational regional energy cooperation. First, Mongolia perceives that its interests are best served by encouraging competition among regional countries that want to participate in energy development projects in Mongolia or supply the country with energy. Mongolia often uses the inherent tensions and competition between its regional neighbors to gain access to capital and expertise and get a better price for its imports and exports. It has generally negotiated on a bilateral basis in its efforts to advance energy efforts, seeking to find the partner that will make the best offer on each project.

Second, Mongolia is a relatively small country in political and economic terms, and it has a fairly small influence on most regional energy markets. Despite its recent growth, Mongolia remains Northeast Asia's smallest and least developed country, with a population of 3 million people and countrywide economic output in 2013 of $17 billion (Central Intelligence Agency, 2013). Mongolia has a per capita GDP of $5,900 in purchasing power parity terms, and 30 percent of the population is classified as poor, with many continuing to practice traditional lifestyles as transient livestock herders living in felt tents (World Bank, 2012). Mongolia faces development hurdles because its territory is vast and its basic infrastructure of roads, railroads, and electricity is poorly developed outside urban areas. Beyond coal, Mongolia's exports remain small, and therefore Mongolia's current impact on energy planning and markets is limited.

Third, Mongolia has thus far been shut out of the growing energy cooperation between China and Russia due to the availability of direct border connections between its neighbors both west and east of Mongolia, and Chinese and Russian fears of ceding control over pipeline infrastructure to a third country. A trans-Mongolian route has been touted as the lowest-cost route for a natural gas pipeline from the Kovykta gas field north of Lake Baikal in East Siberia to the main population centers of China and the Korean peninsula, due to its shorter distance and easy terrain (Paik, 2005). However, China and Russia decided by the early 2000s that any natural gas or oil pipelines should avoid Mongolian territory to reduce the political risk and complication of third-party involvement or control. This decision was reportedly influenced by concerns that a pipeline across Mongolia might offer the United States a lever to potentially influence Russian–Chinese energy cooperation, given Mongolia's close relations with the United States (Mendee, 2014b). Mongolia's exclusion was not in the best interests of Korea, Japan, or Mongolia, because it raised the cost of construction and operation for the line, and excluded Mongolia from the benefits of access to a natural gas supply and potential transit revenues (Paik, 2005).

Mongolian President Elbegdorj has repeatedly called on China and Russia to route proposed pipelines from East and West Siberian gas fields through Mongolia to allow the country to utilize natural gas instead of coal as a power and heating fuel. He pressed both Chinese President Xi Jinping and Russian President Putin on this issue during their visits in August and September 2014. Russia and China have given no public indication that they are considering including Mongolia in their plans, concentrating instead on a dual set of pipelines that both bypass Mongolia. The proposed Altai gas pipeline from West Siberian gas fields has been designed to run through a narrow strip of Russian territory between Mongolia and Kazakhstan to directly link Russia and China, a routing that crosses difficult, mountainous terrain and delivers gas to a lightly settled part of western China. While the western leg is unlikely to be built soon, the eastern leg that will connect Russia's Siberian and Far Eastern gas fields directly to China through the

RFE appears to be moving ahead (Lamphier, 2014). Mongolia currently has no natural gas supply, and seeks to gain access to Russian natural gas to use as a fuel source for power plants and home heating in Ulaanbaatar, which has some of the world's worst air pollution despite being located in the least densely populated country in the world.

Russia's growing interest in developing Asian markets for its energy products may create conditions that support the inclusion of Mongolia into regional oil or natural gas pipeline plans, although it is more likely that a Mongolian pipeline would only be a branch line of an east–west pipeline from Siberia to the RFE. In March 2014, Rosneft President Igor Sechin visited Mongolia and proposed an oil pipeline from Siberia to Mongolia to supply the country with oil on a long-term basis, and hinted at the possibility of a cross-Mongolia oil pipeline to China (Mendee, 2014b). The offer, while raising Mongolian hopes, is probably more reflective of changing market conditions and Rosneft's attempts to lock up a supply deal with a customer that is projecting increasing demand in coming years.

Mongolia will therefore likely only be included in a natural gas or oil pipeline if its neighbors decide it is in their own best interests to include Mongolia in their energy schemes, either to develop a shorter route between Russian fields and Chinese markets, or as an effort to build an alliance with Mongolia. Russia's renewed interest in developing Asian markets for its energy in the wake of the Ukraine crisis, and growing oil and natural gas production in North America, may increase the likelihood that Mongolia may someday be included in the Russian pipeline network, but the Russian and Chinese governments have not endorsed the idea. One proposal for energy transport across Mongolia that did receive the endorsement of its neighbors is the use of the Trans-Mongolian rail line to ship crude oil between Russia and China (Priddy, 2013). Oil shipments along this line occurred prior to the opening of the Eastern Siberia–Pacific Ocean (ESPO) oil pipeline, but then declined. However, the line would need substantial upgrading to handle large volumes of cargo, including oil, but it remains one transit option for increased oil trade in the region.

Mongolia and its two neighbors have developed several joint bilateral projects and proposals in energy fields. China has been Mongolia's primary energy partner despite Mongolian concerns about becoming overly reliant on the Chinese market. Recent agreements between the two states provide evidence that Mongolia intends to follow a more pragmatic approach with regard to energy cooperation with China. A visit to China by Mongolian Prime Minister Altankhuyag in October 2013 and a visit to Mongolia by President Xi in August 2014 resulted in agreements for several new joint projects, including the construction of a cross-border rail line to facilitate coal exports, the signing of a long-term coal agreement covering up to 1 billion tons of coal exports over 20 years, and the development of a coal gasification plant in Mongolia (Kohn, 2013). Mongolia pledged to join China's "Silk Road Economic Belt" and agreed to cooperate in the upgrading of the Trans-Mongolian Railway to develop the overland link between China and Europe.

In all of these agreements, a key goal for Mongolia is to maintain its own ownership and control over assets within Mongolia, as it perceives that foreign ownership would threaten national sovereignty. Therefore Mongolia has been reluctant to allow Chinese firms to directly own coal or railway assets, but is willing to accept Chinese loans or investments in the projects. China appears to have accepted this limitation, taking the view that it is less important who produces or ships the natural resources, as long as the end product is delivered to China. China's main frustration has been the slow rate of development of both mineral production and infrastructure in Mongolia, as the Mongolian government has been unable to enact policies and carry out key projects that would boost Mongolia's production of natural resources. China has the capital and know-how to substantially boost Mongolian production of coal and other resources, as it has shown in the development of resources and infrastructure in Inner Mongolia. However a workable arrangement must be reached that placates Mongolian fears of Chinese domination but facilitates Chinese involvement in developing infrastructure and production capacity.

One energy field where such an arrangement appears to have been reached is crude oil production in Mongolia. Mongolia historically had almost no crude oil production, but oil production has been rising rapidly, moving from almost none in 2005 to more than 5 million barrels produced in 2013, up 50 percent from the year before (U.S. Energy Information Administration, 2014). This increase has been driven almost entirely by PetroChina, a division of Chinese oil giant, the China National Petroleum Corporation (CNPC), which took over a set of oil leases from a Western oil company in 2005. PetroChina has been able to employ seismic technology and drilling crews from its Chinese oil fields at a fraction of the cost of technologies and equipment imported from outside China. The main Mongolian producing oil fields are located in remote areas of eastern Mongolia near the Chinese Daqing oil field, and all the oil produced in Mongolia is exported directly to China by truck. Some concerns have been raised about environmental practices and failures to live up to contract agreements, but no direct efforts have been made to push the Chinese company out of its production rights for oil leases.

Mongolia's willingness to allow a Chinese firm to control oil production, while blocking Chinese ownership of coal assets, reflects the rising volume and value of oil exports and Mongolia's interest in courting China as an alternative supplier of refined oil products to counter Russia's monopoly. In 2013, Mongolia reached an agreement with China for the supply of refined petroleum products in exchange for Mongolia's exports of crude oil to China (Campi, 2013). While infrastructure constraints, such as limited cross-border transfer capacity and China's own desire to utilize refined petroleum products domestically, will prevent China from completely displacing Russia as a refined oil supplier to Mongolia, the two-way flow of oil between Mongolia and China serves the interests of both countries.

Mongolia has also been exploring other options for energy cooperation with China. In March 2014, the Mongolia government set up a working group to explore a project with the Sinopec Group to build a coal gasification project to supply gas for domestic use and potential export to China (Government of

Mongolia, 2014). While such a plant would require billions of dollars to build, the Chinese group is hoping to build on the knowledge learned from the recent opening of the first large-scale Chinese coal gasification plant located in Inner Mongolia. Other opportunities for cooperation between China and Mongolia include proposed projects to build coal-fired power plants in Mongolia to supply both the domestic market and exports of electricity to China, and Chinese interest in exploring and developing uranium deposits in Mongolia.

Because Russia produces many of the same products as Mongolia does, there has been limited interest from Russia in most Mongolian resources. The main energy resource in Mongolia of interest to Russia for import is uranium. Mongolia has the largest deposits of uranium in Northeast Asia and, due to longstanding ties and an interest in finding fields for Russian engagement to balance Chinese investments and power, Mongolia has taken extraordinary steps to offer Russia an opportunity to produce uranium in Mongolia. Russia has no domestic supplies of uranium, and has been seeking new sources of the fuel because of the diminishment of the processed uranium stockpile left over from the dismantling of nuclear weapons after the end of the Cold War.

In 2008 and 2009, Mongolia adopted a new strategy and policy for the development of its uranium resources that focused on cooperation with Russia. At the time, the mining rights to the main uranium deposit in the country, the Dornod deposit, were held by a Canadian firm, which was conducting exploration work and preparing to open a mining operation at the site. The Mongolian government passed a series of laws that first forced the Canadian company to give the Mongolian government a 51 percent share of the mine without compensation, and then led to the cancellation of the Canadian firm's mining license. The Mongolian government then awarded the license to a Russian firm, ARMZ. Many foreign observers saw these moves as a clear case of expropriation of private property by the Mongolian government, and Khan Resources filed a variety of legal actions in Mongolia and international courts, claiming violations of its rights under Mongolian law and international treaties such as the Energy Charter (Stanway, 2010). While the case remains in international arbitration, the Mongolian government has signalled that it plans to continue to work with Russia to develop uranium production, no matter what the court decides.

The actions of Mongolia with regard to uranium seem to undermine Mongolian goals of maintaining national sovereignty and limiting the role of its neighboring countries. However, in this case Mongolia seems primarily motivated by an interest in keeping Russia engaged in Mongolia, to maintain close relations and balance the much larger Chinese investments in the country. Russia does not have the technology or capital Mongolia needs to support the development of its other energy resources, and sees increased Mongolian production of coal, oil, and other energy resources as direct competition to its own production. Mongolia and Russia have explored opportunities to jointly develop Mongolia's rail infrastructure, which is held as a 50/50 joint venture between Russia and Mongolia, but those negotiations have foundered due to the inability of both sides to raise the capital necessary and agree on a workable ownership structure.

In addition to its ties with Russia and China, Mongolia has worked to expand and diversify its energy partnerships, in keeping with its third-neighbor policies. Mongolia has a growing relationship with Japan and South Korea in the energy field, spurred by its need for technology and capital to develop its energy resources and domestic industries. Japan and Korea are seeking commercial opportunities for their companies, and new sources of energy and other natural resources. This mutual engagement was highlighted in March 2013, when Japanese Prime Minister Shinzo Abe chose to visit Mongolia ahead of other regional states, and emphasized the budding energy relationship between the two states. During his visit, Abe told a news conference, "We want to bolster ties with Mongolia with the objective of creating a good makeup of various energy sources. Mongolia is an energy giant, and both countries can create a win-win relationship, with Japan's technological prowess" (Hyashi & Ono, 2013). Since 2012, Mongolia and Japan have been actively negotiating an Economic Partnership Agreement to strengthen trade and investment ties between the countries, and Japan remains the largest bilateral aid donor to Mongolia, financing projects such as power station upgrades and a new international airport in Ulaanbaatar.

Japan is keen to engage Mongolia to help enhance its energy security, and to seek opportunities for its companies to engage in energy development projects. Japanese companies have participated in several important infrastructure projects in Mongolia, including the development of a new coal-fired power plant in Ulaanbaatar. Japanese firms have also been at the forefront of an effort to develop an oil refinery in Mongolia. In 2010, Toyo Engineering and Marubeni announced a $600 million effort to build a refinery in Darkhan, a city in northern Mongolia, to process imported crude oil from Russia (Marubeni Corporation, 2010). This refinery would not reduce Mongolia's overall reliance on Russia as its source of petroleum, but would give the country more flexibility in supply, as it could buy crude oil from a variety of Russian producers rather than relying solely on Rosneft, which supplies more than 90 percent of the refined petroleum products in Mongolia. Mongolia produces crude oil, but is unable to refine and use its domestically produced oil, given the distance between its oil production sites and its population centers. The Japanese oil refinery proposal has been postponed several times, and substantial construction has not yet started, therefore its success and completion date remain uncertain.

A more promising area of cooperation between Mongolia and Japan is in the field of renewable energy. The Japanese National Renewable Energy Foundation, which was established by SoftBank founder Masayoshi Son, has proposed the development of an "Asia super-grid," which would promote the development of renewable wind and solar power in Mongolia and connect the electrical grids of Japan, Korea, China, Mongolia, and Russia (Patton, 2012). SoftBank has partnered with the Mongolian company Newcom to conduct feasibility studies on wind power generation in the South Gobi region near the Chinese border as a first step in the Asia super-grid project. The Asia super-grid is modeled on the Desertec project to produce solar power in North Africa for export to Europe. Mongolian renewable energy has been promoted as a potential clean energy source to reduce China's dependence on highly carbon-intensive coal-fired power, and as a means for Japan to maintain a clean energy supply as it phases out domestic nuclear power production. However, substantial obstacles to an Asia super-grid have been identified, including the closed nature of the Japanese electricity market, the lack of a regional electric power grid, and the political and geographic barriers between Mongolia and Japan (Patton, 2012).

Another joint effort that was touted during Abe's visit was Japanese participation in the development of the huge Tavan Tolgoi coal field in Mongolia (Hyashi & Ono, 2013). This deposit represents the largest untapped global deposit of coking coal, and also contains significant deposits of thermal coal. Japan has been lobbying for its companies to be involved in the development and production of the field. Mongolia is interested in applying Japanese technology and capital resources in the development of the mine, but is most interested in finding ways to export Mongolian coking coal from Tavan Tolgoi to Japan to open an alternative to the Chinese market. Thus far, it has not been economically feasible to ship Mongolian coal to Japan because of the transport costs and bottlenecks involved in trans-shipment across China or Russia. While Japanese–Mongolian cooperation in energy fields has been limited, Prime Minister Abe's visit underscores the interest of both nations in further cooperation.

Mongolia has also been working actively with both South and North Korea on energy-related issues. The Republic of Korea-Mongolia Committee for Energy and Mineral Resources Cooperation was established in 1999, and has held annual meetings since that time to discuss cooperation in the development of coal and uranium deposits, power plants, power lines, and renewable energy. The Korean firm POSCO has announced plans to build a major coal-to-liquids plant in Ulaanbaatar that would allow the country to reduce its reliance on Russian petroleum imports (Oxford Business Group, 2013). Samsung has a major contract to build a coal railway between the largest Mongolian coal mine, Tavan Tolgoi, and the Chinese border. Work on the project has proceeded in fits and starts for several years, but is currently suspended due to the Mongolia government's inability to pay for the work conducted to date. South Korea has also expressed its interest in cooperating with Mongolia on infrastructure projects to support South Korean President Park Geun-hye's Eurasia Initiative to develop transportation networks in the region (Choi, 2013), an initiative that fits Chinese and Russian interests as well.

Mongolia has renewed its ties with its old Communist friend, North Korea, in an effort to explore opportunities to use North Korean ports as an alternative outlet to the sea. In October 2013, President Elbegdorj visited North Korea on a mission primarily aimed at building economic ties between the two states. He noted that North Korean sea ports were the closest to Mongolia, and that Mongolia was interested in cooperating with North Korea to ship Mongolian minerals and energy products such as coal to world markets through North Korea (Kim, 2013). While the infrastructure to ship coal to North Korea is currently lacking, future development of train lines in the region, such as through the GTI, might offer Mongolia a new option to bypass Chinese and Russian ports in the export of coal and other products.

Mongolia's ability to contribute to regional energy cooperation

Mongolia has a demonstrated interest in cooperating with the nations of Northeast Asia on energy development and deposits of a number of resources of interest to countries in the region, including coal, crude oil, shale oil, and uranium. It also has the potential to supply electricity, and the geographic position to serve as a transmission corridor for oil, natural gas, and electricity between Russia and China. Despite these advantages, Mongolia has been unable to effectively develop its energy resources and emerge as a major supplier of energy to the region. The country has been hobbled by both internal and external barriers, including policy confusion, government mismanagement, falling resource prices, and a lack of infrastructure. This section provides an overview of Mongolia's resource endowment and development potential, and highlights some of the internal and external challenges the nation faces with regard to the development of its energy resources and cooperation with its Northeast Asian neighbors.

The primary energy source of interest to regional countries in the near future is Mongolia's vast deposits of both coking coal and thermal coal. Mongolia holds estimated coal resources of more than 150 billion tons, of which 12.2 billion tons are proven, with more than 10 billion tons of thermal coal and 2 billion tons of metallurgical coking coal (Badgaa, 2010). If proven, Mongolia's coal reserves would be comparable to China's and among the largest reserves in the world. More than 200 significant coal deposits have been mapped and tested, many in the South Gobi region of Mongolia near the Chinese border, where Mongolia has a number of active, producing coal mines. Mongolia's exports of coking coal to China have risen five-fold since 2009, with Mongolia at times displacing Australia to become China's largest international coking coal supplier (Steelhome. cn, 2012).

Mongolia is well positioned to become China's primary international supplier of coking coal and a major supplier of thermal coal, given its geographic position, which creates a potential cost and time advantage over other competing producers including Australia, Indonesia, Russia, the United States, and Canada. However, despite these advantages, Mongolian coal shipments to China have been reduced because of falling prices, a lack of infrastructure, and political and management missteps by Mongolia. Mongolia's coal shipments to China fell from 20.9 million tons in 2012 to 18.3 million tons in 2013, and the value of coal shipments from Mongolia plunged 41 percent in 2013 due to sharp decreases in the value of both coking coal and thermal coal (Kohn, 2014).

Several factors have contributed to the slump in Mongolia's coal production and its inability to play a larger role in regional markets. One key issue is the lack of transportation infrastructure in the country, in particular the lack of railroads to export bulk commodity loads such as coal. Mongolia has one trunk railway, known as the Trans-Mongolian Railway, which runs north–south and connects China to the Russian Trans-Siberian Railway. This line is built using the wider Russian-gauge rails, therefore all cargos must be transferred at the Chinese border to access the narrower, Chinese standard-gauge railway. The main Mongolian coal mines are located far from the Trans-Mongolian line, therefore Mongolia exports most of its coal by truck over unpaved roads through the Gobi Desert. Truck transport costs substantially more than rail transport for bulk commodities such as coal, and the unpaved roads create heavy wear and tear on the trucks and severe problems for local residents due to dust and land degradation. Mongolia loses the majority of its price advantage over other coal producers due to its high transport costs.

Construction of new rail infrastructure has been delayed due to debates on its proper routing, whether to construct the lines using the wider Russian gauge or the narrower Chinese gauge, and problems gaining financing for construction. In 2010, Mongolia passed a State Railway Policy aimed at creating a route for Mongolian exports that avoided China, through construction of railways from Mongolia's main coal mines away from the Chinese border to connect with the Russian railway system and facilitate export of natural resources through RFE ports. The policy required use of the wider Russian gauge on all railways in Mongolia. While politically popular, the rail plan adopted by the parliament was not supported by economic conditions, and it has not been implemented in practice. The costs and risks involved in shipping Mongolian minerals from the South Gobi area through Russia to world markets would, at best, have an enormous cost to producers and the nation, and at worst price Mongolian products completely out of world markets. Shipping costs along this route were estimated to be three times higher than direct shipment to China (Warlters, 2009). Mongolia's easiest route to the sea is through Chinese ports, which are 3,000 kilometers closer to Mongolian mines. However, the use of Russian-gauge rails complicates exports through China and places a substantial tax on Mongolian producers.

As part of its new efforts to increase foreign investment and coal production, Mongolia has now reconsidered its rail development plans and started construction on a direct rail line between the Tavan Tolgoi deposit and the Chinese border. Construction is led by the Korean company Samsung and financed by the Mongolian government. Construction is only partially complete; it came to a halt in early 2014 because the Mongolian government does not have the funds to finish the project (News.mn, 2014a). This 240-kilometer rail line will permit the export of 30 million tons of coal per year, and will halve the transportation costs and time compared with shipment by truck. The Chinese coal company Shenhua has been awarded a contract to build a short rail link across the border to connect the Mongolian rail line with the Chinese rail system, facilitating the transfer of coal across the border (Edwards, 2014). This cooperation may be expanded to the entire rail line, from Tavan Tolgoi to the border, and Mongolia is considering the use of the narrow Chinese gauge for the project to reduce border trans-shipment costs (InfoMongolia, 2014a).

Mongolia's ability to effectively cooperate with Russia, China, and other Northeast Asian countries has been complicated and frustrated by domestic political pressures and wrangling within the country. As a democracy with a decentralized power structure, Mongolia has faced challenges in building a stable policy regime to guide foreign investment and engagement. Political parties and leading politicians have used fear of foreign influence as an election issue, while also jockeying for position to benefit personally from deals with particular partners (Mendee, 2014a). The result has been an unstable approach to foreign investment policy and key projects. The government has repeatedly changed foreign investment regulations, as politicians seek to demonstrate their nationalistic credentials at election time by passing legislation that restricts foreign ownership rights, and then reduce the restrictions after the election, when they need to demonstrate progress toward economic development. Elections have also resulted in the cancellation of previously signed agreements and projects as newly elected politicians seek to gain a share of lucrative projects negotiated by previous governments.

Two events related to the development of coal mines in Mongolia highlight the difficulty Mongolia faces in terms of encouraging the foreign investment necessary to develop its natural resources, while also attempting to maintain national sovereignty and balance the interests of its neighbors. The first was the fall 2012 takeover bid by Chalco, a Chinese state-owned aluminum company, to buy a majority stake in a major Mongolian coal mine, Ovoot Tolgoi, which was owned by a Canadian company, SouthGobi Sands. This $900 million takeover bid was the first large-scale attempt by a Chinese state-owned company to buy a major resource deposit in Mongolia. The Mongolian government reacted with alarm and by a rushed passage of a new law on foreign investment, the Strategic Entities Foreign Investment Law (SEFIL), which required parliamentary approval for the sale of any strategic Mongolian mineral assets to foreign state-owned companies (Hook, 2012).

The new law and the uncertainty it created scuttled the takeover bid and seemed to rule out any future investments by Chinese state-owned enterprises (SOEs) in Mongolia, but its impact did not stop there. The unclear provisions in the law implied that almost all foreign investment in Mongolia would be required to go through a government approval process, no matter the home country or structure of the firm making the investment. This created a new level of uncertainty for all foreign investors, raising their risk by increasing the time it might take to complete an acquisition deal, opening deals to government interference, and raising uncertainty as to whether deals would be approved. In October 2013, amid falling foreign investment, Mongolia repealed SEFIL, adopted a new foreign investment law, and stepped up its efforts to woo investors by pledging to maintain a stable and open environment for foreign investment. The new law, however, kept in place restrictions on SOE investments, and foreign investors were slow to react as yet another legislative change made the regime seem more, rather than less, uncertain. Restrictions on SOE investment remove one major source of potential foreign investment for Mongolia and complicate potential deals for other investors that might partner with Chinese SOEs.

A second example, the Tavan Tolgoi coal mine, also illustrates the challenges Mongolia faces as it attempts to reconcile several sometimes competing goals: maintaining national sovereignty, building balanced relations with key foreign states, and attracting foreign investment and capital. Tavan Tolgoi is the largest and most valuable proven coal deposit in Mongolia. It includes several coking and thermal coal deposits located in the South Gobi only 250 kilometers from the Chinese border. The coal fields jointly have 4.5 billion tons of established reserves, including 1.9 billion tons of high-quality coking coal (Warlters, 2009). The Tavan Tolgoi coal fields contain enough coking coal to supply the Chinese import market for more than 100 years and, given their geographic location, they are well positioned to become the primary source of imported coking coal for China, displacing imports from Australia, Indonesia, Canada, and other sources (Warlters, 2009).

The primary Tavan Tolgoi coal fields are 100 percent owned by the Mongolian government through a government-owned company known as Erdenes MGL, but are not yet in large-scale production because issues with the management and development financing of the deposit. Since 2011, the Mongolian government has attempted to finance large-scale operation of the mine through several approaches, including an initial public offering (IPO), a tender process to select operating companies for the mine, the presale of coal, and direct management of production at the mine. All of these approaches have encountered difficulties, and production at the mine has never reached capacity. Operations at the mine were recently halted due to the failure of the Mongolian government to pay the contract operator mining coal there (*Energy Business Review*, 2014).

The Tavan Tolgoi saga offers a glimpse into Mongolian approaches to project development and the challenges major projects have faced. Mongolian government missteps and falling commodity prices have complicated efforts to bring the mine to full production. The original IPO was cancelled due to falling coal prices, but several foreign partners were still interested in playing a role in the development of this world-class deposit. The Mongolian government was reluctant to allow any single foreign company to take a lead role, fearing that choosing one partner might counter their goal of balancing the economic and political influence of their two near neighbors and "third neighbors." Therefore, Mongolia decided to work with three companies from key partner states, including Shenhua Energy from China, Peabody Energy from the United States, and the Russian Railway system, to develop the mine. While the decision clearly had geopolitical aims for Mongolia, it was immediately criticized by Japanese and Korean firms that had been excluded from the deal, and by the companies themselves, which had no experience of working together or no plan to work together (Els, 2011). Attempts were made to bring Japanese and Korean firms into the process and to find a workable arrangement among the partners, but after months of fruitless negotiations no operational plan was reached. This process highlighted Mongolia's interest in engaging countries in the region, but also emphasized that Mongolia is ill-prepared to take a leading role in fostering energy cooperation.

Mongolia also suffers from a poor reputation for honoring contracts, which hurts efforts to raise funds and locate high-quality partners. At Tavan Tolgoi, after failing in its efforts to engage international partners, the Mongolian government decided to take over direct control of the mine. To raise money to run the mine, it entered into a contract with the Chinese firm Chalco, with a $350 million prepayment for the future delivery of high-quality coking coal. Mongolia was unable to deliver this coal, however, after the government redirected the majority of the funds to other purposes, leaving Tavan Tolgoi without working capital to conduct mining operations (Humber, 2013). Production and delivery of coal under the Chalco contract is several years behind schedule, and Mongolia still owes Chalco more than $100 million in undelivered coal (InfoMongolia, 2014b). Mongolia's inability to honor its contractual obligations has hurt its reputation and made many Chinese companies and other potential partners wary of depending on supplies of energy from Mongolia.

Mongolia's challenges with regard to the production and delivery of its most abundant energy source, coal, carry over somewhat to its other potential energy resources, such as conventional and unconventional oil and gas, uranium, and electricity. In most energy fields Mongolia faces complex challenges that will require substantial investments of money, time, and technology. Mongolia's conflicts between its national security goals and efficient production of natural resources, coupled with government mismanagement and a lack of capital, create an environment that makes it difficult to move major projects forward in a timely fashion. Opportunities exist to develop certain Mongolian energy resources, but the country will have to be willing to cede a certain level of control and rights over projects to foreign partners to advance the projects. A number of potential projects that fit this mold are described below.

Oil is one area where Mongolia's production has grown rapidly in recent years, due to Mongolia's willingness to take a relatively hands-off approach to its production. However, while Mongolia's oil production has grown, on a global scale production levels remain low. In 2013, Mongolia produced approximately 5.1 million barrels of oil, a tiny fraction of China's daily imports, and a number that is not expected to grow sharply in coming years (U.S. Energy Information Administration, 2014). The Mongolian Ministry of Energy estimates that Mongolia has proven reserves of approximately 200 million tonnes of oil, with total reserves of 1.6 billion tonnes (National Dispatching Center of Power Systems, 2012). Mongolia also has fairly substantial unconventional oil reserves, such as shale oil, although it has not been produced commercially. According to U.S. government estimates, Mongolia contains risked, technically feasible reserves of 3.4 billion barrels of shale oil and 4 trillion cubic feet (Tcf) of shale gas (U.S. Energy Information Administration, 2013). Shale oil production tends to be very expensive per barrel, and Mongolia must compete with other nations that have much larger shale oil and shale gas reserves, such as Russia, the United States, and China.

Mongolia currently produces no natural gas, and domestic demand is limited to bottled liquefied petroleum gas (LPG), as there are no pipelines or distribution systems in the country. Mongolia has some prospect for coalbed methane and shale gas, and may contain natural gas deposits, but exploration for the fuels has been limited as Mongolia lacks a production and distribution infrastructure (Swedish Trade Council, 2008). Several companies in recent years have touted Mongolia's opportunity to develop its coal resources for coal gasification or coal to liquids, including Korea's POSCO, China's Sinopec, Germany's ThyssenKrup and Bechtel from the United States (Oxford Business Group, 2013). Given the high cost of the gas or liquids produced, most of these projects are touted for their national security rather than economic benefits, a cost Mongolia is not currently able to pay.

A more promising area of production and cooperation for Mongolia is uranium, as Mongolia is one of the few countries in Asia to have substantial deposits of this energy resource. As described earlier, Russia has been Mongolia's long-standing partner in uranium exploration and development, a partnership enhanced through new agreements between the two countries. The international Red Book estimates Mongolia's reasonably assured and inferred uranium resources at 49,000 tonnes uranium (tU) (World Nuclear Association, 2012), but some reports indicate that untested deposits may raise total reserves in the country to 1.39 million tons, the largest in the world (Sachs, 2009). Northeast Asia is not generally well endowed with uranium resources, and the largest suppliers are Australia and African countries, although Kazakhstan is emerging as a supplier in Asia.

The Dornod deposit is by far the largest and most advanced uranium project in Mongolia, and the only one likely to enter significant production within a five-year time frame. ARMZ has estimated that Dornod contains at least 50,000 tonnes of uranium reserves, and that production of approximately 1,000 to 2,000 tU per year is possible by 2015 (World Nuclear Association, 2012). Given the interests of both the Russian and Mongolian governments in pursuing nuclear cooperation, ARMZ will likely lead the development of the Dornod mine, although development may be delayed by the continuing international legal action by Khan Resources. Exploration has also continued at several other sites for uranium exploration and mine development. Companies from several countries, including Canada, China, Japan, France, and India, hold exploration licenses for uranium prospects in Mongolia. However, the Nuclear Energy Law, which gives the Mongolian government an automatic 51 percent share in most uranium deposits in Mongolia, is a major obstacle to the successful development of uranium mines.

In terms of energy resources, electricity generation and transmission offer Mongolia its best opportunity to become involved with a wider regional market. Mongolia's system of electricity production and distribution largely dates from the Soviet era, but a significant expansion has been proposed to meet Mongolia's growing domestic needs and potential for export to China, Japan, and the Koreas. Several new power plants have been proposed for the South Gobi region near the Chinese border with a focus on mine mouth coal-fired power plants that would supply electricity to Mongolia's mining industry and export electricity rather than coal to China. The Mongolian government has projected that Mongolia has the ability to export over 4 gigawatts (GW) of electricity to China in coming years as mines and power plants are developed (Khashchuulun, 2010).

In the short run, Mongolia is likely to increase its electricity imports from both Russia and China to meet growing domestic demand, but in the longer run, Mongolia may serve as an electricity producer and exporter to China and the region through the development of both coal-fired power plants and renewable power sources such as wind and solar. Mongolia has one of the world's largest endowments of wind power potential, with estimated wind power capacity of more than 4,300 GW, a figure that dwarfs Mongolia's domestic energy needs and even exceeds China's total installed electricity capacity (Elliot, 2001). Mongolia's solar potential is also huge, given its large land mass and low population density. Many of the areas of highest wind and solar potential are located near the Chinese border, and some observers have touted the potential for Mongolia to develop its wind and solar resources for export to China, Japan, and South Korea (Borford-Parnell, 2010).

While Mongolia has tremendous potential as a renewable energy supplier, renewable power production on a large scale in Mongolia also faces numerous domestic and international challenges. Mongolia has only one large-scale renewable project, a 50 megawatt (MW) wind farm near Ulaanbaatar. Mongolia's domestic capacity to support wind and solar power is limited due to the unpredictable nature of most renewables, the low retail price of domestic power, the availability of cheap coal, and the lack of transmission infrastructure. Renewable power is of interest to regional countries such as Japan that might be willing to pay the high costs of project development and the resulting high electricity prices; however, there is a lack of existing administrative and transmission infrastructure to support the export of electricity from Mongolia across China to Japan or South Korea.

In addition to power production, Mongolia has been cited as a potential transmission route for hydropower exports from Russia to China and other Northeast Asian countries (Hyun-jae, 2003; Asia Pacific Energy Research Centre, 2004). Large-scale export of power from Russia to China, however, would require the development of new transmission infrastructure. Siberia contains some of the largest hydropower resources in the world, and substantial opportunities exist to link these resources to markets in China, Korea, and Japan. Companies including RusHydro and the En+ group in Russia are developing new hydropower dams along the Angara River, which flows north from Lake Baikal near Irkutsk. These dams will have a capacity of more than 3 million MW, and plans have been developed to export the power from these new dams to the Beijing area in China along a 1,400-kilometer power line crossing central Mongolia (Nishimura, 2012). The trans-Mongolian route would be advantageous to minimize the distance between the production and consumption locations of electricity, due to the cost of transmission lines and the degradation and loss of electrical power that occurs during transmission.

Despite the economic advantages, however, it is unclear whether the Russian and Chinese governments would be willing to allow transmission lines to cross Mongolian territory, or whether the two countries would route transmission lines around Mongolia. Russia recently completed a major new electrical power line across the Amur River in the RFE, significantly expanding Russia's capacity to export electricity to northeastern China. The new power line allows up to 7 billion kilowatt-hours of electricity to be exported to Heilongjiang province, and plans call for up to 60 billion kilowatt-hours a year to be delivered from Siberia and the RFE to China by 2020 (Nishimura, 2012). Electricity from the RFE can be distributed to other parts of northeastern China through the Chinese state electrical grid. Russia lacks the transmission capacity, however, to transmit Siberian hydropower to the RFE. Russia and China could develop the infrastructure necessary to send Siberian electricity to the Far East and then directly into China, bypassing Mongolia. However, in contrast to natural gas or oil, electricity loses power during long-range transmission, increasing the cost of sending Siberian electricity on the longer route around Mongolia to China.

Electricity can also easily flow in any direction along transmission lines, a feature that would facilitate load balancing and electrical grid optimization among Russia, Mongolia, China, and potentially other Northeast Asian countries, if a major trans-Mongolian electrical transmission line were built. Such a line would increase the capacity for regional cooperation in electricity, and would be part of a wider grid with multiple cross-border connections between Russia, Mongolia, and China. Therefore the advantages of routing a major transmission line from Russia to China across Mongolia are higher for electricity than for oil or natural gas, and the risks in terms of Mongolia potentially interfering in the trade are lower, making the project potentially more acceptable to both China and Russia. The effort, however, would require a substantial financial commitment to build the transmission infrastructure, and a long-term agreement between Russia, China, and Mongolia with regard to the price of electricity, transmission fees, and other key issues. Serious negotiations on transmission rights and agreements have yet to occur, therefore any significant role for Mongolia in the Northeast Asian electricity market, either as a supplier or conduit for power, is likely decades away.

Conclusion

Mongolia emerged as an energy supplier for Northeast Asia during a time of strong international demand for resources and relatively high prices. Lower commodity prices and Mongolian government missteps have set Mongolia back in its quest to ramp up its energy exports, and the country has failed to find a role in the growing energy trade between Russia and China. Given its infrastructure deficit and a lack of capital and expertise, in the near future the country will be challenged to regain its coal export volumes and expand energy production in a significant way. Despite these challenges, in the longer run Mongolia has several advantages that support the country's engagement in regional energy export and cooperation. Many of Mongolia's energy resources, including coal, uranium, and oil, are located close to the Chinese border, and no significant geographic barriers block their development for export. Mongolia's resource endowment is complementary to regional needs, opening the door for cooperative development initiatives, such as those discussed during Prime Minister Abe's visit in 2013 and Chinese President Xi's visit in 2014. Mongolia's new pragmatism toward foreign investment and cooperation with its neighbors offers some hope that the country will be able to overcome its history of government policy and management missteps.

In order to move forward and play a larger role in regional energy matters, Mongolia must first develop a workable approach to foreign involvement in energy and infrastructure projects in the country. Mongolia needs access to foreign capital and technology to support the development of energy resources and the related infrastructure such as roads, railroads, and the electrical grid. The Mongolian government has legitimate concerns about maintaining national control over strategic assets in the country, but it needs to be careful to ensure that the policies it adopts with regard to foreign investment do not push out foreign investors and put off Chinese buyers. The moves made by the Mongolian government in 2013 and 2014 to repeal the most onerous provisions of its foreign investment laws and to invite foreign investors back to the country are steps in the right direction. However, Mongolia will need to demonstrate the enduring stability of its new laws and the ability to be a trustworthy partner in major projects before foreign investors will be willing to take major risks and finance projects in the country.

The decline in foreign investment in Mongolia, in particular from Western companies, has put the country in the awkward position of having to turn to its neighbors, in particular China, for development funding, while also seeking to limit its neighbor's influence on its economy. China stands ready to finance and build the infrastructure necessary to increase Mongolia's energy output. In return, Mongolia has sought China's assurances that it will provide Mongolia with access to the sea and permit trans-shipment of Mongolian cargos via China's rail system, without special tariffs or barriers. Mongolia and China signed several agreements on these issues during the Chinese president's visit in August 2014 (Khuder, 2014). In practice, these measures will be hard for Mongolia to utilize, as the low price of coal and high cost of shipment make it uneconomical in most cases to ship bulk cargos from Mongolia to other countries. Mongolian cargos are also likely to be disadvantaged in their movement through an already overburdened Chinese rail system.

While Mongolia's transport agreements with China may have little practical impact on the ability of Mongolia to expand its export markets, they may serve a more important domestic purpose by making it politically acceptable to cooperate with China in development of infrastructure and natural resource deposits. Mongolia will hold a parliamentary election in 2016, and the issue of Chinese involvement in Mongolian resource development will be a major issue. The fall in foreign investment and slowdown in the Mongolian economy has forced the Mongolian government to reconsider its "resource nationalist" positions as it seeks new sources of revenue and project financing. Increased cooperation with China offers the country the easiest and fastest path to development, but also poses risks for politicians who might be accused of selling out the nation's interest for personal gain. Mongolia and China must therefore continue to work together to find investment structures acceptable to both sides. Chinese investors want to ensure the security of their investments in Mongolia and guarantees around the long-term supply of natural resources. Mongolia needs assurances that Chinese firms will pay appropriate world prices and promote value-added processing in Mongolia.

Several opportunities for collaboration appear to be in the works. In 2013, China's largest coal company, Shenhua, announced an agreement to buy 1 billion tonnes of coal from the Tavan Tolgoi mine over the next 20 years, with the price set based on international prices for coal (Kohn, 2013). Such long-term agreements provide a level of assurance to both sides, and open the door for cooperation on infrastructure development to insure efficient production and delivery of the coal. New infrastructure would support the development not just of the Tavan Tolgoi mine, but also other coal deposits in the South Gobi area. As was discussed, however, in the case of the pre-payment contract signed by Chalco and the wrangling over the SouthGobi Sands mine, significant hurdles remain in the implementation of such deals. Mongolia has a poor track record in terms of meeting its delivery obligations and developing the necessary infrastructure. Mongolia will need to grow more comfortable about allowing Chinese companies such as Shenhua to play a more direct role in resource production and infrastructure construction. Shenhua's agreement to build the cross-border portion of the new railway from the Tavan Tolgoi mine might be expanded to include the entire line to the mine. Shenhua's involvement might focus on financing and construction, with ownership remaining with the Mongolian government or another regulated Mongolian entity that ensures that the railway line is open for use by all mines in the South Gobi region.

Within this framework, it will be important to create opportunities to engage firms from Russia, Japan, Korea, and other third neighbors in the construction and operation of mines and railways to balance Chinese influence. In particular, Mongolia will need to find ways to engage Russia, with the most likely partnership involving expanded cooperation in railways. While the railways from the mines to China should be built on Chinese-gauge rails to reduce shipment costs, Mongolia and Russia have significant opportunities to expand Mongolia's trunk railway system, which remains a Mongolian–Russian 50/50 joint venture. This railway might handle some bulk natural resource cargos, but can also serve as a transit corridor to facilitate trade between Russia and China, such as expanded shipments of Russian oil and Chinese cargos transiting Russia to Europe. Japanese and Korean firms might engage in the construction and operation of mines and infrastructure, while continuing to explore opportunities to export Mongolian natural resources to these countries.

A second field where Mongolia may be able to enlarge its energy participation is through the development of a regional electric grid. Electricity has the unique quality of being the only energy source both produced and consumed by all countries in Northeast Asia. A regional grid would help all countries balance power loads and increase system efficiency and reliability. On net, Mongolia should be able to emerge as a supplier of electricity to the region through the development of new coal-fired power plants and renewable energy projects. The country might also serve as a central transmission corridor and hub within a wider system. The relatively small Mongolian market has limited capacity to support a significant expansion of power plants and renewable energy, and therefore a regional strategy is crucial to allow Mongolia to develop its electrical supplies. Regional initiatives such as the Asia super-grid and the development of transmission lines for the delivery of Russian hydropower to China would bring co-benefits to the country by helping to both expand and diversify Mongolia's domestic energy supply.

To facilitate this outcome, Mongolia will need to become more active in efforts to develop bilateral and regional agreements on electricity pricing and supply. The regional electricity task force under the Energy Charter Treaty might provide one avenue for cooperation, and Mongolia can make the issue a key discussion point in bilateral and multilateral meetings with regional countries. To date, Mongolia has largely approached energy issues with its Northeast Asian neighbors on a bilateral and project basis. This approach makes sense given the country's geographic constraints and desire to find ways to engage a variety of partners in specific projects. Electricity, however, offers one energy field where a regional approach makes economic and political sense for all participating countries because all the countries of Northeast Asia can benefit from an integrated electrical grid on both the supply and demand side, while reaping benefits from increased efficiency and reliability. The relatively high benefits and low costs and risks of regional cooperation in electricity might provide an avenue for Mongolia to take a stronger role in the development of a regional energy regime.

References

Asia Pacific Energy Research Centre. 2004. *Electrical Power Grid Interconnections in the APEC Region*. Tokyo: Institute of Energy Economics.

Badgaa, G. 2010. *Current Status of and Prospects for Energy Resource Development of South Gobi in Mongolia*. Online: www.keei.re.kr/keei/download/seminar/080703/s1-4.pdf (accessed September 12, 2012).

Borford-Parnell, N. 2010. Synergies of Scale: A Vision of Mongolia and China's Common Energy Future. Online: www.worldenergy.org/documents/congresspapers/158.pdf (accessed August 2, 2012).

Campi, A. 2013. Sino-Mongolian Oil Deal Undercuts Russian Role. *Asia Times*, May 15.

Central Intelligence Agency. 2013. *CIA World Factbook*. Online: www.cia.gov/library/publications/the-world-factbook/ (accessed March 4, 2013).

Choi, H. 2013. Park Seeks "Eurasia Initiative" to Build Energy, Logistics Links. *Korea Herald*, October 18. Online: www.koreaherald.com/view.php?ud=20131018000620 (accessed July 4, 2014).

Edwards, T. 2014. China's Shenhua to Invest in Cross Border Rail Link from Mongolia. Reuters, April 9.

Elliot, D., Schwartz, M., Scott, G., Haymes, S., Heimiller, D., and George, R. 2001. *Wind Energy Resource Atlas of Mongolia*. Washington, DC: National Renewable Energy Laboratory.

Els, F. 2011. Building the World's Largest Coal Mine Turning into a Diplomatic Disaster. *mining.com*, July 28. Online: www.mining.com/building-the-worlds-largest-coal-mine-turning-into-a-diplomatic-disaster/ (accessed March 21, 2012).

Energy Business Review. 2014. Macmahon Suspends Operations at Mongolia's Tavan Tolgoi Coal Mine. *Energy Business Review*, August 21.

Gambrel, D. 2014. Russian Coal Exports in the Pacific Rim. *Coal Age*, April 14.

Government of Mongolia. 2014. Government of Mongolia Resolves to Build the "Coal Gasification" Plant in Collaboration with China's Sinopec Group. *Infomongolia*, March 10.

Hook, L. 2012. Chalco Abandons Mongolia Coal Mine Deal. *The Financial Times*, September 3.

Humber, Y. 2013. Tavan Tolgoi Pays Chalco Higher Rate on Loan as Coal Resumes. *Bloomberg News*, April 26.

Hyashi, N. and Ono, K. 2013. Abe Strikes Energy Deal with Mongolia in a Bid to Curb China's Clout. *Asahi Shimbun*, March 31.

Hyun-Jae, D. 2003. Energy Cooperation in Northeast Asia: Prospects and Challenges. *East Asian Review* 15(3): 85–110.

InfoMongolia. 2014a. A Draft Bill Mongolia's Railroad to Have Both Narrow and Broad Gauges is Presented. *InfoMongolia*, April 30. Online: www.infomongolia.com/ct/ci/7773 (accessed June 4, 2014).

InfoMongolia. 2014b. Remaining US$130 Million Debt to Chalco Not to be Covered in June. *InfoMongolia*, May 2.

Jacob, P. 2011. Mongolia: Ulaanbaatar Subjected to Moscow's Energy Arm Twisting. *Eurasianet*, July 25.

Jones, A.W. 2009. Mongolia Sitting on a Goldmine. *Washington Times*, August 2.

Khashchuulun, C. 2010. *Development Policies of Mongolia, Incorporating Mining as a Growth Engine*. Ulaanbaatar: National Development and Innovation Commission Government of Mongolia.

Khuder, B. 2014. About Documents Signed During Chinese President's Visit. *Montsame*, August 22.

Kim, S. 2013. Mongolia Sees Trade Boost by Using North Korean Ports. *Bloomberg News*, October 30.

Kohn, M. 2013. China's Shenhua Agrees to Buy 1 Billion Tons of Mongolian Coal. *Bloomberg News*, October 29.

Kohn, M. 2014. Mongolia's Export Income Falls 2.6% in 2013 as Coal Sales Slump. *Bloomberg News*, January 12.

Kohn, M. and Humber, Y. 2014. Mongolia Seeks Economic Lifeline with Pivot to China, Russia. *Bloomberg News*, August 19.

Lamphier, G. 2014. Russia–China Natural Gas Deal Could Put a Crimp in B.C.'s LNG Export Plans. *Edmonton Journal*, May 15.

Marubeni Corporation. 2010. Darkhan, Mongolia Oil Refinery Project Framework Agreement with Mongol Sekiyu Corporation. Online: www.marubeni.com/dbps_data/news/2010/100929f.html (accessed May 15, 2014).

Mendee, J. 2011. *Anti-Chinese Attitudes in Post-Communist Mongolia: The Lingering Negative Schemas of the Past*. Vancouver: University of British Columbia.

Mendee, J. 2014a. Foreign Policy Implications of Mongolian Crony Democracy. *Eurasian Daily Monitor*, March 12.

Mendee, J. 2014b. Rosneft Pipelines To and Through Mongolia. *Eurasian Daily Monitor*, May 1.

National Dispatching Center of Power Systems. 2012. *Mongolia Energy Policy*. Online: eneken.ieej.or.jp/data/4480.pdf (accessed August 20, 2014).

News.mn. 2014a. "New Railway" Project Temporarily Halted. *News.mn*, April 16.

News.mn. 2014b. V. Putin to Visit Mongolia. *News.mn*, August 5.

Nishimura, D. 2012. Russia Now a Key Power Supplier for China. *Asahi Shimbun*, June 20.

Oxford Business Group. 2013. *New Uses for Coal in Mongolia*. Online: www.infomongolia.com/ct/ci/6874 (accessed May 3, 2014).

Paik, K.-W. 2005. *Pipeline Gas Introduction to the Korean Peninsula*. Seoul: Korea Foundation.

Patton, D. 2012. Japanese Group Hopes Mongolia Can Act as Desertec of Asia. *Recharge News*, March 13.

Priddy, B. 2013. Transneft Opposes Rosneft Plans to Increase Chinese Oil Supply via Kazakhstan. *Oil & Gas Eurasia*, April 5. Online: www.oilandgaseurasia.com/en/news/transneft-opposes-rosneft-plans-increase-chinese-oil-supply-kazakhstan/page/0/1#sthash.MmIYRGN5.dpuf (accessed March 3, 2014).

Sachs, R. and Agvaanluvsan, U. 2009. *Fueling the Future: Mongolian Uranium and Nuclear Power Plant Growth in China and India*. Palo Alto, CA: Stanford University Press.

Sant Maral Foundation. 2012. *Politbarometer*. Ulaanbaatar: Sant Maral Foundation.

Shi, T. 2014. Xi Upgrades Mongolia Relationship as Bilateral Trade Grows. *Bloomberg Businessweek*, August 22.

Stanway, D. 2010. Doing Business in Mongolia a Tightrope Walk. Reuters, May 26.

Steelhome.cn. 2012. Mongolia's Coal Exports up 19% on Year in First Seven Months. Online: http://newsen.steelhome.ca/2012/08/07/n656337.html (accessed August 27, 2012).

Swedish Trade Council. 2008. *Private Sector Opportunities in the Oil, Gas and Coal Sectors in Mongolia*. Beijing: Swedish Trade Council.

Task Force on Promoting Regional Electricity Cooperation Between Central and South Asia. 2010. *Ulaanbaatar Declaration on Promoting Regional Energy Cooperation*. Online: www.encharter.org/fileadmin/user_upload/Conferences/2010_July_9/Declaration_ENG.pdf (accessed August 27, 2012).

UNDP China. 2009. *United Nations Development Programme China*. Online: www.undp.org.cn/modules.php?op=modload&name=News&file=article&catid=14&topic=35&sid=4421&mode=thread&order=0&thold=0 (accessed September 7, 2012).

U.S. Energy Information Administration (EIA). 2013. *Technically Recoverable Shale Oil and Shale Gas Resources: An Assessment of 137 Shale Formations in 41 Countries Outside the United States*. Washington DC: EIA/ARI.

U.S. Energy Information Administration (EIA). 2014. Mongolia Oil Production (1980–2013). Online: www.eia.gov (accessed May 1, 2014).

Warlters, M. 2009. *Southern Mongolia Infrastructure Strategy*. Washington, DC: The World Bank.

Working Group on Energy Planning and Policy. 2010. *Five Year Strategy (2010–2014) to Implement the Intergovernmental Collaborative Mechanism on Energy Cooperation in North-East Asia*. Bangkok: Economic and Social Commission for Asia and the Pacific.

World Bank. 2012. *Mongolia Quarterly Economic Update*. Ulaanbaatar: World Bank.

World Nuclear Association. 2012. *Uranium in Mongolia*. Online: www.world-nuclear.org/info/infl125-mongolia.html (accessed August 8, 2012).

Xinhua. 2014. Mongolian President Says Ready to Further Promote Ties With China. *Xinhua*, August 19.

7 Dilemmas and prospects for Russian–Northeast Asian energy security

Adam N. Stulberg

Russia's energy foray into Northeast Asia is both concerted and befuddling. On the one hand, Moscow conspicuously reinvigorated its energy presence with the opening of the Eastern Siberia–Pacific Ocean (ESPO) pipeline in December 2009, which provides a direct link between potentially huge sources of new east-facing oil production and the world's fastest-growing regional market. As evidenced by the push to implement projects leading up to and following the 2012 Asia-Pacific Economic Cooperation (APEC) meeting in Vladivostok, the Kremlin also relies on these energy prospects as a method to establish itself as a key player in the broader Asia-Pacific integration process and to propel regional energy governance and development of East Siberia and the Russian Far East (RFE). As reflected by President Medvedev's endorsement of the 2012 APEC Leaders Declaration at that APEC summit, Moscow trumpets strong support for region-wide energy infrastructure investment—especially pertaining to "clean" nuclear energy, natural gas liquefaction, low-emission energy supply, and emergency notification procedures—as the bulwark for advancing collective interests in sustainability, efficiency, predictability, and transparency of regional energy markets.[1]

On the other hand, Russia's expanding energy footprint stokes anxiety about the prospects for conflict. As discussed in Chapter 2 by Mikkal E. Herberg, there are mounting concerns about a rise in Russian resource nationalism. In this respect, Russia's own pivot of strategic and diplomatic resources to Asia (the "Asian pivot") raises the specter of Moscow brandishing its energy superpower stature and state control over national energy firms to limit options for regional energy security cooperation and to exploit differences among import-dependent European and Northeast Asian customers for political advantage. Veiled threats to redirect flows of oil and gas from Europe to Asia amid the 2014 crisis with Ukraine seemed to affirm such anxiety (Cohen, 2009; Heritage, 2014). Yet Russia faces daunting challenges in wooing Northeast Asian energy partners and spearheading regional energy regime formation. The apprehension evinced by policymakers from Moscow to Vladivostok about China's holdings and trading in the RFE, as well as its energy offensive to secure equity stakes with Central Asian suppliers and bickering over the terms of Russian energy imports, betray mounting tensions between Beijing's strategy of "going out" and Moscow's determination to "go east." Just as Moscow has consistently refrained from supporting Beijing's boundary and resource disputes in the East and South China Seas, and has cultivated independent energy ties with Japan and Southeast Asian states that Chinese leaders regard as meddlesome, China has harassed Gazprom's offshore exploration with Vietnam. Notwithstanding complementary supplier and customer interests, therefore, it is clear that Russia and China pursue respective energy security, often at the other's expense. Accordingly, there are mounting concerns among policymakers and investors across Northeast Asia that Moscow is simply too untrustworthy, ambitious, insecure, and/or weak internally to engage in large-scale bilateral or multilateral energy security cooperation (Blank, 2011).

This chapter explicates Russia's energy engagement with Northeast Asia, exposing flawed projections of Moscow's inevitable marginalization and its lapse into competitive resource nationalism. In short, there is both more and less to Russia's Asian pivot than accounted for by either traditional integrationist or great power approaches to regional energy relations. Notwithstanding rhetorical platitudes, the promotion of Northeast Asian governance is not the focal point of Moscow's eastern energy strategy; its interests lie primarily with stimulating energy development in the RFE to undergird Russia's competitive advantages—commercially and strategically—across the region. At the same time, Russia's ability to manipulate Asian markets varies, leaving it with modest capacity to realize these commercial and strategic ambitions. Specifically, Moscow's strategic energy interaction is largely conditioned by market and domestic regulatory factors that in combination either accentuate or mitigate regional security dilemmas, with attendant consequences for fueling conflict or advancing commercial interests in Russia's oil and gas relations with Northeast Asian states and firms. Although opaque national regulatory systems complicate bargaining and sow mutual frustration, all of the parties have something to gain and incur little political risk by undertaking pragmatic commercial cooperation in the oil sector. However, Russia has neither the market power nor domestic leverage to arbitrarily exploit the growing oil import dependency of Northeast Asian customers or to spearhead regional governance. Conversely, gas relations are marred by a more intense security dilemma, whereby no single party is prone to take political risks on a deal.

Moscow's market power and regulatory effectiveness position it to break into Northeast Asian markets with high-margin overland deliveries, as well as to manipulate Central Asian supply and raise the costs to China of fundamentally antagonizing Russia's regional gas interests. Yet this stature and the opacity surrounding Chinese economic and strategic interests conspire against large-scale, long-term commercial deals as the bedrock for regional energy cooperation, as well as limit the capacity of state parties to avert costly political disputes over competition for new supply. The upshot is that distinct balances of market and institutional conditions in respective oil and gas sectors have created powerful incentives for commercial and strategic posturing, thus restricting Moscow's capacity to play a prominent role in Northeast Asian energy governance, irrespective of shifts in strategy for developing the RFE.

This chapter unfolds in four parts. The first section reviews Russia's renewed interests in expanding energy cooperation with Northeast Asia as part of initiatives to develop the RFE, and the attendant constraints on Moscow's resource nationalism. The second section explicates the market and domestic institutional conditions that shape Russia's energy security dilemmas in the region. The third part briefly illustrates this argument as it bears on Moscow's success in breaking into emerging Asian markets via cooperation on the ESPO pipeline, and on political competition with China for development of Russian and Central Asian gas. The conclusion discusses practical implications for regional energy governance amid changing Russian and Northeast Asian landscapes.

Russia's eastern energy vector

Russia's 2009 National Security Concept for the first time codified energy as a prominent national security issue. Energy security—defined in terms of stable demand for Russian energy, competitiveness of domestic producers, and prevention of national energy shortages—is singled out for strengthening Moscow's stature in the rough-and-tumble of international relations. With energy scarcity forecast as a touchstone for future conflict, the document directs the leadership to retain control over natural resources and preserve Russia's advantageous position as an international energy supplier, with explicit objectives of "developing its own reserves and having access to others" (Rustrans.wikidot.com, 2012). That Russian officials have reacted arbitrarily to divisive contract negotiations and repeatedly disrupted exports also reveals the lengths to which Moscow will go to get its way, irrespective of the cost to its reputation as a reliable supplier and regardless of the instability imposed on vulnerable downstream customers (Larsson, 2006; Trenin, 2008).

Russia's declared expansion of energy ties with key players in East Asia figures prominently in this strategic calculus. At the crux are projections for accelerating discovery and production from the four oil and gas centers in East Siberia and the RFE—Irkutsk, Krasnoyarsk, Yakutsk, and Sakhalin—which could hold nearly 20 percent and 50 percent of national oil and gas reserves, respectively.[2] The national energy strategy, in particular, estimates that new oil development will constitute 50 percent of national production and that output from these eastern fields will exceed that from mature fields in European Russia by 2030.[3] Notwithstanding considerable geological and commercial uncertainty associated with tapping this potential, Russia's eastern energy wealth represents the brightest light amid rising depletion rates (60 to 75 percent) of existing large fields in West Siberia. Coupled with the Kremlin's determination to spur economic and political development in the RFE, mounting activism of state-owned energy companies to unlock new reserves in the region, and a push for diversifying Russia's international customer base to reduce dependence on established European markets and unreliable NIS transit states, Moscow seems primed to embrace an "eastern vector" projected to constitute more than 30 percent and 50 percent, respectively, of its total oil and gas exports by 2050 (Poussenkova, 2009; Henderson, 2011a; Paltsev, 2011; Mares & Larys, 2012).

At the same time, Russian officials and policy insiders eye the promise of stepped-up energy cooperation with Japan and South Korea for diversifying regional exports beyond the Chinese market, gaining a foothold in new markets in Southeast Asia and the United States, and playing an integral role in the dynamic Asian-Pacific face of globalization (Lavrov, 2006; Baev, 2008; Russian National Committee of the Council for Security Cooperation in Asia Pacific, 2010).

Yet Russia has consistently prioritized construction of a new energy infrastructure for socio-economic development at home over promotion of Northeast Asian energy governance. In short, Russia's newfound energy wealth animates different faces of Moscow's resource nationalism for building up the RFE and broadening the country's competitive footprint in regional integration. Under Vladimir Putin's first presidency, the emphasis was on addressing a confluence of challenges attendant to mounting insecurity presented by dramatically declining socio-economic trends and general degradation of the inhospitable RFE (e.g., the "Siberian Curse"), Russia's creeping dependency on China, and appreciation of the region's importance as a "future energy storehouse and source of leverage in Asia" (Blank, 2011, p. 7; see also Hill & Gaddy, 2003; Christoffersen, 2010; Petro, 2011).

This fostered an autarchic, if not paranoid, approach to establishing a regional energy infrastructure as a bulwark for accelerating protectionist political and economic development in the RFE and asserting Moscow's approach to engaging non-Western institutions in competitive multilateral balancing across the Asia-Pacific region. At the nub of this vision was the Eastern Gas Program in 2007, which stipulated development of an "integrated gas production, transmission, and supply system" in East Siberia and the RFE, with the aim of both satisfying domestic demand in the region and securing increased gas deliveries to East Asia. Together with the 2003 Energy Strategy to 2020, this mandated Gazprom's central coordinating role over domestic supply and monopoly over exports in order to minimize competition between Russian projects and to optimize competitive advantages in East Asian markets (Gazprom, 2008–14; see also Gazprom website and Kalashnikov et al., 2005).

The convergence of strategically competitive domestic and foreign policy agendas was affirmed by successive regional development programs and in statements by leading diplomats from 2005 to 2009. For some, the very stature of Russia's civilization and integrity as an independent great power in Asia turns on "successful internal reconstruction of the RFE," buoyed by national development of oil and gas projects in Siberia and Sakhalin Island and the related rents that accrue from East Asian energy exports and diplomacy.[4]

The particular fusion of domestic and foreign priorities embedded in Russia's eastern energy strategy, however, shifted during the subsequent tandem leadership of President Dmitry Medvedev and Prime Minister Putin. In response to the deleterious impact of the global financial crisis on the credibility of Western-centric approaches to regional integration, as well as declining socio-economic trends in the RFE (both below the Russian national average and in comparison to China's dynamic growth), disappointing performance of successive government-sponsored regional development projects, and the threat of Russia's further marginalization in Asian economic integration, the Kremlin backed away from relying on a competitive energy strategy for autarchic development of the RFE. Medvedev explicitly blamed the "humiliating," "burdensome," and "nostalgic" habit of relying on the export of raw materials for driving centuries of backwardness, undermining the country's global economic competitiveness, and diverting attention to an "impossible" task of exercising leadership via control of oil and gas markets. Instead, he asserted that the keys to modernizing the country—and the RFE, specifically—rest with invigorating the "so-called intelligent economy, creating unique knowledge, exporting new technologies and innovative products."[5]

Central to Moscow's eastern modernization program is a national energy strategy oriented primarily toward attracting foreign investment to boost environmentally and economically efficient production and export infrastructure (Medvedev, 2009). The revised Russian Energy Strategy, for example, calls for East Siberia to emerge as the country's second-largest oil and gas production region by 2030, and for the Far Eastern district to become self-sufficient and an important additional source of exports directly to the Asia-Pacific region (Ministry of Energy of the Russian Federation, 2010). Russia's vast eastern energy potential was dubbed a lure for large-scale Asian investment in the RFE that, in turn, could boost Moscow's otherwise low profile in regional economic institutions and facilitate multilateral partnerships across the Asia-Pacific region. By promoting such development, Moscow at once pushed to attract investment to build up the eastward-oriented energy infrastructure, leverage its emerging energy strength as a gateway for diversifying its export profile in East Asia, and mitigate asymmetric economic dependence on China (Lavrov, 2011; see also discussion in Lee & Novitskiy, 2010; Lukin, 2011; Kuhrt, 2012). This, in turn, provided grist for advancing Moscow's tangible priorities of expanding free trade, promoting the liberalization of investment, establishing reliable supply chains and transport links, and fostering innovation under its leadership of APEC in 2012 (Ivanov, 2011). Thus, in contrast to the strategically competitive orientation of the earlier Russian posture, there was a shift in 2009 to a state-directed strategy that emphasized bartering commercial energy deals in the RFE to become a full-fledged participant with shared responsibilities for managing risks in complementary regional political and economic organizations (Ministry of Energy of the Russian Federation, 2010; President of Russia, 2011; Pronina, 2011).[6]

Notwithstanding these policy pronouncements, the Kremlin has remained ambivalent about deepening energy ties with Northeast Asian customers and prone to bouts of both cooperative engagement and competitive power plays within the region. The leadership publicly oscillates between paranoia about becoming a "resource appendage" to expanding Asian (especially Chinese) markets, and reliance on regional energy engagement to stimulate foreign investment and development (Danchenko *et al.*, 2010; Kuhrt, 2012). The Kremlin regards Northeast Asia neither as a panacea for solving the modernization problem, nor as a foil to balance established supply relations with Europe. As underscored by Lavrov, the country's western and eastern vectors of energy integration are mutually reinforcing, as Russia depends on the former for internal development that, in turn, is crucial for joining the integration process unfolding in the Asia-Pacific region (Lavrov, 2006). Indeed, subsequent commentary suggests that, if anything, the leadership favors strategic energy cooperation with the West. As revealed in a 2010 leaked foreign policy document, the modernization program requires forging partnerships with the United States and Europe that can deliver the foreign investment and technology that friendly nations in the developing world and Asia allegedly cannot. Only by establishing commercially inspired modernization alliances with advanced economies of the West are Russia's energy and foreign policies expected to yield the benefits for economic and global competitiveness that the leadership covets. By contrast, China's rise necessitates close scrutiny and containment, both regionally and within international fora.

With his return to the presidency in 2012, Putin reaffirmed that developing "the enormous resource potential of Siberia and the RFE" remains a strategic priority and holds the key to bolstering Russia's competitive position with the integration of Northeast Asian markets (eng.kremlin.ru/news, 2013) In a historically unprecedented tactical shift, the Kremlin recentralized power by creating a Ministry for the Development of the Russian Far East to consolidate implementation of all federal programs, including large-scale investment in energy infrastructure projects. Frustrated by continued bureaucratic gridlock and mounting fiscal waste, Moscow subsequently augmented large-scale state spending with efforts to stimulate regional investment. The latter included the introduction of tax breaks for local export industries (while retaining mineral taxes on local oil and gas investment to boost federal coffers), as well as plans to relocate central offices of federal organs to the regions and to form a state corporation to channel state funds to designated "fast-track" development zones across the RFE. These initiatives underscored Moscow's determination to guide cross-border trade and investment while retaining close state control of regional energy development programs, even at the risk of retarding local development, failing to arrest Russia's yawning trade imbalances with Northeast Asian partners, and stunting regional investment and market integration, to its competitive disadvantage (*Eurasia Review*, 2013; Medetsky, 2014; Richardson, 2014).

Notwithstanding the derivative interest in regional energy security cooperation, Russia's projected energy trade with Northeast Asia constitutes a residual opportunity, even under optimistic scenarios for energy development in East Siberia and the RFE. To date, Europe has been the destination for the bulk of Russia's oil and gas exports (up to 80 percent), which, in turn, represent approximately 20 percent and 40 percent, respectively, of total EU-27 imports. While the national energy strategy officially calls for boosting Russia's deliveries to East Asia from 4 percent to nearly 30 percent of overall energy exports by 2030, oil deliveries will still likely constitute only 10 percent of regional demand by 2030 under optimistic scenarios, with supply from the Middle East and Africa continuing to meet the lion's share of rising import demand. Moreover, this increase will be gradual and require significant start-up investments in new infrastructure (Ministry of Energy of the Russian Federation, 2010; Henderson, 2011a).[7] That Russia has experienced delays in developing its eastern fields and related pipelines, and also faces mounting competition from Central Asian oil and gas suppliers, further suggests that such plans may be overly optimistic.

Finally, Russia's resource nationalist determination is typically ascribed to aggressive intentions, domestic institutions, legacy infrastructure, and resource endowments. Yet the Russian government does not operate in a strategic vacuum. The Kremlin's ability to realize its ambitions, and the outcomes of its energy posture, stem largely from what it expects other states and firms to do and how these actors indeed behave. The calculations and related energy outcomes, therefore, are shaped by the interaction of national preferences and visions for energy security, as well as by environmental conditions, including market and political factors, that are beyond Moscow's direct control.[8]

Russia's energy security dilemmas

Russia's strategic context presents a basic paradox for its foreign energy dealings, as the same policies calculated to promote stable and affordable energy flows can trigger energy security dilemmas. What one state does to enhance its own security and to bolster its commercial capacity, even for purely defensive or benign purposes, can fuel the fears of other states, generating spirals of mutual suspicion and hostility that, in the end, can make both states less secure.[9] In this regard, efforts to bolster mutual energy security or to temper escalating strategic competition can be exceedingly difficult because of the uncertainty imposed by strategic circumstances and tension between commercial and political motives and policy behavior.[10]

The general tenor of Russian–Northeast Asian energy relations reflects this strategic predicament. Extra-commercial energy conflict is both more common and inadvertent than would be expected by countries with otherwise complementary natural resource portfolios. The uncertainty and risks stoked by mutual pursuit of energy security at times fuel strategic suspicions that, in turn, spill back into energy competition and hamper progress toward regional governance. Under certain circumstances, the net impact of Russia's energy resurgence, Asia's growing import dependence, the increasingly state-dominated shape of regional energy plays, and shifting geostrategic outlooks is a predatory approach to resource nationalism, defined by zero-sum competition and costly, if not inadvertent, escalation of commercial rivalry into strategic energy conflict. Notwithstanding common energy interests, the nature of the situation facing both Russian suppliers and Northeast Asian customers can compel them to take politically competitive steps (Herberg, 2010).[11] Conversely, other circumstances augur well for mitigating such bargaining problems, allowing mutual interests in delivering energy and institutionalizing cooperation to prevail, confining competition to a commercial plane (Garrison, 2009).

The variation in strategic energy interaction between Russia and Northeast Asian states, therefore, raises several core questions: Under which conditions are

Russia's competitive commercial plays likely to escalate into strategic conflict with its emerging Northeast Asian partners? Are these conflicts intentional or avoidable? Alternatively, can those conditions that temper strategic conflict augur well for strengthening regional energy security governance? Answers turn on the intensity of energy security dilemmas, as derived from prevailing market standing and the character of domestic regulatory systems associated with respective states.

Russia's market power in Northeast Asia

Market power—as defined by relative shares of global production, exports, and consumption, and access to critical energy infrastructure—determines the range of international advantages available to a national energy sector by exploiting accessible resources and vulnerabilities of rival suppliers, customers, and transit states. Accordingly, the stronger the market power of a state (i.e., the greater the asymmetry between interacting parties), the more unstable the strategic energy context. Stronger parties enjoy cheap opportunities to leverage commercial advantages for strategic gain. This can include arbitrarily altering the value of specific energy transit options, setting volumes and prices, beating rivals to markets, taking preventive action, and manipulating the risks of preferred energy deals for other states and firms (Stulberg, 2007). By contrast, weaker parties are both more dependent and less trusting of stronger states. The weaker the market power, the more vulnerable international customers are to supply disruption, suppliers are to unfavorable competition and market capture, and transit states are to more cost-effective alternatives and arbitrary renegotiation of tariffs and offtake. Confronting such vulnerabilities, weaker parties are especially prone to gambling on preventive, if not aggressive, action.[12]

By the numbers, Russia maintains a formidable footprint in global energy markets. Proven oil reserves constitute roughly 5.6 percent of the global total. Russia holds the largest proven, conventional natural gas reserves, at 23.9 percent of the world's inventory. Furthermore, it is home to nearly 10 percent of global oil exports, and is the leader of global gas exports, at roughly 50 percent. Although the oil sector experienced a sharp decline (–46 percent) in production following the Soviet collapse, levels subsequently recovered to their peak, with Russia becoming the largest single oil exporter in 2010. By contrast, Russia's gas production has remained relatively stable since the Soviet collapse (notwithstanding several 10 percent shifts from and to its peak), and it was not until 2008 that it relinquished status as the world's largest producer (BP, 2011).[13]

Despite its re-emergence as one of the world's top two oil and gas producers (behind the United States since 2012), Russia is not a global energy hegemon, and it faces significant market and infrastructure constraints on converting these resources into a sustainable strategic instrument in relations with Northeast Asian customers. Based on the size of proven reserves, legacy development, production rates, export penetration, and technical dimensions to the gas trade, Russia clearly enjoys status as a natural gas power, with incremental supply advantages in established European and Eurasian markets. It is capable of delivering gas at lower marginal costs, as well as diverting or stifling large-scale pipeline supply to regional customers in the short term. These structural advantages, however, are severely circumscribed in emerging Northeast Asian markets owing to steep start-up costs of construction and a preoccupation with returns on investment associated with new pipelines and liquefaction infrastructure. Russia's clout is further tamed by the increasing prominence of integrated markets for liquefied natural gas (LNG) and the rising potential of unconventional gas offered by more established Southeast Asian, Australian, North American, East African, and Middle Eastern suppliers to Northeast Asia (Hill, 2004; Goldthau, 2008; Stevens, 2009). Moreover, Russia remains a price-taker in integrated global oil markets. It possesses neither the reserve, production, nor export capacities to act as a swing producer on par with Saudi Arabia, irrespective of the geographic proximity and transit security presented by potential direct overland links to Asian markets (Victor & Victor, 2003).[14] This significantly limits the prospects for wielding an "oil weapon" against regional customers, irrespective of the determination of Saudi Arabia and other Persian Gulf suppliers to expand their dominant market shares in Northeast Asia.

In addition, Moscow's ability to maintain its stature in both sectors is tenuous, due to a swelling gap between domestic production and rising domestic and export demands. Russia faces a welter of long-term structural challenges that include: rapidly declining production rates at super-giant legacy fields in West Siberia; repeated delays in opening new, remote, and relatively smaller greenfields in East Siberia and the RFE (which are also separated from existing national pipeline networks); elevated domestic energy intensity of the country's economic growth; aging national refining and pipeline infrastructure; and prolonged upstream investment shortfalls (and relative preoccupation with downstream acquisitions) (Sagers, 2006; Milov, 2008; Mankoff, 2009). These challenges are especially acute for Russia's eastern hydrocarbon resources, which are situated under permafrost and complicated geological conditions, thus leading to higher exploration, production, and export costs. The competitive disadvantages of these fields are compounded by the fragile ecosystem and general underdevelopment of the surrounding provinces, as well as by Moscow's dependence on securing greater access to foreign investment, capital, technical knowledge, and managerial experience to deliver these new and especially difficult-to-unlock reserves (Poussenkova, 2009, pp. 143–4). Accordingly, Moscow must overcome significant geological, infrastructural, and financial barriers to realize its market potential in the oil and gas sectors, let alone to make use of an effective energy lever in relations with Northeast Asia (Shevtsova, 2009).[15]

Regulatory opacity and diverging interests in Russia's energy landscape

Simultaneously, discrete national choices for promoting energy security (and ultimately outcomes) are influenced by a second defining feature—the transparency of respective domestic regulatory systems.[16] The delineation of national regulatory authority establishes domestic rules of the game—rights to own and access resources and pipeline, set prices, tax, and export—that, in turn, directly define domestic energy stakeholders, specify transaction costs of formulating national energy policies, and shape bargaining among international parties. Clearly established regulatory authority among state and private actors, in particular, aligns stakeholder interests and enhances respective capacity to exploit commercial versus strategic opportunities in an energy sector. Regulatory transparency both reduces information asymmetries and bolsters the credibility of signals, making it easier for outsiders to disentangle economic from political motives, thus being less prone to conflate commercial with strategic vulnerability. Because policy preferences are transparent and compliance with national preferences can become mutually rewarding, domestic policymakers, firms, and international interlocutors alike can readily identify potential allies, assess the costs of building supportive coalitions, monitor the internal workings of the national regulatory system, and target policies accordingly. Conversely, opaque regulatory processes obscure stakeholders and encourage opportunism among domestic state and private actors, in turn blurring commercial and strategic interests. This aggravates the "bluffer's dilemma" confronting the state: simultaneously increasing incentives to conceal parochial intentions while raising the costs of marshaling the country's energy capabilities. Thus, regulatory opacity undermines the credibility of national policies or efforts to reassure other states and firms, as well as accentuating prospective foreign partners' fears and worst-case planning for energy security (Jentleson, 1986).

The general institutional context of policymaking complicates Moscow's capacity to realize its strategic energy objectives. Although Russia has experienced a conspicuous "re-statization" of the energy sector since 2004, the government has remained weak institutionally, with the energy policymaking process captured by rival corporate and political interests. State ownership of Russian energy resources also has not enabled Moscow to transcend market constraints on energy diplomacy, and has come at a high price in terms of the strategic effectiveness of the sector. Not only have economic rents been diverted from national welfare to parochial political agendas via opaque mechanisms of state ownership (and corporate governance), but inchoate property rights and the poor investment climate (especially in the RFE) mar the outlook over the medium and long terms. Accordingly, investment (domestic and foreign) and production rates have steadily declined (with total debts rising) among state energy companies compared to Russian private oil and gas firms.[17] Similarly, Moscow's backsliding on initial fiscal liberalization and privatization schemes in the oil sector neither affected the shares of Russian energy in international markets nor reduced the vulnerability of the sector (or of project financing) to the vicissitudes of global financial markets. As discussed below, the very lack of political transparency and arbitrariness of the Kremlin's renationalization has limited the state's regulatory capacity in the oil sector, including effective oversight of access to the national pipeline system and techniques for developing eastern fields (Poussenkova, 2009, p. 142; Milov, 2008).[18]

As Russia interacts with Northeast Asian customers, the two conditions of market power and regulatory opacity combine to vary the prospects for international conflict, irrespective of resource scarcity, complementary portfolios, or national inclinations and policies. This generates alternative contexts that shape Russia's ability to realize narrow commercial, political, and/or strategic energy ambitions within Northeast Asia. At one extreme are highly intense energy security dilemmas marked by mutual incentives for predation. Asymmetries in market power and interaction among opaque regulatory processes create windows of opportunity for stronger parties and windows of vulnerability for weaker parties; together, these forces make it especially difficult to contain the escalation of commercial energy competition into political conflict, even among benignly motivated actors and with third-party intervention. The uncertainty and risks attendant in such conditions both accentuate instability and militate against reassurance, as all of the parties can renege on their promises without paying significant domestic political costs. Defensive- or commercially minded actors, in particular, cannot credibly signal their intentions in upholding mutually beneficial energy governance without significantly increasing their vulnerability (Montgomery, 2006, pp. 157–67). Conversely, situations marked by symmetrical market power and transparent regulatory processes can facilitate Russia's commercial energy cooperation. Here, none of the parties possesses the capacity or incentive to gamble on arbitrary extra-commercial plays. While energy conflict can arise, it results more from costly, premeditated, and aggressive intent than from missteps or commercial miscues. Ironically, under such conditions, the need to formally institutionalize regional cooperation may be less pressing from an international security perspective but more propitious for redressing collective governance issues for the parties. In between these extreme conditions are strategic contexts distinguished by either market power asymmetries or mixed institutional settings, giving rise to moderately intense energy security dilemmas. Although more stable than one extreme and more tragic than the other, such conditions are primed to stoke commercial competition and intransigence. Yet commercial plays need not lapse inadvertently into strategic energy conflict and can be leveraged to promote common concerns. By engaging third parties or implementing domestic reform to solve for respective market disparities or for one party's regulatory opacity, Russia and its Northeast Asian partners can craft respective policies to reassure each other enough to realize mutual energy security interests.

Russia's Northeast Asian energy gambits

The variation in intensity of the security dilemmas confronting the Russian government in its energy dealings with Northeast Asia accounts in part for the mixed success in forging partnerships in the oil and natural gas sectors. On the one hand, the combination of weak market standing and opaque regulatory systems in both Russia and China has, ironically, augured well for cementing joint oil development and pipeline deals. Although the strategic context has been ripe for competitive posturing over contract terms and stoking mutual misperceptions, the opportunities for modest gains from cooperation generally outweigh the risks. While muddled regulatory authority in Russia and China shakes mutual confidence as negotiating partners, the opportunistic circumstances reduce the stakes of bilateral confrontation and contain the potential adverse strategic consequences of commercially competitive policies for each party. The absence of clear market power among the trade partners, however, makes it difficult for the parties to transcend narrow interests and institutional uncertainty to capitalize fully on mutual interests and opportunities to make substantive progress toward regional energy governance.

On the other hand, the historical market vulnerability associated with piped gas from Russia and mixed authority relations among government offices and national energy firms in China conspire against long-term bilateral natural gas deals. Such conditions have been conducive to accentuating mistrust and converting competitive commercial plays into episodic political rivalry, notwithstanding otherwise common interests in unlocking Eurasian reserves and diversifying the Northeast Asian energy trade. Yet, because Japan and South Korea do not depend on imports of piped gas, but are large consumers of LNG and possess more transparent regulatory institutions, their natural gas ties to Russia lack both the intensity and instability that hamper Sino-Russo gas relations, creating opportunities for modest bilateral commercial cooperation in the sector. To date, however, this constellation of factors has militated against turning the growing regional gas trade into the bedrock for energy security governance.

Against the odds: Russia, China, and the ESPO

January 1, 2011 marked the end of the first phase of construction and commercial opening of the ESPO pipeline. Russia began regular shipments of 300,000 barrels per day (bpd) of crude oil from the West Siberian pipeline system across East Siberia to Skovorodino in the RFE (roughly 1,700 miles), which, via a 45-mile connector, links up to the Chinese pipeline system through a spur to Daqing in Manchuria. This development added to the 300,000 bpd of oil exported across Asia (30 percent Japan, 29 percent South Korea) via rail from Skovorodino to the dedicated ESPO export terminal at Kozmino on the Pacific coast. Although construction accelerated in 2009 with the $25 billion Chinese loan to Rosneft and Transneft (with specified repayment from the revenue of future deliveries), the opening of the ESPO represented the culmination of negotiations over routes, terms of delivery, volumes, pricing, and financing that began in earnest in 2001.[19] With completion in 2012 of the second stage of the ESPO (from Skovorodino to Kozmino), which expanded delivery capacity to 1.6 million bpd, the Russian government projects that the pipeline will generate $47 billion annually for the federal budget by 2015, with overall revenue approaching $200 billion over the expected lifetime (Mares & Larys, 2012, p. 439).

Furthermore, China's growing import demand led to a subsequent deal in 2013 worth an estimated $270 billion, whereby Rosneft agreed to supply the China National Petroleum Corporation (CNPC) with 365 million tons of oil over

25 years in return for China's pre-payment to Rosneft of approximately $70 billion.[20] Thus, the different segments of the ESPO provided impetus for deepening Rosneft's penetration of downstream markets across Northeast Asia, with the construction of an additional refinery in Kozmino to service regional export markets, as well as memoranda of understanding (MoUs) for the joint construction of a major refinery/petrochemical complex in Taijin and operation of a network of more than 500 service stations across China.[21] Accordingly, the ESPO is widely heralded as a momentous springboard for Russia's eastern energy vector.

On the surface, the ESPO represents an especially curious breakthrough for Russian–Northeast Asian energy relations. The twists and turns of negotiations over sourcing, routes, financing, and pricing were fodder for political battles between the Kremlin and private oil companies, as well as the source of acrimony among Moscow, Beijing, and Tokyo for over a decade. In 2003, for example, shortly after the joint presidential declaration on Sino-Russian energy cooperation that embraced commitments by both Transneft and the Russian private company, Yukos, to construct a pipeline to deliver 5 billion barrels of oil to the Chinese border, the Kremlin approved a rival proposal to build a longer and more expensive route to the Pacific Ocean with Japan. Boldly exploiting competition between Tokyo and Beijing for locking in Russian deliveries, the Kremlin shunned talks with Beijing in favor of hinting at $14 billion in soft loans for pipeline construction, as well as additional Japanese investment to underwrite development of East Siberian fields in Yakutsk and Irkutsk, and general access to markets across the region and the United States. Yet in a predatory *volte-face* merely a year later, the Kremlin arrested Yukos's principal shareholder for tax evasion and forced the auction of the company's prized extraction assets to state-backed companies, as well as scotching the deal with Japan in favor of a revocable commitment to construct the pipeline to Skovorodino (Gulick, 2007, pp. 215–22).

Similarly, after signing an initial loans-for-oil deal with China in 2005, which effectively enabled Rosneft to purchase a Yukos subsidiary, the Russian state oil company insisted on reducing the agreed interest rate and arbitrarily revising the price formula in response to changes in oil market conditions that made it more profitable to sell to European consumers. This frustrated the Chinese, because in the process Rosneft threatened not to renew the supply contract, a precondition for construction of the ESPO spur to China (Danchenko *et al.*, 2010, pp. 43–4). Furthermore, Chinese and Russian officials were engaged in a seemingly intractable dispute over project financing, with the former adamant about securing a floating, market-based interest rate while the latter demanded a fixed, below-market interest rate. As noted by one Chinese oil executive, commercial negotiations during 2008–9 were especially tense, as "every fraction of a percent was disputed" (quoted in Danchenko *et al.*, 2010, p. 45).

In addition to protracted contract disputes, the rationale for constructing the ESPO remained commercially suspect. Rising production and operational costs and lingering uncertainty about the scale of Russia's eastern resources undercut the economic basis for the pipeline.[22] This was compounded by oil consumption rates in Russia that outpaced the growth of indigenous production but were dwarfed by even higher rates of demand growth for oil in China and Japan. Notwithstanding common interests in diversification and building direct overland pipelines, there has been a conspicuous disconnect between Russia's drive to add export capacity to East Asia, limited available throughput, and Moscow's growing preference for increasing exports of refined products over crude oil.[23] Consequently, the commercial prospects for undertaking construction of the ESPO have been highly dubious, with planned capacity for 2030 simply too large to support without costly buildup of the eastern transit infrastructure, redirection of dwindling West Siberian crude, and new incentives to offset the significant exploration costs and risks of the eastern oil field reservoirs. Moreover, such prospects are highly vulnerable to fluctuations in global oil prices beyond the control of Russian or Northeast Asian parties (Vatansever, 2010).[24]

Notwithstanding conspicuous political, economic, and geological problems, Russia, China, and Japan managed to strike a balance between their competitive and cooperative interests to initiate commercial operation of the landmark ESPO. Viewed through the lens of the prevailing energy security dilemma, the strategic context was especially propitious for transcending the commercial uncertainty and containing related risks. In particular, none of the parties wielded enough market power to incite fears of aggressive resource nationalism. Ironically, as Russia became the world's largest daily producer and exporter of crude oil in 2009 and 2010, respectively, it accounted for at most only 16 percent of the global integrated oil market, with marginal swing capacity (IEA, 2011, pp. 283–302). Its footprint in Northeast Asia was particularly modest, as China turned to Russia for less than 10 percent of its projected imports (U.S. Energy Information Administration, 2010a).[25] Similarly, Japan relied on Russia to meet only 6 percent of its imports, and maintained the world's largest national stockpile, which could insulate it from severe disruptions for up to six months (Itoh, 2010; U.S. Energy Information Administration, 2010b).[26] While all three parties had common stakes in construction of the ESPO that would satisfy respective demand and supply security concerns, no single state was rendered more vulnerable to the others.

With little to lose and prospects for diversifying direct overland oil deliveries enhanced by relatively weak and symmetrical market power, state and corporate players in all three states were opportunistic toward the ESPO. Russian state and commercial actors did not have strong incentives either to ingratiate or strongly alienate respective Chinese and Japanese partners. Rather, emphasis was placed on keeping options open and wooing preferred financing arrangements for construction of the ESPO up to Skovorodino, as well as on securing multiple commitments for throughput from emerging Northeast Asian customers. Coupled with temporary tax breaks for exploration and production from new eastern fields, this posture effectively reduced the significant up-front domestic investment, preserved Asian outlets for Russian crude, restricted foreign equity in lucrative and strategic reserves, and otherwise boosted the commercial appeal of the costly East Asian export project (Henderson, 2011a, pp. 16–21). The downturn in global prices during the second half of 2008, which reduced demand in the established

European market and adversely affected the financial standing of Rosneft and Transneft, only slightly modified these incentives. While it added commercial pressure to advance the ESPO, the focus remained on locking in foreign custom-ers via commitments for building the trunk line and short connector to China, while increasing rail exports and preserving a future option of phased develop-ment of the Kozmino extension (Gulick, 2007, p. 221; Garrison, 2009, pp. 69–76; Danchenko *et al.*, 2010).

By the same token, the drop in oil prices and tight global credit conditions enhanced China's leverage in bilateral negotiations over construction of a direct ESPO connector. This not only strengthened the appeal of Beijing's loans-for-oil offers with Russia, but also fostered opportunities to negotiate creative financing arrangements with other suppliers (e.g., Brazil, Venezuela, and Kazakhstan). It also enabled China to hedge its bet with Moscow, diversifying the commercial and political risks of the country's growing oil import dependence, and providing an important safeguard against disruption of sea-based deliveries from the Middle East.[27]

Similarly, the ESPO presented relatively modest gains and a bargaining chip for Tokyo. Given constraints on available throughput and significant costs of underwriting construction of a long pipeline to the Pacific Ocean compared with existing Russian rail deliveries, Japan could readily afford to float alterna-tive financing proposals with various contingencies, including demands for equity stakes in East Siberian fields and permission to sell respective oil to multiple customers at spot prices. Neither dependent on Russian pipeline deliveries nor compelled to accept single purchaser terms, Japanese negotiators also had little to lose by upping the ante with Moscow, demanding the return of the Kurile Islands as a precondition for the soft loans that were offered (Gulick, 2007, pp. 220–1).

Simultaneously, bargaining between Russia and China over the ESPO was constrained by respective regulatory opacity. As described elsewhere, Russia's oil sector was marred by a "recombinant" property rights structure, governed by overlapping fiscal authority and blurred relations of ownership and control spread among numerous federal, regional, quasi-state, and private actors. This effectively obfuscated decision making and economic power, covered up intra-elite rivalry, enhanced the practical autonomy of bureaucrats and firm managers, and reduced industry responsiveness to specific foreign policies. The instability fostered by this system came to a head in 2003–4 with the pursuit of rival eastern pipeline options by Transneft and Yukos, and the predatory dissolution of the latter that confused both Chinese and Japanese partners. The situation was compounded after 2004 with the dramatic re-statization of the sector that empowered multiple state stake-holders to pursue preferred Northeast Asian deals (Stulberg, 2007, pp. 75–81; Poussenkova, 2009, pp. 145–7; Luong & Weinthal, 2010, pp. 178–80).

Transneft's support for constructing the ESPO to Skovorodino with a link to the Chinese border, for example, was countermanded by the state railway monopoly, which had its own designs on increasing market share for oil exports via Pacific Ocean terminals. The arbitrariness surrounding the allocation of throughput rights and requirement for domestic producers to subsidize the costs of constructing the ESPO undermined investor confidence in commitments to construct the ESPO and its extensions (Poussenkova, 2009, pp. 144–5; Ahn, 2010; Danchenko et al., 2010, p. 10; Vatansever, 2010, p. 14). Similarly, the fluid revenue-based character of Moscow's tax breaks, combined with the 2010 reintroduction of the 45 percent export tax on sales below 15 percent rate of return and President Putin's reluctance to extend additional tax breaks to the oil and gas sector at the end of 2013, perpetuated uncertainty over cost recovery and muddied incentives for new field exploration for Russian producers (Henderson, 2011a, pp. 64–5).

The situation was compounded by institutional uncertainty in China. The national regulatory system has been marred, in particular, by an imbalanced information advantage of administrative agencies over executive bodies in the oil sector, as well as by unclear division of responsibility among rival party, ministerial, local, and national oil companies with competing demand- versus supply-side mandates. National decision making also has been frustrated by the absence of a high-level planning body to integrate broad energy policies, and the indecisiveness of state financial support for the competitive international plays by Chinese national oil companies. This regulatory opacity has presented both Russian and Chinese partners with considerable uncertainty about the significance of commercial versus strategic interests for the other side (Downs, 2009; Garrison, 2009, pp. 27–39; Overland & Broekhus, 2009).

Although market relations were propitious for Russian and Chinese leaderships to realize commercial opportunities with only modest risks of being exploited by the other, the ambiguity of respective decision making spurred mutual frustration and mistrust about the stability of negotiated commercial contracts. Chinese officials, for example, consistently bemoaned repeated cost overruns, as well as the indecisiveness and sluggishness with which Moscow embarked on development of East Siberian fields and construction of the ESPO. Fatigued by the incoherence of Russian policymaking, fluidity of interlocutors, and lack of political transparency (what the Chinese called "legal nihilism"), Chinese energy officials became increasingly resigned to a tortuous and limited commercial energy relationship, characterized by "one step forward, two steps back" (Danchenko et al., 2010, p. 12; Jakobson et al., 2011). By the same token, Russian officials remained wary about the credibility of Beijing's commitments to uphold commercially compelling pricing and supply terms. There was little confidence in Beijing's political capacity and will to follow through on engaging Russian oil firms in the domestic downstream market, notwithstanding the general warming of economic and political relations (Danchenko et al., 2010, p. 12; Itoh, 2011).

The mutual suspicions came to the fore quickly, only several months after initial deliveries of oil to China via the ESPO. This was manifest in a public dispute over tariffs, with China shortchanging Rosneft and Transneft, claiming it unfair that it pays the same duties on deliveries at its border as the premium charged for exports at Russia's Far Eastern port of Kozmino. The Russian government insisted that China honor its contract commitments, and the Russian state energy companies threatened to sue the Chinese partner in an international court. Both sides accused the other of adopting unfair practices; arbitrarily violating agreed price discounts, transit fees, and supply commitments; and interfering in national energy policymaking. Yet for all of the acrimony, the crisis was defused in 2012 as China agreed to pay its debt at a slight discount (Adelaja, 2011b; Helmer, 2011; *Kommersant*, 2011).[28] Most notably, however, the sides employed the bilateral energy negotiating mechanism (ENM) to transcend the institutional morass that stymied intergovernmental policymaking and negotiations up to that point. Specifically, the ENM enabled both sides to elevate decision making directly to vice premiers who wielded significant executive and corporate authority to cut through the respective administrative uncertainty. Accordingly, after several rounds of haggling, a compromise was reached in early 2012 whereby Rosneft and Transneft would provide a "country" discount to the CNPC, China's national gas company, costing roughly $3 billion, while the CNPC agreed to repay the debt for supply of oil from the beginning of 2011 (approximately $134 million). Although the risks were sufficiently low, and an extragovernmental instrument was put in place to enable the parties to step back from escalating the price dispute into a political conflict, the episode nonetheless reflected deep-seated institutional and commercial challenges that stand to perpetuate bickering and confound mutual energy security aspirations tied to the bilateral oil trade (Downs, 2011; Christoffersen, 2012).[29]

Fits and starts in Russia's eastern gas diplomacy

In comparison to the oil sector, Russia's gas trade with Northeast Asia has been conspicuously nettled. Notwithstanding complementary energy profiles and the opportunity presented by overland transit from Russia to avert Asia's "Malacca dilemma" with sea-based natural gas imports, long-standing promises of joint development and export of natural gas have largely failed to materialize. Unlike with the ESPO, the parties have proved indecisive, as well as less adept at employing the ENM, transcending deep suspicions and commercial rivalries to cement mutually beneficial gas deals and, in some cases, at avoiding episodic political turbulence.[30] Furthermore, Russia's gas relations with Chinese national energy companies have been more prone to these problems than have development projects involving Japanese and South Korean partners.

From 2004 to mid-2012, Moscow and Beijing succeeded only at inking framework agreements on Gazprom's future sales of natural gas to China. Although both presidents heralded the beginning of a new era in strategic partnership—capped by the codification of huge deals, including delivery of up to 68 billion cubic meters (bcm) per annum over the next 30 years from both West and East Siberian fields to meet 85 percent of China's projected import needs after 2015—the ability to reach a commercially viable compromise provided frustratingly elusive for both sides. Over ten years of talks, price ostensibly was the main point of contention, with Russia demanding European prices for its exports and China insisting first on prices comparable to domestic coal prices and then to LNG prices benchmarked to other regions. Yet, even when Moscow relaxed its earlier position in favor of a price formula linked to an Asian oil basket, China refused to compromise publicly on a reference price.[31] Beijing also remained deeply suspicious of Moscow's slow pace in developing eastern gas fields and pipelines. The intransigence in contract negotiations persisted, despite Russia's subsequent concessions for a joint Sino-Russo investment company to secure a controlling stake for up to 60 bcm in East Siberian reserves. Similarly, since 2006, Moscow has tendered successive proposals for pipelines to China without verifying the scientific or economic viability of the projects, granting significant equity stakes in new fields, committing to specific transit routes, or addressing Beijing's main concerns of increasing gas deliveries to its eastern provinces from fields in East Siberia and Sakhalin (Henderson, 2011b; Mares & Larys, 2012, pp. 443–4).[32] The reticence of both sides to consider the other's concessions and the repeated airing of arbitrary proposals not only stymied implementation of prospective gas deals but undermined confidence in each other as negotiating partners. Moscow's posture, for example, is attributed to political ambitions aimed at leveraging talks about delivering West Siberian gas to China to intimidate European customers and preserve profits amid Beijing's pressures on price, while China's diffidence conveys a commitment to lock in East Siberian imports at Japan's expense (Overland & Broekhus, 2009; Itoh, 2010, p. 25; Blank, 2011, p. 17; Henderson & Stern, 2014).

At the same time, the competition for Eurasian gas has been strategically precarious, notwithstanding mutual Russian, Central Asian, and Chinese interests in avoiding conflict. In stark contrast to the sluggishness of Sino-Russo gas developments, in 2009 China and Turkmenistan formally opened the Central Asian Pipeline to deliver 20 bcm of gas from Turkmenistan and Kazakhstan (and eventually Uzbekistan) to Xinjiang. This was followed by China's $4 billion loan-for-energy deal with Turkmenistan. The deal paved the way both for Ashgabat to negotiate increases in deliveries from 30 bcm to 65 bcm annually to eastern China by 2015 (with a future link to Hong Kong), and for the CNPC to acquire rights to develop the giant South Yolotan gas field. Moreover, the speed of negotiating and implementing these pipeline, credit, and development ventures with Central Asian suppliers came at the direct expense of Russia's early deliveries to China.[33] By comparison, progress on Russia's rival Prikaspiyskii pipeline with Turkmenistan and Kazakhstan stagnated, seemingly mired in corruption and bad faith. This effectively undermined both the credibility and practical significance of Moscow's subsequent commitments to purchase 30 bcm from Ashgabat and to construct a link to untapped reserves in eastern Turkmenistan (Baev, 2009; Garrison, 2009; Kim, 2010). Accordingly, Turkmenistan's success in constructing the first direct overland transit route to China, which circumvented Russia's extraterritorial export network, was a blow to Moscow's dominant energy stature in the post-Soviet space. The episode sparked a welter of nationalist "Sinophobic" commentary and political handwringing in the Kremlin about China's rise and the general ebbing of Moscow's influence across both Eurasia and East Asia. This sentiment was aptly captured by one Russian commentator, who opined that the "Kremlin lacks either strength or willingness to put up a fight for Central Asia" (*Kommersant*, 2009, as referenced in Kim, 2010, p. 34; Danchenko *et al.*, 2010, pp. 5–7).

The variable riskiness of the strategic context has compounded difficulties in regional bargaining. To date, this has been characterized by asymmetries in market power between Russia and its Northeast Asian partners on issues of piped gas. As mentioned above, Russia is a natural gas superpower, possessing the largest proven and probable reserves in the world. This stature is accentuated by Gazprom's near monopoly on the existing Russian and Central Asian pipeline system, which, in combination with the remote location of gas fields in Turkmenistan, Kazakhstan, and Uzbekistan, renders its consent crucial for monetizing Eurasian supplies to extraregional consumers. This affords Russian suppliers significant market power over exports from Eurasia, especially via overland pipelines to Northeast Asian customers.[34]

China's market standing is very different. Although Beijing has not traditionally relied on natural gas as a significant component of its national energy mix, it became a net importer in 2007, and domestic demand is expected to treble by 2035. To meet this shortfall, China has turned to boosting indigenous and unconventional supply, and complementing increased imports of LNG (and construction of new terminals at home) with overland deliveries from Russia and Central Asia. Accordingly, both the prospective costs and risks of committing early to Moscow for long-term supply are moderately high in comparison with the pace of China's steadily growing demand and availability of favorable alternative domestic and foreign benchmark sources of supply (Itoh, 2010, p. 26; Kim, 2010, p. 24; Jakobson *et al.*, 2011, pp. 33–8; Lelyveld, 2011; Tunsjo, 2013, pp. 165–70; Zoller, 2013).

By contrast, Japan and South Korea rely on imports to satisfy nearly all of their natural gas consumption. Yet as the number one and two importers of LNG, respectively, they are not prone to becoming directly vulnerable to pipeline supply from Russia (U.S. Energy Information Administration, 2010b, 2010c).[35] Working with Russia, therefore, does not present the same commercial or political risks that confront China's future import dependence.

Moreover, unlike the opaque institutional setting for oil transactions, Russia's natural gas bargaining with Northeast Asian customers is complicated by variable national regulatory systems. On the one hand, the Russian gas system is centralized and clearly delineated. The state retains a majority stake in the world's largest gas company, Gazprom, which is responsible for more than 80 percent of national production and nearly 10 percent of GDP. Gazprom also enjoys monopoly control over the nation's entire chain of development, production, processing, transmission, and exports.[36] This posture was enhanced in 2011 as Gazprom secured controlling rights to develop the huge Kovytka field, which, when combined with its majority shares in the Sakhalin-2 and Sakhalin-3 gas reserves, complemented its export monopoly of Russian pipeline and LNG deliveries to Northeast Asia.

Although the state's majority stake does not ensure control over the company, due in large part to divergent interests in price and an opaque corporate governance structure, it can meaningfully affect the firm's operations.[37] This has been reinforced by clearly defined federal authorities to set domestic wholesale and retail prices; to ensure supplies for domestic consumption by households and industry; and to impose royalty fees, export tariffs, and quotas. Accordingly, the Russian state is well poised to align domestic stakeholder interests with its foreign policy ambitions in the gas sector, and is thus capable of sending clear and credible signals to foreign interlocutors (Stulberg, 2007, pp. 68–71; Mankoff, 2009; Pirani *et al.*, 2009).

On the other hand, the respective institutional setting in Northeast Asia varies. In China, lines of executive and administrative authority over national gas policy remain ambiguous, as in the oil sector. Administrative bodies operate on the same plane with rival ministries with much larger staffs. Consequently, they lack sufficient authority to coordinate the fractured interests among bureaucratic rivals, commissions, state-owned gas companies, and regional authorities. Moreover, they compete against the influence of top executives of the three principal state-owned oil and gas companies, who are also members of the Central Committee of the Chinese Communist Party. As noted by several scholars, China's policymaking in the gas sector is marred by a collage of various policy pieces rather than a coherent policy (Downs, 2007; Garrison, 2009).

Conversely, the regulatory structures for overseas gas exploration, production, and imports in South Korea and Japan are clearly delineated. The Korea Gas Corporation (KOGAS), in which the state holds controlling equity stakes, retains a virtual monopoly on the purchasing, import, and wholesale distribution of natural gas (U.S. Energy Information Administration, 2010c). Although private companies are the prime actors in Japan, reforms enacted in the late 1990s have effectively streamlined oversight and competition (U.S. Energy Information Administration, 2010b).

Together the prevailing market and institutional conditions can account for two distinct features of Russia's gas diplomacy toward Northeast Asia. The first pertains to the conspicuous impasse in gas relations with China compared with Russia's ventures with South Korea and Japan. Whereas the risk and opacity associated with Moscow's dealings with China conspire against cooperation, both the reduced vulnerability to Russia's supply and mutual transparency augur well for advancing financially sound joint commercial ventures. As suggested by preliminary cooperation with Gazprom on the construction of an LNG plant linked to Russia's Sakhalin-2 and Sakhalin-3 fields, connector to the Primorsk region, and potential pipeline extension to external markets in South Korea, engaging Russia (especially in nonstrategic fields) offers the prospects for commercial gain without accentuating political risks of dependence (Takeda, 2008; Itoh, 2010; Henderson & Stern, 2014).[38]

Second, the efficacy of Sino-Russian gas relations has been compromised by the moderately intense energy security dilemma, especially in dealing with Central Asian suppliers. The reaction to a 2009 pipeline explosion, which turned a technical issue into a political one, illustrates the inadvertent tensions associated with this strategic context. For Russia, both the potency and efficiency of its market stature at piping gas proved to be a liability for sustaining favorable commercial relations. This posture simply made claims of innocence incredible, as

Ashgabat dismissed Gazprom's apologies for a "technical accident" as "irrational and irresponsible." Ashgabat blamed Moscow for purposefully turning off the valve (spiking transmission pressure) in an effort to shirk its commitment to purchase larger volumes from Turkmenistan (at nearly European prices) because of a downturn in global demand. Accordingly, Ashgabat not only delayed consenting to Russian development of its new and coveted onshore gas fields, but openly flaunted independence by soliciting a German firm to develop Turkmenistan's off-shore fields, jump-starting a dialogue with Azerbaijan on a prospective trans-Caspian pipeline to deliver additional gas to Western markets, and turning to China for the loan to develop the South Yolotan gas field. Coupled with shortfalls in Gazprom's financing, this effectively stunted Russia's plans for advancing the Prikaspiyskii pipeline, while bolstering the promise of the Central Asian Pipeline to China. Ashgabat also responded by actively pursuing Iranian and South Korean investment in the Turkmen gas sector to promote further diversification.

Unclear about Turkmen and Chinese motivations but empowered by its market stature, Moscow was willing initially to escalate tensions and lay down political markers regarding its preferred direction for Central Asian supplies by reducing the amount and price it would pay for the Turkmen gas it purchased. Although not a devastating blow, this raised the risks of antagonizing relations with Ashgabat and Beijing. Notwithstanding Moscow's denial of wrongdoing and ultimate success at defusing the crisis with commitments to increase the annual purchase of 30 bcm of Turkmen gas at a commercial loss, the fear and confusion generated by the market weakness and opacity within the Turkmen and Chinese regulatory systems, respectively, had a boomerang effect on Russia's gas diplomacy. Rather than accentuating the costs of building a pipeline between Turkmenistan and China, mere intimation of Moscow's heavy-handedness effectively increased the prospective payoffs of taking risks on diversification for Ashgabat and Beijing, thus inflating the costs to Moscow of exerting its significant market power.

Implications

This chapter suggests that nothing is straightforward about Russia's energy engagement with Northeast Asia. The ability to realize complementary interests among the world's fastest-growing hydrocarbon supplier and its customers varies with market and institutional conditions that inform strategic bargaining in the oil and gas sectors. This illuminates several practical considerations for future approaches to regional energy governance.

First, it underscores that Russia's reliance on an energy pillar to reinvigorate its regional stature and orchestrate new divisions of responsibility for managing interdependent economic and political relations in Northeast Asia remains limited. First and foremost, Moscow's commitment to expending political capital to make substantive progress toward implementing new rules of the road for regional energy governance, per se, has been circumscribed by a growing focus on development of the RFE and shifting approaches to enlarging its commercial and strategic footprint. That said, opportunities for bilateral oil ventures offer little in terms of noncommercial advantages or the basis for Moscow to become a regime-setter. By contrast, Russia is poised to break into new regional gas markets with development of new pipelines to China and act as a spoiler to rival commercial initiatives. Yet this very stature, together with the challenges presented by limited demand for piped gas by Japan and Korea, and China's hedging strategy and political opacity, narrow the scope for regional governance and increase the prospects for inadvertent escalation of commercial competition. Similarly, progress in working with one set of customers or at consummating a specific bilateral deal is not readily transferable, complicating issue linkage and efforts to build regional energy regimes from the bottom up. Each side's confidence in the others as negotiating partners in the ESPO also is not likely to unlock or to restrict opportunities in the gas sector; the obstacles to a Sino-Russo gas deal are sizeable and require significant changes beyond narrow commercial compromises on price.

Second, the strategic context for Russia's energy forays into Northeast Asia is not static. With the growing promise of shale and unconventional gas exploration across the globe, the industry stands at the precipice of transformation. Should trends hold, the gas sector may reflect the dynamics of the integrated oil trade, reducing the significance of overland pipelines, and thus Russia's regional market power (Johnson & Stromquist, 2014). However, this opening of the gas market can reduce the risks of commercial cooperation with Russia. With viable financing arrangements, it could increase Russia's LNG transactions and accelerate eastern field development. While the former will not play to Russia's strategic or market advantages, it could provide the reassurance needed to reduce the stakes and break the logjam over prices, thus enabling Moscow and Beijing to realize ambitious commercial plans for an overland pipeline.

Finally, attention to the prevailing strategic context reveals that institutions do indeed matter for unlocking the prospects for regional energy security. Yet, unlike relations in Europe that feature efforts to forge international energy charters and norms to protect supply, demand, and especially transit security discussed in Chapter 8 by Carla Freeman, the focal point for institutional reform should rest squarely on enhancing the transparency of respective national regulatory systems. Relative market power and bargaining strength matter so much in shaping bilateral Russo-Sino deals and the risks of inadvertent escalation of commercial gas rows are so great because the credibility and capacity engendered by opaque regulatory systems in both countries are so weak. Accordingly, the Kremlin would be wise to rethink formation of still another state megacorporation with additional authority to issue tax breaks and mining licenses that effectively exacerbates regulatory uncertainty in the oil sector.[39] By the same token, the increasing domestic market share of independent gas companies in Russia, coupled with their engagement with China in joint development in new LNG projects and the Kremlin's decision at the end of 2013 to partially liberalize exports, may stimulate new Russian stakeholders in promoting investment and effective LNG price mechanisms across Northeast Asia (Lunden et al., 2013; Mitrova, 2013). Similarly, policymakers across the region should strive to clarify authority and oversight mechanisms—such as easing restrictions on foreign direct investment, deregulating domestic prices, enhancing third-party access to national pipelines, creating new and transparent production sharing agreement (PSA) arrangements, reforming tax structures to stimulate investment in refining and greenfield projects in East Siberia and Sakhalin, and delineating state and private authority— in order to allow commercially viable and self-enforcing agreements to take hold. While this may not root out risks of future energy conflicts, it will go a long way toward distinguishing commercial from strategically offensive intentions, averting costly blunders, and easing the flow of financing and technologies so that parties across Eurasia and Northeast Asia can forge regional governance mechanisms to advance common energy security interests.

Notes

1 Russian President Medvedev also ordered a concerted effort to start gas supplies via a new intra-Far Eastern pipeline before the opening of the APEC summit (APEC, 2012).
2 *The Russian Energy Strategy to 2030* estimates that East Siberian fields (including Yakutia, Irkutsk, and Krasnoyarsk) hold roughly 11 percent and 38 percent of the nation's oil and gas reserves, respectively. The Far East centers (including Sakhalin and Okhotsk) are claimed to be home to 9 percent and 11 percent of oil and gas reserves, respectively. The estimates, however, are problematic and contested by different Russian state agencies, academics, and private firms. Projections vary widely, as only a small portion of conventional reserves has been explored (and tremendous uncertainty surrounds Russia's potential unconventional gas resources); there are different scenarios for extraction; different state agencies are motivated to report and highlight only partial assessments; and debate rages over expected recovery rates, with as much as 75 percent of the reserves classified as least reliable. See discussion in Poussenkova (2009, pp. 134–5) and Henderson (2011a).
3 In 2009, production from the four East Siberian and Far Eastern oil centers totaled less than 500,000 bpd or less than 5 percent total national production (U.S. Energy Information Administration, 2010d). By comparison, the *Energy Strategy* calls for 3 billion tons of "new" oil to be pumped at optimal levels from these four reserves, constituting nearly 20 percent of Russia's total gas production by 2030. Similarly, it projects that Russian gas production in these four centers will ramp up to 132–152 bcm, surpassing production from established fields in the European part of the country to represent 15 percent of total gas production by 2030.
4 See, especially, commentary in Lavrov (2006, pp. 8–10), Wishnick (2006), and Rozman (2008).
5 See, especially, speech by President Dimitry Medvedev (Medvedev, 2009).
6 As several scholars note, this nuanced change in approach to regional energy security cooperation was mirrored by a shift away from traditional insecurity about Russia's position in East Asia and the influx of Chinese immigrants and local traders, as well as a growing sense across the RFE that closer regional economic engagement is highly desirable (Sullivan & Renz, 2010). Though at the time of writing Putin's second presidency remains in its infancy, continuity rather than change seems more conspicuous in the approach to regional governance. The early priority placed on development of the RFE and Siberian provinces by attracting global energy majors,

as well as investment from Northeast Asian and APEC regional players, for example, suggests that the renewed commitment to state-promoted reindustrialization aims to give impetus to the modernization program championed by Medvedev (Petro, 2011).

7 The prospects for realizing an optimal 30 percent of the Chinese, Japanese, and South Korean markets will rest on the acceleration of Russia's infrastructure development, reduction of deliveries to Europe, construction of Caspian bypass pipelines to established European markets, and the indefinite postponement of Iraqi gas development. For a more sanguine assessment of Russia's potential to support increased gas flows abroad, including projections that nearly 50 percent of its exports can be shipped to Asia by 2050, see Paltsev (2011).

8 Typically, the success at wielding an "energy weapon" is constrained by market and political factors related to supply and demand elasticities, concentration of reserves/output/consumption, possibilities for resource and supplier/customer substitution, strategic importance of the resource, and global patterns of supply and consumption. See discussion in Garrison (2009).

9 For seminal work on international security dilemmas, see, especially, Jervis (1978), Glaser (1997), and Booth and Wheeler (2008).

10 That respective states may embrace benign conceptions of resource nationalism provides little relief, as information asymmetries, market disparities, and expectations of future harm can undermine the ability of states to communicate their intentions or reassure others. However, should Russian or Asian policymakers be able to discern aggressive/greedy political ambitions from commercial impulses and to send costly signals that convey benign intent, they can extract themselves from the fatalistic logic of mutual insecurity. This can be accomplished by crafting policies that reassure others with similarly defensive energy concerns or by demonstrating resolve in the face of an unambiguously belligerent adversary (Kydd, 2005; Montgomery, 2006).

11 For discussion of an analogous dynamic afflicting Russian–European energy relations, see Monaghan (2006).

12 On the incentives for offensive action and international mistrust between strong and weak parties, see, especially, Sechser (2010).

13 For slightly different figures, see Renaissance Capital (2008). By 2008, U.S. natural gas production exceeded that of Russia, owing to increased shale volumes.

14 The outlook for oil is further muddled as Russia is projected to hit its peak oil production (9.5–10 mmbd) between 2012 and 2017 (assuming that new megaprojects are readily brought on line), with output declining steadily to 6 mmbd. If Russia continues along this current trajectory, with depletion rates at 4 percent at existing fields, oil production is expected to plateau by 2012. On Saudi Arabia's growing Asian focus, see, especially, Jaffe and Elass (2007).

15 Russian and foreign sources project that the oil and gas sectors will require nearly $400 billion each in accumulated investment through 2030 (Goldthau, 2008; Milov, 2008).

16 For detailed discussion of this line of argument, see, especially, Stulberg (2007).

17 See discussion in Stulberg (2007) and Pleines (2009). Recent figures tend to obfuscate this trend, as the state-owned oil company, Rosneft, posted a large increase in crude oil output. This mostly reflected an accounting shift, however, as the surge in output was driven by the addition of upstream assets previously owned by the private firm Yukos that were acquired in the forced bankruptcy auction in 2007. That said, Rosneft has been the beneficiary of significant nonmarket competitive advantages over rival Russian private oil firms, owing to exclusive access to pipelines, strategic and off-shore fields; application of special bankruptcy procedures; Putin's close personal association with the corporate leadership; and the Kremlin's lobbying on behalf of the state

company in foreign markets. See discussion in Renaissance Capital (2008, p. 26) and Poussenkova (2013).

18 On the character and consequences of Russia's dramatic shift in ownership and fiscal structure of the oil structure, see, especially, Luong and Weinthal (2010).

19 The 20-year, $25 billion loan-for-oil deal (extended by the China Development Bank) allocated $15 billion to the Russia state-owned oil company, Rosneft, and $10 billon to the national pipeline operator, Transneft. Rosneft received 60 percent of the loan and agreed to supply 180,000 bpd of oil, while Transneft received 40 percent of the loan to complete the pipeline connector for Skovorodino to the Chinese border and agreed to deliver an additional 120,000 bpd (purchased from Rosneft under a separate agreement). The agreement calls for the price of oil to be set each month based on the market quotes for the new blend, which, as of 2010, sold at a premium to benchmark Dubai crude (Downs, 2011, pp. 39–42; Platts Special Report, 2011).

20 In October 2013, Rosneft agreed to supply an additional 10 million tons per year of crude to Sinopec for ten years, which was worth roughly $85 billion in trading volume.

21 The maximum capacity of the second stage of the ESPO provides for 300,000 bpd to be shipped to China, and 600,000–700,000 bpd to be exported across the Pacific from the Kozmino terminal. In addition to the follow-on deals with Rosneft, a contract was signed for the Russian private oil company, Lukoil, and Sinopec, to develop another East Siberian field to supply 3 million tons of crude oil. Moscow and Beijing also signed MoUs pertaining to the development of Russian natural gas, coal, gold mining at the June 2009 summit. By the end of 2013, Russia secured at least six routes for delivering oil to Northeast Asian customers (ESPO, ESPO–China spur, truck, rail, through Kazakhstan, from Sakhalin), with key importers via the ESPO including Japan (31 percent), China (24 percent), the U.S. (22 percent), South Korea, Singapore, the Philippines, Thailand, and Malaysia. See Paik (2014).

22 By many estimates, the ESPO was not commercially profitable from inception, costing Transneft and the federal budget more than $1 billion per year, due to the enormous initial outlays combined with the difficulties of securing supply, high cost of delivering oil to Asian markets, and lower prices paid by Chinese consumers. That said, various Russian regions have obtained fairly high revenues from taxes. See discussion of the strategic versus commercial advantages of the ESPO in Mares and Larys (2012, pp. 442–3).

23 By 2009, for example, Rosneft sold more than 40 percent of its total refined product exports to Asian customers (Henderson, 2011a, p. 34). Also, whereas the volume of domestic oil production increased by more than 28 percent in 2010, the volume of refined products available for domestic consumption dropped by 20 percent, prompting national gasoline shortages within the world's leading oil producer. This irony prompted Russian Prime Minister Putin to threaten to strip domestic oil companies of access to export pipelines and lucrative foreign markets if they fail to meet respective obligations to modernize domestic refineries and boost sales of refined products (Adelaja, 2011a).

24 One systematic analysis of the main corporate players reveals that Russia maintains sufficient eastern production potential to support plans for the ESPO by a general 2020 time frame, but only under advantageous above-ground conditions (Henderson, 2011a, p. 34).

25 China relies on the Middle East and Africa for more than 80 percent of its crude oil imports, one-third of which is provided by Saudi Arabia and Angola.

26 Japan receives as much as 80 percent of its imports from the Middle East, and has embarked on efforts to diversify the residual imports from Southeast Asian and African suppliers, as well as from Russia.

27 By some accounts, Beijing leveraged the favorable interest rates of the 2009 loan to lock in a significant price discount for long-term deliveries that were especially advantageous given the higher cost of production from smaller fields in the RFE. See discussion in Danchenko *et al.* (2010, pp. 12–13), Mares and Larys (2012, p. 442), and Tunsjo (2013, pp. 174–6).

28 Under the deal reached in 2012, Rosneft and Transneft offered the Chinese partner a $1.50 per barrel discount on crude shipments from November 2011, while the Chinese state oil company agreed to pay its outstanding debt since early 2011.

29 By mid-2013, there were signs that this compromise agreement was beginning to fray, with the Russian Prosecutor's Office investigating both alleged violations and the "legality" of subsequent contracts involving Chinese customers. See Poussenkova (2013, p. 20).

30 It is interesting to note that, at the eighth meeting of the ENM (immediately following resolution of the 2011 oil price dispute), the Russian and Chinese vice premiers detailed favorable prospects for expanding upstream and downstream oil cooperation, but made only passing reference to hopes for resolving lingering obstacles to bilateral gas negotiations (Ministry of Foreign Affairs of the People's Republic of China, 2012).

31 The June 2011 talks between the two presidents stalemated over different price formulas resulting from Russian demands of $350 per thousand cubic meters compared to China's offer to pay $235 per thousand cubic meters. Although nearly all of the commercial elements of the contract were in order, the parties nonetheless failed to come to terms over minimum volumes and delivery dates, suggesting that political will rather than technical differences were standing in the way of codifying the gas supply contract. Moreover, China gradually abandoned its earlier position of tying gas import prices to coal, agreeing to market prices for LNG, including for deliveries from Sakhalin and via a future Arctic passage (Adelaja, 2011b; Lelyveld, 2011; Tunsjo, 2013).

32 For example, the Altai pipeline, with capacity to deliver 30 bcm from West Siberia to China's West–East Pipeline, has been held up due to differences over pricing, notwithstanding the signing of successive framework agreements and bilateral commitments on volumes and start-up dates since 2006. It was only in March 2013 that Putin formally conferred priority development to the eastern route to deliver 38 bcm per year for 30 years over Gazprom's preferred Altai pipeline from West Siberia. Yet even after this declaration, haggling over price continued, and Russia and China failed to finalize the pipeline agreement. See Paik (2013).

33 Turkmenistan's deliveries arrive proximate to the entry point of Russian gas from West Siberia, as well as enjoy relative price and netback advantages. Not surprisingly, Beijing's price offerings to Russia are close to what it pays for the cheaper Central Asian supply (Henderson, 2011b, pp. 190–1).

34 Some argue, for example, that Russia purposefully accedes to, if not subtly manipulates, early Central Asian supplies to China as a way of reducing future competition in established European markets or setting a precedent with price discounts for West Siberian exports (Henderson, 2011b, p. 24; Tunsjo, 2013, p. 191).

35 Japan, for example, receives only 4.3 percent of its domestic consumption of LNG from Russia, as opposed to nearly 40 percent from Indonesia and Australia.

36 Although the government has officially committed to deregulating domestic prices by 2015, it has successfully postponed this goal and demonstrated only sporadic progress since 2007. Accordingly, the unregulated gas market in Russia accounted for only 25 percent of total domestic gas sales in 2011, the original target date for complete deregulation. Notwithstanding calls for liberalizing third-party access to at least 10 percent

of national pipeline system since 2007, Gazprom has practically withheld capacity in the absence of price deregulation (Pirani, 2011, p. 12).

37 Where Gazprom generally favors higher domestic prices and sitting on reserves within its extensive portfolio, the state and regional leaderships remain committed to increasing investment in new field development in the RFE and preserving strategic sales at a discount to domestic consumers. Similarly, Gazprom's arbitrary intervention in development of the Kovytka gas field and the gas giant's decision to buy Central Asian gas at the expense of exploring the Chayandinsk field in Sakha suggest the limits to direct state control. In both incidents, Gazprom's behavior undermined the negotiating credibility of federal and provincial authorities, as well as the coherence and appeal of prospective field development, pipeline deals, and commercial contracting with potential Northeast Asian energy investors and customers (Danchenko *et al.*, 2010, p. 10; Medetsky, 2011).

38 Rather, the commercial viability of pipeline deliveries from Russia to the Korean Peninsula turns on the prospects for integrating North Korea into the transaction, an issue beyond Moscow's direct control via its market power or otherwise.

39 As noted by the former finance minister, this directive, which exempts the state corporation from federal legislation, distorts investor confidence in the sector by countermanding national tax and tariff policies and obfuscating authority among federal and agencies. It undermines the business climate in the region, as "at any moment another player with special preferences, special administrative resources and special access to finances may come to the market" (*Sputnik News*, 2012).

References

Adelaja, T. 2011a. Where Did All the Crude Go? Can Russian Prime Minister Vladimir Putin and His Government Avoid a Fresh Fuel Crisis? *Russia Profile*, July 11.

Adelaja, T. 2011b. A Chinese Game: Russia and China Set Aside Their Differences in Pursuit of Greater Economic Goals. *Russia Profile*, June 2.

Ahn, S.H. 2010. Framing Energy Security Between Russia and South Korea? Progress, Problems, and Prospects. *Asian Survey* 50(3): 591–614.

APEC. 2012. *Declaration at the Conclusion of the 20th APEC Economic Leaders Meeting in Vladivostok, ANNEX B—Strengthening APEC Energy Security*. Online: http://apec.org/Press/News-Releases/2012/~/link.aspx?_id=8D5E334F90E6452FBA341CA50ED2C934&_z=z (accessed September 4, 2013).

Baev, P. 2008. Asia-Pacific and LNG: The Lure of New Markets. In: K. Barysch (ed.) *Pipelines, Politics, and Power: The Future of EU–Russia Energy Relations*. Brussels: Center for European Reform, pp. 83–92.

Baev, P. 2009. China Trumps Gazprom. *Moscow Times*, December 17.

Blank, S. 2011. *Toward a New Chinese Order in Asia: Russia's Failure*. NBR Special Report, March, Volume 26. Seattle, WA: National Bureau of Asian Research

Booth, K. and Wheeler, N. 2008. *The Security Dilemma: Fear, Cooperation, and Trust in World Politics*. New York: Palgrave Macmillan.

BP. 2011. *BP Statistical Review of World Energy*. London: BP.

Christoffersen, G. 2010. Russia's Breakthrough into the Asia-Pacific: China's Role. *International Relations of the Asia Pacific* 10(1): 61–91.

Christoffersen, G. 2012. Multiple Levels of Sino-Russian Energy Relations. In R.E. Bedeski and N. Swanstrom (eds.) *Eurasia's Ascent in Energy and Geopolitics*. New York: Routledge, pp. 149–54.

Cohen, A. 2009. The Flawed Energy Superpower. In G. Luft and A. Korin (eds.) *Energy Security Challenges for the 21st Century*. Santa Barbara, CA: ABC-CLIO LLC, pp. 91–108.

Danchenko, I., Downs, E., and Hill, F. 2010. *One Step Forward, Two Steps Back? The Realities of a Rising China and Implications for Russia's Energy Ambitions*. Policy Paper 22. Washington, DC: Brookings Institution.

Downs, E.S. 2007. China's Energy Bureaucracy: The Challenge of Getting the Institutions Right. In M. Median (ed.) *Shaping China's Energy Security: The Inside Perspective*. Paris: Asia Centre, pp. 64–89.

Downs, E.S. 2009. Who's Afraid of China's Oil Companies? In C. Pascual and J. Elkind (eds.) *Energy Security: Economics, Politics, Strategies, and Implications*. Washington, DC: Brookings Institution, pp. 73–102.

Downs, E.S. 2011. *Inside China, Inc.: China Development Bank's Cross-Border Energy Deals*. Washington, DC: Brookings Institution.

eng.kremlin.ru/news. 2013. *Presidential Address to the Federal Assembly*. Online: http://eng.kremlin.ru/news/6402 (accessed June 4, 2014).

Eurasia Review. 2013. The Russian Far East and China: Thoughts on Cross-Border Integration. *Eurasia Review*, November 11.

Garrison, J.A. 2009. *China and the Energy Equation in Asia: The Determinants of Policy Choice*. New York: Lynne Rienner.

Gazprom. 2008–14. *Eastern Gas Program*. Online: www.gazprom.com/press/news/east-program/ (accessed July 17, 2014).

Glaser, C.L. 1997. The Security Dilemma Revisited. *World Politics* 50(1): 171–201.

Goldthau, A. 2008. Resurgent Russia? Rethinking Energy Inc. *Policy Review* 147, February–March: 53–63.

Gulick, J. 2007. Russo-Chinese Energy Cooperation: Stepping Stone from Strategic Partnership to Geo-economic Integration? *International Journal of Comparative Sociology* 48(2–3), April: 203–33.

Helmer, J. 2011. Russia, China Clash Over Oil Price, Supply. *Asia Times*, May 5.

Henderson, J. 2011a. *The Strategic Implications of Russia's Eastern Oil Resources*. Oxford: Oxford University Institute for Energy Studies.

Henderson, J. 2011b. *The Pricing Debate over Russian Gas Exports to China*, NG 56. Oxford: The Oxford University Institute for Energy Studies.

Henderson, J. and Stern, J. 2014. *The Potential Impact on Asia Gas Markets of Russia's Eastern Gas Strategy*. Oxford Energy Comment, February 14. Oxford: The Oxford University Institute for Energy Studies.

Herberg, M. 2010. The Rise of Energy and Resource Nationalism in Asia. In A.J. Tellis, A. Marble, and T. Tanner (eds.) *Strategic Asia 2010–11: Asia's Rising Power and America's Continued Purpose*. Seattle, WA: National Bureau of Asian Research.

Heritage, T. 2014. Putin Looks to Asia as West Threatens to Isolate Russia. Reuters, March 21. Online: www.reuters.com/article/2014/03/21/us-ukraine-crisis-russia-insight-idUSBREA2K07S20140321 (accessed June 15, 2014).

Hill, F. 2004. *Energy Empire: Oil, Gas, and Russia's Revival*. London: The Foreign Policy Centre. Online: http://fpc.org.uk/fsblob/307.pdf (accessed May 14, 2010).

Hill, F. and Gaddy, C. 2003. *The Siberian Curse: How Communist Planners Left Russia Out in the Cold*. Washington, DC: Brookings Institution.

International Energy Agency (IEA). 2011. *World Energy Outlook 2011*. Paris: OECD/IEA.

Itoh, S. 2010. *The Geopolitics of Northeast Asia's Pipeline Development*. National Bureau of Asian Research Special Report. Seattle, WA: NBR.

Itoh, S. 2011. *Russia Looks East: Energy Markets and Geopolitics in Northeast Asia.* Washington, DC: CSIS.

Ivanov, I. 2011. *About Russia's Chairmanship of APEC 2012.* Moscow: Russian APEC Study Center.

Jaffe, A.M. and Elass, J. 2007. *Saudi Aramco: National Flagship with Global Responsibilities.* Houston, TX: The James A. Baker III Institute for Public Policy, Rice University.

Jakobson, L., Holtom, P., Knox, D., and Peng, J. 2011. *China's Energy and Security Relations with Russia: Hopes, Frustrations and Uncertainties.* Stockholm: SIPRI.

Jentleson, B.W. 1986. *Pipeline Politics: The Complex Political Economy of East–West Energy Trade.* Ithaca, NY: Cornell University Press.

Jervis, R. 1978. Cooperation Under the Security Dilemma. *World Politics* 30(2): 167–214.

Johnson, R. and Stromquist, E. 2014. *The Russian Gas Sector: A Political Risk Case Study.* Houston, TX: The James A. Baker III Institute for Public Policy, Rice University.

Kalashnikov, V.D., Bardal, A.B., and Khmelnitskim, V.V. 2005. Toplivo-Energeticheski I Transportni Kompleks Regiona. In: *Dalni Vostok I Zabaikale V Rossii I ATR. Dalnevostochni Mezhdunarodni Ekonomicheski Kongres [Regional Energy and Transport Complex, The Far East and Zabaikal in Russia and the Asia Pacific Region].* Khabarovsk: Russian Academy of Sciences, Far Eastern Branch, Economics Research Institute.

Kim, Y. 2010. *Central Asia's Great Game and the Rise of China.* Paper presented at the 2nd International Conference of the HK Russia·Eurasia Research Project: Beyond Russian and Becoming Eurasian, Hanyang University, Korea, May, pp. 9–41.

Kommersant. 2011. Rosneft–CNPC Conflict Threatens Russia's Largest Oil Supply Deal. *Kommersant,* March 18.

Kuhrt, N. 2012. The Russian Far East in Russia's Asia Policy: Dual Integration or Double Periphery. *Europe–Asia Studies* 64(3), May: 471–93.

Kydd, A.H. 2005. *Trust and Mistrust in International Relations.* Princeton, NJ: Princeton University Press.

Larsson, R.L. 2006. *Russia's Energy Policy: Security Dimensions and Russia's Reliability as An Energy Supplier.* Stockholm: FOI.

Lavrov, S. 2006. The Rise of Asia, and the Eastern Vector of Russia's Foreign Policy. *Russia in Global Affairs* 3, July–September. Online: http://eng.globalaffairs.ru/number/n_6865 (accessed March 25, 2013).

Lavrov, S. 2011. Russia's Policy in Asia Pacific: Towards Peace, Security, and Sustainability. *Strategic Review.* Online: www.mid.ru/brp_4.nsf/0/0783A1264F6F63FA442579D7005 25C04 (accessed December 12, 2012).

Lee, J.-Y. and Novitskiy, A. 2010. Russia's Energy Policy and Its Impacts on Northeast Asian Energy Security. *International Area Review* 13(1), Spring: 41–60.

Lelyveld, M. 2011. Gas Deal Delayed Again. Radio Free Asia, *Commentaries: Energy Watch.* Online: www.rfa.org/english/commentaries/energy_watch/deal-06272011103259.html (accessed July 3, 2012).

Lukin, A. 2011. Russia and the Emerging Institutional Order in the Asia-Pacific Region. *Estudios Internacionales* 170: 141–56.

Lunden, L.P., Fjaertoft, D., Overland, I., and Prachakova, A. 2013. Gazprom vs. Other Russian Gas Producers: The Evolution of the Russian Gas Sector. *Energy Policy* 61: 663–70.

Luong, P.J. and Weinthal, E. 2010. *Oil Is Not a Curse: Ownership Structure and Institutions in Soviet Successor States.* New York: Cambridge University Press.

Mankoff, J. 2009. *Eurasian Energy Security.* New York: Council on Foreign Relations.

Mares, M. and Larys, M. 2012. Oil and Natural Gas in Russia's Eastern Energy Strategy: Dream or Reality. *Energy Policy* 50: 436–44.

Medetsky, A. 2011. Gazprom Expands Interests in Far East. *St Petersburg Times*, March 9.

Medetsky, A. 2014. Some Government Agencies Could Move East. *The Moscow Times*, February 6.

Medvedev, D. 2009. Go Russia. Official Site of the President of Russia. Online: http:/eng. news.kremlin.ru/transcripts/298/print (accessed June 9, 2010).

Milov, V. 2008. *Russia and the West: The Energy Factor*. Washington, DC: CSIS.

Ministry of Energy of the Russian Federation. 2010. *Energy Strategy of Russia for the Period up to 2030*. Moscow: Ministry of Energy of the Russian Federation. Online: www. energystrategy.ru/projects/docs/ES-2030_%28Eng%29.pdf (accessed May 30, 2011).

Ministry of Foreign Affairs of the People's Republic of China. 2012. Wang Qishan and Dvorkovich Hold the Eighth Meeting of Chinese and Russian Energy Negotiators. Online: http://fmprc.gov.cn/eng/zxxx/t939622.htm# (accessed October 5, 2013).

Mitrova, T. 2013. *Russian LNG: The Long Road to Export*. IFRI Russie.Nei.Reports, December, Volume 16. Paris/Brussels: Institut Français des Relations Internationales.

Monaghan, A. 2006. Russia–EU Relations: An Emerging Security Dilemma. *Pro et Contra* 10(2–3), March–June: 16–31.

Montgomery, E.B. 2006. Breaking Out of the Security Dilemma. *International Security* 31(2), Fall: 151–85.

Overland, I. and Broekhus, E. 2009. Chinese Perspectives on Russian Oil and Gas. In J. Perovic and R.W. Orttung (eds). *Russian Energy Power and Foreign Relations: Implications for Conflict and Cooperation*. New York: Routledge.

Paik, K.-W. 2013. The Role of Russian Gas in China's Energy Supply Strategy. *Asia Europe Journal* 11(3): 323–38.

Paik, K.-W. 2014. *Sino-Russian Relations: From the Energy Sector Perspective*. Oxford: Oxford Institute for Energy Studies.

Paltsev, S. 2011. *Russia's Natural Gas Export Potential up to 2050*. Cambridge, MA: MIT Joint Program on the Science and Policy of Global Change.

Petro, N.N. 2011. Russian Foreign Policy, 2000–2011: From Nation-State to Global Risk Sharing. *PECOB's Paper Series* 12, June.

Pirani, S. 2011. Liberalization Heralds Change in the Gas Market. *St Petersburg Times*, March 9, p. 12.

Pirani, S., Stern, J., and Yafimava, K. 2009. *The Russo-Ukrainian Gas Dispute of January 2009: A Comprehensive Assessment*. Oxford: Oxford Institute for Energy Studies.

Platts Special Report. 2011. *Russian Crude Oil Exports to the Pacific Basin—An ESPO Update*. New York: Platts.

Pleines, H. 2009. Developing Russia's Oil and Gas Industry. In J. Perovic, R.W. Orttung, and A. Wenger (eds) *Russian Energy Power and Foreign Relations: Implications for Conflict and Cooperation*. New York: Routledge, pp. 71–86.

Poussenkova, N. 2009. Russia's Future Customers. In J. Perovic, R.W. Orttung, and A. Wenger (eds) *Russian Energy Power and Foreign Relations: Implications for Conflict and Cooperation*. New York: Routledge, pp. 132–54.

Poussenkova, N. 2013. *Russia's Eastern Energy Policy: A Chinese Puzzle for Rosneft*. IFRI Russie.Nei.Visions, April, Volume 70. Paris/Brussels: Institut Français des Relations Internationales.

President of Russia. 2011. Modernization to Top the Agenda of Russia's 2012 APEC Presidency. Online: www.kremlin.ru (accessed August 9, 2012).

Pronina, L. 2011. Medvedev to Trade Energy for Investment on China Trip. *Bloomberg News*, April 12.

Renaissance Capital. 2008. *2008 Oil & Gas Yearbook*. Online: http://rencap.com (accessed June 9, 2009).

Richardson, P. 2014. Russia's Turn to Asia: China, Japan, and the APEC 2012 Legacy. *Russian Analytical Digest*, March 31.

Rozman, G. 2008. Strategic Thinking About the Russian Far East: A Resurgent Russia Eyes its Future in Northeast Asia. *Problems of Post-Communism* 55(1), January/February: 41–3.

Russian National Committee of the Council for Security Cooperation in Asia Pacific. 2010. Going East: Russia's Asia-Pacific Strategy. *Russia in Global Affairs*, December.

Rustrans.wikidot.com. 2012. Russia's National Security Strategy to 2020 (translated version). Online: http://rustrans.wikidot.com/russia-s-national-security-strategy-to-2020 (accessed November 20, 2013).

Sagers, M.J. 2006. The Regional Dimension of Russian Oil Production: Is a Sustained Recovery in Prospect? *Eurasian Geography and Economics* 47(5): 505–45.

Sechser, T.S. 2010. Goliath's Curse: Coercive Threats and Asymmetric Power. *International Organization* 64: 627–60.

Shevtsova, L. 2009. *The Medvedev Presidency: Russia's Direction and the Implications for Foreign Policy*. Houston, TX: James A. Baker III Institute for Public Policy, Rice University.

Sputnik News. 2012. Kudrin Slams Russia's Far East Mega Plan. *Sputnik News*, April 24.

Stern, J. 2009. Russian Gas Balance to 2015: Difficult Years Ahead. In S. Pirani (ed.) *Russian and CIS Gas Markets and their Impact on Europe*. Oxford: Oxford University Press, pp. 79–86.

Stevens, P. 2009. *Transit Troubles: Pipelines as Sources of Conflict*. A Chatham House Report. London: Royal Institute of International Affairs.

Stulberg, A.N. 2007. *Well-Oiled Diplomacy: Strategic Manipulation and Russia's Energy Statecraft in Eurasia*. Albany, NY: State University of New York Press.

Sullivan, J. and Renz, B. 2010. Chinese Migration: Still the Major Focus of Russian Far Eastern/Chinese North East Relations. *The Pacific Review* 23(2), May: 261–85.

Takeda, Y. 2008. Russia's New Political Leadership and Its Implications for East Siberian Development and Energy Cooperation with North East Asian States. *Russian Analytical Digest* 33(8), January: 5–8.

Trenin, D. 2008. Energy Geopolitics in Russia–EU Relations. In K. Barysch (ed.) *Pipelines, Politics, and Power: The Future of EU–Russia Energy Relations*. Brussels: Centre for European Reform, pp. 15–24.

Tunsjo, O. 2013. *Security and Profit in China's Energy Policy: Hedging Against Risk*. New York: Columbia University Press.

U.S. Energy Information Administration (EIA). 2010a. *Country Analysis Brief: China*. Washington, DC: EIA.

U.S. Energy Information Administration (EIA). 2010b. *Country Analysis Brief: Japan*. Washington, DC: EIA.

U.S. Energy Information Administration (EIA). 2010c. *Country Analysis Brief: South Korea*. Washington, DC: EIA.

U.S. Energy Information Administration (EIA). 2010d. *Country Analysis Brief: Russia*. Washington, DC: EIA.

Vatansever, A. 2010. *Russia's Oil Exports: Economic Rationale Versus Strategic Gains*. Carnegie Papers 116. Washington, DC: Carnegie Endowment for International Peace.

Victor, D.G. and Victor, N.M. 2003. Axis of Oil? *Foreign Affairs* 82, March–April: 47–61.

Wishnick, E. 2006. Russia and CIS in 2005: Promoting East Asian Oil Diplomacy, Containing Change in Central Asia. *Asian Survey* 46(1), February: 69–78.

Zoller, M. 2013. *Does China Need Russian Gas?* Research Paper 1/2013, April. Prague: Association for International Affairs.

8 Building an energy cooperation regime in Northeast Asia

Carla P. Freeman

Introduction

This chapter considers what it would take to build an energy cooperation regime in Northeast Asia. Energy is a growing source of insecurity in the region. Led by the Chinese economic juggernaut, regional energy demand continues to rise, outstripping current regional capacity to meet it. There are intensifying rivalries within the region between China and Japan over access to Russian gas, a scramble for Mongolian coal and potential oil reserves, and rival claims for offshore oil or gas reserves. Perceptions of growing resource nationalism on the part of Russia, the region's top energy producer, and concerns that Moscow will seek to use its energy endowment for political ends complicate the picture. Regional competition for energy resources extends into energy-rich areas of the world where Northeast Asian national oil companies (NOCs) may jockey for oil concessions and contracts. Fears about the vulnerability of the seaborne fossil fuel imports on which the region is increasingly dependent to disruptions of the sea lines of communication (SLOCs), moreover, contribute to naval expansion by countries in the region. Energy security worries have also impelled aggressive unilateral strategies by countries in the region to develop indigenous energy resources where possible, often at significant environmental costs. Some analysts have raised concerns that the industrial policies supporting "green" energy development by countries in Northeast Asia are engendering a neo-mercantilist rather than a cooperative dynamic even in this area of energy relations in the region (Lee, 2013, p. 237).

Cooperation within Northeast Asia to meet energy needs could mitigate insecurities about access to energy resources and yield numerous dividends. The political stakes involved for the region's governments in maintaining confidence in the delivery of adequate energy services within national borders are high. Reducing the role of energy as a factor in the region's increasingly tense geopolitical atmosphere would be a significant contribution toward regional security writ large. Moreover, cooperation around energy would enable the maximization of regional complementarities as well as the development of new resources. More specifically, regional cooperation could address many of the issues explored in other chapters in this volume, including those issues driving fears of insufficient energy supply in oil and gas markets, falling low-cost reserves, the arrival of new, thirsty consumers on the energy scene, inadequate investments in new resources, and region-specific issues, such as the "Asian price" (Goldthau & Witte, 2010, p. 9). In addition, regional cooperation in investment for the development of new renewable and low-emissions energy sources—and transportation systems that are not so dependent on petroleum— along with energy-saving technology, could play a critical role in helping the region meet its energy needs along a more climate-friendly path.

These are compelling reasons for countries in the region to cooperate for improved energy security, yet most experts remain pessimistic about the prospects for regionalism in Northeast Asia on security issues of any kind.[1] Competitive behavior among countries in Northeast Asia is reinforced by a litany of historically rooted and geopolitical insecurities. These include a deficit in mutual trust associated with the traumas of Japanese imperialism and great-power rivalries; American ambivalence toward regional cooperation among the region's powerful countries, alongside its hub-and-spokes alliance system; the lack of full diplomatic normalization between some states in the region; divergent political ideologies and levels of development; and intensifying nationalism in countries in the region, to name some of them (Rozman, 2004; Calder & Ye, 2008; Cha, 2011).

At the same time, the statist approach to energy security that dominates national energy policies in the region complicates cooperation. China's historical experience with the political and economic challenges of life under an oil embargo during the Korean War is among the factors that make oil and petrochemicals, along with armaments, power generation and distribution, telecommunications, coal, aviation, and shipping, among the sectors of its economy over which the Chinese leadership has said it will retain "absolute control" (Kong, 2011, p. 59). Japanese and South Korean behavior also suggests a growing preference for more state-driven approaches to securing international supplies of energy (Goldthau & Witte, 2010, p. 12). Korea's 2010 *Overseas Energy Development Plan* triples the proposed overseas equity production share of the country's oil and gas consumption, for example (Dow Jones, 2010), and Japan's state-backed Japan Bank for International Cooperation (JBIC) has continued to be involved in the direct acquisition of overseas upstream resources (Vivoda & Manicom, 2011, p. 231). As Chapter 6 by Charles Krusekopf describes, resource nationalism is growing in Mongolia, even as it transforms into an energy supplier. The privatization of Russia's oil industry initiated immediately after the collapse of the Soviet Union has largely been reversed, with both Russia's oil and gas sectors now under state control, with state-run companies Rosneft producing most of Russia's oil and Gazprom controlling the balance of Russia's gas reserves and generating most of Russia's natural gas output. As Adam Stulberg observes in Chapter 7 on Russia's energy "foray" into Northeast Asia, Moscow defined energy security for the first time in 2009 as a national security issue.

Nonetheless, this pattern contrasts with an alternate global trend. International energy flows are becoming more decentralized and more market-oriented, with the global market driving the bulk of oil purchases and movement toward a global market for gas (Goldthau & Witte, 2010, p. 12). In addition, the increasingly urgent realities of climate change are forcing new international discussions about how to design and implement global incentives to encourage the growth of regular supplies of greener, more sustainable, and lower-carbon energy resources, particularly without disrupting market-driven investment in more traditional energy supplies. Emerging alongside these developments are new mechanisms and institutions to support the development of more market-driven flows of energy, as well as a proliferation of institutions related to transborder energy cooperation (Hirst & Froggatt, 2012).

These patterns and activities suggest that it is worth looking beyond dominant assumptions shaped by perceptions of the barriers to regionalism in Northeast Asia to consider what energy cooperation in the region might look like. If, for example, as was the case among Organisation for Economic Co-operation and Development (OECD) countries in the wake of the oil price shocks of the 1970s when the International Energy Agency (IEA) was created, the necessary political will could be mustered for the creation of a Northeast Asian energy cooperation regime, what form might it realistically take? To arrive at some preliminary answers to this question, this analysis compares intergovernmental institutions involved in energy issues in Northeast Asia to a set of the core characteristics associated with the existing international energy cooperation regime. This enables the construction of a "balance sheet" assessment of the features of an energy cooperation regime that are found among Northeast Asian energy institutions and the ones that are missing. A key challenge of this analytical strategy is that, while there is an extensive literature on international organizations, there is no definitive work on energy regime fundamentals (Esakova, 2012). With reference to work on international regimes by Victor and Raustiala (2004) and Keohane and Victor (2010), this chapter begins by scanning the existing international energy institutions that are functioning effectively to support international energy cooperation today and "unpacking" them to identify their fundamental functional elements and features. The second section inventories the region's energy cooperation institutions and describes their basic features. The third section carries out a balance sheet exercise, assessing the collection of energy cooperation arrangements involving the region to see which core elements and related features of an international energy cooperation regime they most closely embody. These go in the "assets" side of the assessment. This accounting then allows identification of those areas that may be seen as "deficits," or weaknesses, in the existing constellation of institutions for energy cooperation in which countries in Northeast Asia play a role. The fourth section considers how, given the context shaping regional energy dynamics, these deficits may be redressed to improve regional energy cooperation for energy security. Recognizing that it applies a simplistic conceptualization of the idea of a regime complex, this chapter seeks to stimulate refinements of its analysis, at the same time as the concept of a regime complex is itself further refined.

International energy institution fundamentals

The fragmented nature of the institutions that have emerged for energy governance at the international level complicates identification of the fundamental elements or features of an energy cooperation regime. This fragmentation reflects multiple factors, not the least of which is the nature of energy itself. Each energy type has distinctive characteristics as an object of market activity, as a focus of national security, and as a source of negative externalities. International institutions for energy cooperation have emerged largely to manage issues concerning discrete energy types and related issues. Some global institutions, those designed to tackle complex transnational issues on a global scale, including the United Nations (UN), the World Trade Organization (WTO), and the World Bank, offer governing structures for energy and energy-related issues. However, these generally address the broader context for energy relations among states. Supplementing these universal membership bodies, there are additional multilateral institutions that have a specific focus on energy, organized for the most part around energy type. Not including the two major international nuclear energy institutions, which are not considered in this chapter, there are seven key international energy multilaterals (IEMs) in total. Oil production and pricing, for example, is dominated by the Organization of Petroleum Exporting Countries (OPEC), forged in 1960 by five major oil-producing countries for this purpose. OPEC's membership has since grown to 12 countries, collectively controlling 80 percent of global reserves. On the consumer side of the energy dynamic, the International Energy Agency (IEA), a treaty organization, was formed among OECD countries first and foremost to manage an emergency response to oil price shocks. It has been called a "club" due to its restrictions on membership to OECD countries. OPEC and the IEA have served as the dominant sources of rules coordinating energy since they were created. Their remit has broadened to include the promotion of dialogue among energy consumers, enhancing information sharing about energy data, and, in the case of the IEA, improving the coordination of energy policies.

As OPEC and the IEA have evolved in response to changing international energy dynamics, new groupings organized around different functions and types of energy emerged, beginning in the 1990s. The International Energy Forum (IEF), formed in the 1990s, gathers energy ministers from around the world with a mission of promoting dialogue between energy consumers and producers, and enhancing the quality and transparency of data specifically on oil. It has 89 member states, all of which signed its charter. The Energy Charter Treaty (ECT) is a unique, legally binding treaty designed to regulate trade, investment, dispute settlement, and transit among other areas of energy cooperation. It was designed in response to the new opportunities for Eurasian energy cooperation that arose after the collapse of the Soviet Union. However, despite a substantial international membership (currently 49 countries have ratified the treaty), Russia's unwillingness to ratify the treaty and its continued focus on European–Russian gas trade are among the factors that have inhibited its potential to become a truly global tool for facilitating energy trade and investment. The Gas Exporting Countries Forum (GECF), established in 2001, includes 12 leading natural gas-producing countries as full members, with five countries with the status of observer members. The International Partnership for Energy Efficiency Cooperation (IPEEC) was founded in 2009 to "accelerate the adoption of energy efficiency policies and practices" (IPEEC, 2014). The International Renewable Energy Agency (IRENA) came into force in 2010 with the aim of promoting a more rapid transition to the use of more sustainable energy resources. There is also considerable collaboration among these institutions. On the data-sharing front, for example, the secretariats of several organizations (the IEA, IEF, and OPEC), as well as other entities involved in collecting and analyzing energy data, collaborate in the Joint Oil Data Initiative (JODI).

Work by Victor and Raustiala (2004) and Keohane and Victor (2010), among others, suggest that states develop and participate in international regimes based on their national interests. These interests change as relations, including power relations, among states, and on the part of the actors within them that influence states' interests, change. One consequence is that international regimes are shaped by path-dependent processes. This observation leads to an understanding that the international regimes that increasingly emerge to address international issue areas are not single, fully integrated institutions with comprehensive rules. Rather, they may be an array of partially overlapping institutions that may all play different roles in the governance of a transnational issue area. A collection of international institutions with even loosely interlocking rules and modes of coordination can function across a single issue area as what Victor and Raustiala were the first to label a "regime complex" (Victor & Raustiala, 2004, p. 279). Viewed through a "regime complex" frame, we can examine the array of energy institutions described above as a single "international regime complex." As constituent parts of the complex, these institutions perform discrete but perhaps also duplicative and overlapping functions within the particular issue area of energy security. This means that, on the energy demand side, these institutions seek to help consumers ensure uninterrupted access to adequate supplies of energy at a reasonable price; on the energy supply side, this means a key goal is to enhance the "security of demand" for energy exports, which generally are the principal source of suppliers' fiscal revenues (Yergin, 2006, p. 71). By definition, the principal actors of these international energy institutions are governments. But the role of states in their membership also reflects the critical importance of energy supply to countries' economic growth and national security, in combination with other features of energy, such as its monopoly characteristics and the high barriers to entry of energy markets. It is governments, or states, that therefore play the central role in setting and enforcing the "rules of the game" for the energy cooperation the complex seeks to structure, with decisions taken and acted upon collectively by states participating in the institutions (see Andrews-Speed, 2011; Goldthau & Witte, 2011). The energy regime complex thus approximates or reaches toward the regulatory role that a state would perform for a single country in seeking to provide a set of rules and incentives to foster cooperation by multiple energy-consuming and-producing countries (see Goldthau & Witte, 2010, p. 7).

In reality, this complex of IEMs remains far from coherent in terms of its coverage of energy issues and patchy government membership, as well as weak in terms of its implementation and enforcement capacity. Nonetheless, despite its fragmentation, if analyzed as a single international regime for global energy, six core features and a seventh fundamental characteristic can be unpacked from its complex of structures:

1   It sets binding rules as well as standards to lower market barriers and reduce investment risks. In this area, supplementing the WTO at the global level on trade in energy goods and services, among the IEMs, the ECT includes binding protections for foreign energy investors and obligations by member countries to promote reliable international transit flows, for example (see Energy Charter, 2014).

2   It helps ensure stable demand and a reasonable rate of return for energy-exporting states. Here, OPEC is the model, with the GECF potentially developing its capabilities in this direction.

3   It addresses energy market failures through coordinating responses among states and by promoting emergency preparedness. This is a function performed by both the IEA and IEF on the consumer side. Notably, the IEA has binding obligations for members vis-à-vis its emergency preparedness system, which involve regular reviews by technical experts to verify compliance.

4   It seeks to improve the quality and transparency of data available. This is a function most energy institutions provide to some degree. Leading activities in this area include the IEA's *World Energy Outlook*, among other publications, the IEF, and the JODI, which involves collaboration among the secretariats of several organizations (the IEA, IEF, and OPEC), as well as other entities involved in collecting and analyzing energy data.

5   It lowers transaction costs through functions such as producer–consumer dialogues. This is an explicit mission of the IEF, but OPEC also holds bilateral dialogues with consumers, and the GECF also indicates that increasing the "meaningful dialogue between gas producers and gas consumers" is among its core objectives.

6   It helps manage the negative externalities associated with producing, transporting, and using energy by setting standards and inducements for collective action, from information sharing, to technology networks, and financing. These are functions that most of the institutions in the regime complex perform but are inherent to the missions of IPEEC and IRENA.

As indicated above, these six core functional features rest on a characteristic fundamental to energy governance—that is, the critical role that governments play in energy issues. In addition to their role as vital inputs for economic security and the monopoly characteristics of energy resources mentioned above, energy resources are finite national resources requiring government oversight. Additionally, the negative externalities associated with energy production and consumption carry broad policy repercussions, requiring complex policy responses that generally involve trade-offs by governments (Andrews-Speed, 2011, p. 7). The importance of the state's role in energy governance means that a fundamental feature of an energy regime is membership by governments willing to sign on to rules and accept enforcement mechanisms that require the derogation of some measure of sovereignty over policy related to a key strategic resource (Andrews-Speed, 2011, p. 7; see also Goldthau & Witte, 2010).

Institutions in the regime complex also exhibit a number of core structural features that give the complex as a whole its functionality—many of these features are common to any effective international organization. In practice, these structural features are more or less developed across all constituent institutions in the regime. These structural features include:

- A membership structure for states with clear parameters for membership. OPEC's exclusive producer country membership offers one example.
- Institutional capacity as an additional feature. This includes a staff and a steady stream of support, which enable institutions to perform their core functions. For example, the IEA has a secretariat and several functional offices and directorates, as well as a governing board. It receives much of its funding from assessed contributions based on a formula agreed upon by its members.
- Convening capacity and routinized meetings, such as the OPEC annual meeting and the IEA Ministerials held every other year, are an additional feature.
- Procedural capacity, including, most importantly, a process that institutionalizes collective decision making by member countries for new rules or actions serving the mission of the institution is an additional characteristic. Within the IEA, decisions are finalized through a voting process, requiring unanimity or a majority vote on the activation of emergency measures and other procedural matters respectively.

These core functional features of an international energy regime and supporting structures and their relationship to the seven international energy institutions forming the regime complex described above are captured in Figure 8.1.

An inventory of regional energy cooperation mechanisms in Northeast Asia

Although Northeast Asia lacks a single, overarching energy cooperation institution, all countries in the region participate in mechanisms or groupings related to energy relations at various levels of the international system. At the global level, for example, five countries in Northeast Asia now belong to the WTO—China, Japan, South Korea, Russia, and Mongolia. Only North Korea is an outlier (Korea Energy Economics Institute, 2004; Asian Development Bank, 2006; World Bank and AusAid, 2010). All countries in the region are UN members and, as such,

Core features		IEA	IEF	OPEC	GECF	ECT	IPEEC	IRENA
Functions								
Set rules for market openness/investment protection			X			X		
Stabilize demand/prices for suppliers				X	X			
Coordinate responses to market failures			X	X				
Improve quality and transparency of data		X	X	X	X	X	X	X
Coordinate communication among producers and consumers and between the two groups			X			X		X
Manage negative externalities			X	X			X	X
Membership parameters	Mitigate risk							
Permanent technical staff								
Budget support	Lower transaction costs							
Procedural capacity								
Convening capacity								

INTERNATIONAL COOPERATION — Act collectively / Derogate sovereignty

Energy Security

ENERGY SUPPLY and DEMAND

Figure 8.1 Energy regime fundamentals.

they interact with UN energy governance institutions, from the Energy Branch of the UN Environmental Programme (UNEP) to the inter-agency grouping UN-Energy to the UN Framework on Climate Change and related activities, among other UN bodies.

Countries in the region are also members in some of the IEMs discussed above. However, membership is uneven and does not reflect the region's weight in either global energy demand or supply. Two countries, Japan and South Korea, are members of the IEA; notably, they are the only two countries in the region eligible for membership under current IEA rules, which, again, limit membership to states in the OECD. Given the importance of the two countries to international energy issues, however, China and Russia, along with India, are a particular focus of the IEA Standing Group on Global Energy Dialogue. In contrast to the IEA, the IEF's open and inclusive approach to participation has enabled membership of China and Russia, as well as Japan and South Korea, in the IEF. Two states in the region have also ratified the ECT: Japan was among the ECT's earliest members, with some Japanese officials advocating broader regional membership in the treaty to enhance regional energy integration (Toyama, 2006). Mongolia acceded to the ECT in 1999, perceiving it as a valuable tool in developing its energy resources and facilitating its role as an energy transit country, as did many former Soviet bloc countries (Swedish Trade Council, 2008, p. 18). As noted, energy relations between Europe and Russia were a key factor in the ECT's inception; however, in 2009 Moscow decided to suspend its provisional commitment to ECT principles. In addition to these institutional relationships, with the exception of North Korea, the region's oil-consuming countries all engage in dialogue with OPEC through the IEA and IEF, as well as through separate bilateral dialogues; there is a special China-OPEC Roundtable, for example. Despite its importance as a global energy supplier, Russia has not pursued membership in OPEC but often attends its meetings and routinely engages with OPEC through a biannual High-Level Russia-OPEC Dialogue (Goldthau & Witte, 2011, pp. 31–40). Russia, with its vast gas reserves, is a key member of the GECF. China, Japan, Russia, and South Korea are all members of the IPEEC. China, Japan, Mongolia, and South Korea are members of IRENA; Russia has indicated it will join the grouping (Meza, 2014).

The membership, or participation, of regional states in these IEMs contributes to improved international conditions for energy relations in several respects. It enhances data about energy, provides opportunities for information sharing around national energy policies, and offers mechanisms through which at least some countries in the region may choose to negotiate energy-related disputes. However, these institutions lack the focus on improving energy cooperation and energy flows for energy security within the region that would be inherent in a discrete Northeast Asian energy regime. Indeed, the pattern of membership in international institutions reflects and may reinforce perceptions of divisions among countries in the region along economic and political lines. The IEA is a particular case in point. It represents the world's top energy consumers, yet its membership requirements mean that China, the world's largest energy consumer, is excluded.[2]

At the regional level, there are also institutions and organization to promote energy cooperation, among which there is broad membership from countries in Northeast Asia. These are the focus of the discussion below. Table 8.1 identifies eight principal institutions or mechanisms. Recognizing that these groupings, with only two exceptions, are not exclusive to Northeast Asian countries but are regional (principally East Asian) institutions in which multiple Northeast Asian countries interact together routinely on the issue of energy security, it is useful to explore this collection of institutions by framing them as a regional regime complex. The selection process uses a component of what some theorists might identify as a basic factor in assessing regime "density" or links among a complex's constituent elements, which is the membership of countries from Northeast Asia (Orsini *et al.*, 2013, p. 33). The institutions are both examined in terms of participation of countries in the region within them and analyzed in terms of their principal activities. These descriptions then serve as points of reference for the analysis of the extent to which they embody the components of an energy regime and promote energy cooperation for energy security in the region.

The Intergovernmental Collaborative Mechanism on Energy Cooperation in North-East Asia

Of the eight regional mechanisms identified, only one grouping on energy issues is aimed at promoting cooperation on energy in Northeast Asia. After the failure of the Korean Peninsula Energy Development Organization (KEDO), which was designed to implement the 1994 U.S.–DPRK Agreed Framework, the Intergovernmental Collaborative Mechanism on Energy Cooperation in North-East Asia (ECNEA) is alone in having a discretely Northeast Asia focus, including Mongolia, North Korea, South Korea, and Russia as members and involving both China and Japan. Meetings of this forum, which was organized by senior officials of the four member-country governments, have been held under the auspices of the UN Economic and Social Commission for Asia and the Pacific (UNESCAP) since 2005. The mechanism was created to help facilitate regional projects on energy cooperation, from energy trade to investment in equipment to sharing information. Russia pledged a financial contribution of $2.4 million over the 2011–12 period to UNESCAP, in large part in support of the "further facilitation of a mechanism for continuous intergovernmental dialogue in the energy sphere with the aim to develop co-operation in energy resource development" (Mitrova, 2010, p. 34). Again, China participates in the grouping but is not a full member, while Japan has remained an observer. Most analysts suggest that neither China nor Japan has seen the grouping as much more than a useful forum for exchanging information about regional energy issues, reflecting a preference for pursuing their energy relations with regional energy suppliers, Russia and Mongolia, independently on a bilateral basis. Without their involvement, the mechanism has failed to gain organizational momentum (Lee & Novitskiy, 2010, p. 56; Wang & Wang, 2010, p. 44). UNESCAP is serving as its interim secretariat and chair of its two working groups, one on energy planning and policy, the other on coal

(UNESCAP, 2013). One report suggested that disagreements over energy pricing have been a source of challenges in engaging broader regional membership (GTI, 2013b). China principally takes part in joint research projects and, again, Japan attends meetings only as an observer. North Korea participates only irregularly. A five-year strategy for the grouping from 2010 to 2015, which hoped to galvanize broader regional participation for the creation of "an enabling policy and market environment for regional energy cooperation" and "enrich[ing] energy cooperation activities among North-East Asian countries" (UNESCAP, 2013), has effectively failed to move the grouping beyond the role of a forum for research and data collection on regional energy issues.

Asia-Pacific Economic Cooperation activities

As noted above, however, in addition to ECNEA, there are several groupings for energy cooperation. These extend beyond the narrow geographic scope of this volume, spanning the wider East Asian region, but including at least two Northeast Asian countries among their members; the average number approaches four Northeast Asian countries. There are seven principal bodies along these lines; most of these are embedded within broader regional bodies for multilateral cooperation, and two subregional groupings (see Table 8.1). The oldest of these structures, established in 1990—just a year after APEC was formed—is the Energy Working Group (EWG) within the Asia-Pacific Economic Cooperation (APEC) group. The EWG includes China, Japan, and South Korea, as well as Hong Kong and Taiwan, among its members. It has a secretariat with program staff to manage its subsidiary working groups, which include groups on energy types, exploration, and energy data, among others. Supported by the Tokyo-based Asia-Pacific Energy Research Centre (APERC), in place since 1996, EWG has a track record of helping facilitate information sharing, including training and development of best practices or guidelines for

Table 8.1 Regional energy institutions

Body	Subsidiary energy grouping
UNESCAP	ECNEA
APEC	EWG, APERC, APEC Energy Ministerial, ESI
ASEAN+3	Oil Market and Natural Gas Forum; ASEAN Senior Officials Meeting on Energy (SOME) Plus Three Energy Policy Governing Group (EPGG); Energy Security System
EAS	Energy Ministerials; ECTF
SCO	Energy Club
CAREC	Energy Sector Program
GMS	GMS Energy Roadmap for Expanded Energy Cooperation
GTI	Energy Board

the management and reform of certain energy sectors (Small-Scale Sustainable Infrastructure Development Fund (S3IDF) and Nexant, 2005, pp. 3–22). Early activities of the EWG and APERC responded to concerns about the volatility in energy markets related to the first Gulf War of 1990, and other conflicts involving energy-supplier countries. APEC activities included the 3Es Initiative, adopted by APEC leaders in 1995 to promote energy security through cooperation on sustainability issues involving energy supply and the environment and to develop shared, though nonbinding, energy objectives for member states (APEC, 2014, pp. 9–10). In cooperation with the IEA and ASEAN beginning in 2011, APERC also launched a series of "Oil and Gas Security Exercises." Aims of these exercises include testing domestic energy systems for emergency preparedness; developing scenarios for oil and gas supply- and demand-side disruptions; and accumulating information and mobilizing capable experts in the APEC region. APERC has done extensive research on best practices for energy stockpiling, including the feasibility of joint oil stocks among APEC states, although concrete steps toward reaching agreement on proposals have yet to be taken as of the time of writing (APEC, 2014, p. 12).

Along with the EWG, APEC also convenes the APEC Energy Ministerial meetings, which seek to find common ground and commitments among APEC member countries on issues related to energy security. Agenda items have included discussions on member countries phasing out fossil fuel subsidies and specific goals for reducing energy intensity levels. Other initiatives include efforts to develop frameworks to accelerate investment in the development of additional natural gas supplies (APEC, 2007, p. 1).

These activities have contributed to information exchanges around energy security, but have also reflected the limits of APEC's institutional capacity. APEC offers an institutional space for interaction among regional leaders and energy officials on energy policy and related issues, but leaves it to member countries to adopt the regulatory or other policy actions needed to act upon the common goals that may emerge from these dialogues. Discussions about removing market barriers for energy trade and investment and facilitating cross-border infrastructure networks for gas within the region, including pipelines and liquefied natural gas (LNG) trade, have been part of regular discussions among APEC members. This is not to say that there have been no APEC-organized initiatives specifically designed to enhance regional energy security. Through APEC's Energy Security Initiative (ESI), launched in 2001, for example, APEC has served as a key vehicle for significant efforts at collaboration among the organization's 21 member countries—only five of which are members of the IEA—to help the region improve its preparedness for potential energy supply disruptions. Activities have included joint exercises on oil data gathering, natural gas trade, and oil supply emergency responses. Other initiatives involve knowledge sharing on green energy and energy-efficiency technologies and associated best practices (Noor, 2012). The ESI has also explored dialogues on maritime security and energy issues. Concrete outcomes have included the Real Time Emergency Information System (RTEIS), which uses an Internet platform as a vehicle for data sharing via a bulletin board and real-time communication on energy issues (through a chat room). New initiatives within RTEIS as proposed by Russia include the development of so-called "rapid response networks" for critical infrastructure related to counterterrorism (APEC, 2008).

ASEAN+3 *activities*

Energy has also been a focus of diffuse activities within ASEAN+3 (ASEAN with the three Northeast Asian countries of China, Japan, and South Korea). Among the ASEAN+3 activities on energy security is the ASEAN+3 Natural Gas Forum. Launched in Shanghai in 2004, China continues to lead what has morphed into the Oil Market and Natural Gas Forum, focused on investment in new resources. ASEAN+3 has also recently become a participant in the ASEAN Forum on Coal (ASEAN, 2011). There is an ASEAN Senior Officials Meeting on Energy (SOME) Plus Three Energy Policy Governing Group (EPGG) as well, which dates from 2003 (Phuong, 2013, p. 21).

ASEAN+3 energy programs include an "oil stockpiling roadmap." This initiative arose following the U.S. decision to strike Iraq in 2003 amid growing concerns among ASEAN member countries about disruptions to oil supply; of the ASEAN states, only Brunei and Malaysia remain net oil-producer countries. International trends, such as declining oil stocks among members of the IEA, as well as decreases in OPEC's spare capacity, have only reinforced these concerns within ASEAN. The roadmap, which was not formalized until 2008, rests on a set of principles consistent with those of the ASEAN charter: voluntary and *nonbinding* agreements; mutual benefits; mutual respect, including respect for bilateral and regional cooperation; and a step-by-step approach with long-term perspective. Discussions on implementation have helped focus regional governments on the importance of both stockpiling and joint sharing arrangements for energy security. As IEA members, Japan and South Korea already have these arrangements; as noted, China has about a 30-day supply stockpiled. Other ASEAN+3 countries, including Indonesia (which has just 23 days of commercial stock, rather than strategic reserves), have weak to nonexistent emergency stocks. Nonetheless, despite a growing sense of urgency within the ASEAN+3 grouping on the need for putting stockpiling and energy-sharing arrangements into place as rapid increases in demand for oil have been met by imports, there has been only limited progress toward implementation. An ASEAN Petroleum Security Agreement (APSA) dating from the 1980s took nearly three decades to be ratified by all ten ASEAN states. It includes an agreement on Coordinated Emergency Response Measures (CERM), which has yet to be operationalized. Plans are to make CERM an institution with a regulatory council, a compliance committee, a secretariat, a coordinating body, an industry advisory group, and an implementing body with membership from each of the ASEAN member states. The CERM will be triggered when a member country's energy supply falls short of a minimum of 10 percent of regular domestic consumption for 30 consecutive days. All member countries are obligated to help supply the oil and gas needs of the country in distress, but countries contribute at a level negotiated bilaterally, trying to do so at the level of 10 percent of the normal domestic requirement of the country facing the shortfall (Sihite, 2013). It is unclear what role China, Japan, and South Korea would play in the CERM. To date, what has been established in the area of energy security for the +3 grouping is an ASEAN+3 Energy Security System, launched in 2007, which includes a chat room and bulletin board. An ASEAN+3 Energy Security Forum held in February 2014 followed previous ASEAN+3 meetings of energy ministers in calling upon member states to invest in a joint oil stockpile (Reap, 2014).

The East Asia Summit

The East Asia Summit (EAS) also plays a role in regional energy cooperation through its support for energy dialogue among the region's ministers. EAS comprises ASEAN+3 nations plus Australia, India, and New Zealand, and, with the November 2011 meeting, Russia and the United States. From its first meeting in 2005, the EAS included enhancing energy security among its goals. First convened in 2007, the Energy Ministers Meeting (EMM) has organized several "work streams" for energy cooperation: energy efficiency and conservation; energy market integration, which includes market deregulation; and biofuels (EAS EMM, 2013). An EAS Energy Cooperation Task Force (ECTF) manages these work streams, with each work stream co-chaired by two or more EAS member countries. With substantial support from Japan, the Economic Research Institute for ASEAN and East Asia (ERIA), which has a broad mission of providing research and policy guidance on East Asian integration, has functioned as a research unit for EAS energy activities (Yoshimatsu, 2014, p. 132). The EAS's 2007 Cebu Declaration on East Asian Energy Security expressed a commitment to "explor[ing] possible modes of strategic fuel stockpiling such as individual programmes (*sic*), multi-country and/or regional voluntary and commercial arrangements" (ASEAN, 2007). However, this expression of intent has remained just that: To date the EAS has undertaken no concrete steps toward either emergency energy planning or oil stockpiling activities, which, notably, are not included among the ECTF's work streams (Cutler, 2014).

The Shanghai Cooperation Organization

The Shanghai Cooperation Organization (SCO) Energy Club is an energy cooperation framework within the SCO that is still a work in progress. The SCO itself was formed in 2001 in Shanghai by China and Russia. Its current membership does not extend to all countries in Northeast Asia; it comprises China and Russia, along with the Central Asian states of Kazakhstan, Kyrgyzstan, Tajikistan, and Uzbekistan. There are also five observer states, Afghanistan, India, Iran, Mongolia, and Pakistan; additionally, Belarus, Sri Lanka, and Turkey are dialogue partners. In 2014, Mongolia reportedly formally registered its interest in becoming a full member of the SCO (Anon., 2014).

Countries participating in the SCO include some of the world's largest energy consumers—namely, China and India—but also some of the most energy-rich countries in the world. Collectively, SCO members control a quarter of global oil reserves, more than half the world's gas reserves and uranium reserves, and more than one-third of the world's coal. Following a proposal introduced by Russia in 2004, SCO members agreed on a set of statutes for the organization in 2007, but only signed a memorandum of understanding (MoU) for the Energy Club in late 2013 (Anon., 2013b). Analysts have a range of expectations for the club. Optimists anticipate that it involves coordination in a number of areas that could result in the institutionalization of cooperative processes in multiple areas of energy relations. The speculation is that there could be a joint mechanism for implementation of SCO member countries' energy policies, coordination of investment plans, and information and data exchange. Some expect the club to become a supranational rule-maker for energy in the region, which could create new conditions for the development of energy and transportation infrastructure, as well as energy investment—what some have called a new "energy space" for the region (SCO, 2013).

However, skeptics see the club very differently. Rather than contributing to the development of a regional "energy space," they see it as an effort by Moscow to construct an "energy bloc," favoring its state-run energy companies. Analysts with this view observe that Russia has stalled China's proposals for a common market among SCO countries, preferring its own initiatives, including the Eurasian Union, which excludes China (Weitz, 2014). China, for its part, has indicated a preference for having the club serve as a vehicle for facilitating energy relations in the region, which would fundamentally be conducted through bilateral, not multilateral, agreements (Boland, 2011, p. 19; Pron, 2014, p. 65).

Progress toward the development of the SCO Energy Club has been stymied by a number of factors, including disagreements among member countries over the impact of additional flows of financing into energy infrastructure in the region. Some countries in the region perceive opportunities in the SCO Energy Club's potential role as a promising new platform for structuring energy infrastructure project financing that will increase access to diverse funding streams within the region (Bhutta, 2013). However, others, Uzbekistan in particular, have resisted the development of an SCO Energy Club precisely for this reason. It has concerns that additional investment flows toward dam construction could benefit the upstream hydro-rich Tajikistan and Kyrgyzstan economies, while damaging its agricultural production (Pron, 2014, p. 63; Weitz, 2014).

The memorandum signed by SCO members on the creation of the SCO Energy Club in late 2013 suggests that, for the near term, it is likely to serve principally as a forum for discussion of issues related to energy. It is unclear if it will acquire capacities beyond that. Indeed, some expect that, given divisions over its functions among the SCO's full members, particularly Uzbekistan, the club could well develop in the absence of consensus such that membership would not be required of all six (Anon., 2013b; SCO, 2013). Some observers of the SCO suggest that such a development would be consistent with the "constrained potential" of the organization as a whole, which reflects a deadlock among member states over granting the SCO the "independent power or resources" it would need to be a source of collective action on any security issue (Weitz, 2014).

Central Asia Regional Economic Cooperation

Finally, China and Mongolia are the two Northeast Asian countries in the ten-member Central Asia Regional Economic Cooperation (CAREC) grouping. CAREC was established in 1997 with key support from the Asian Development Bank (ADB) with the goal of reducing poverty through improved regional policy coordination focused on infrastructure development. Japan may also be considered an indirect participant in CAREC, given its substantial role in the ADB as its largest shareholder, along with the United States. In addition to the ADB, the World Bank, the European Bank for Reconstruction and Development, the Islamic Development Bank, the UN Development Programme (UNDP), and the International Monetary Fund (IMF) provide regular support to CAREC. The ADB's CAREC unit houses CAREC's program secretariat. Energy infrastructure and policy coordination have been key issue areas for CAREC, whose official aims in the energy area explicitly focus on energy security, including promoting "the balanced development of the region's energy infrastructure and institutions, and stronger integration of the region's energy markets to make available adequate volumes of commercial energy to all in a reliable, affordable, financially sustainable, and environmentally sound manner," and promoting economic growth through trade in energy (CAREC, 2013a). CAREC's Energy Sector Coordinating Committee meets twice a year, supplementing CAREC's annual ministerial meetings and the somewhat more frequent Senior Officials Meetings. It guides planning, oversees implementation, and has the authority to make decisions on regional initiatives (programs, projects, or activities) that involve two or more countries, which may relate to billions of dollars in loans, grants, and technical assistance to member countries related to regional electricity grids, oil and gas pipelines, and hydropower resources development and sharing in the region (CAREC, 2013b).

Despite the projected benefits from proposed projects, progress in project implementation in the energy area has been slow. There are many possible reasons. In the area of hydropower, for example, cooperation through CAREC has been constrained by a decision to exclude the topic of water resource management and allocation from the organization, at the request of both China and Uzbekistan (Linn, 2012, p. 16). After years of delay, however, work is moving ahead on two projects, one in the electricity sector, the other involving a gas pipeline. In the area of electricity, a favorable board vote in the World Bank in March 2014 made it possible to get an electricity transmission project, which will bring electricity to Pakistan from unused existing capacity in Tajikistan and Kyrgyzstan, underway. The gas pipeline project is the long-awaited Trans-Afghan Pipeline Initiative (TAPI) pipeline, which will convey gas a distance of 1,735 kilometers, stretching from Turkmenistan to Afghanistan, Pakistan, and India. An agreement was reached in July 2014 among the four countries involved (Krist, 2014).

The Greater Mekong Subregion

In addition to these broader regional structures or initiatives, there are two subregional efforts with substantial energy dimensions of note. The first is the Greater Mekong Subregion (GMS) Economic Cooperation grouping, also supported by the ADB. With ADB assistance, Cambodia, China (represented in the GMS by Yunnan Province and Guangxi Zhuang Autonomous Region), Lao People's Democratic Republic (Lao PDR), Myanmar, Thailand, and Vietnam formed the GMS to improve economic cooperation with each other. The GMS has a substantial and expanding energy focus, responding to both sustained energy poverty in the region and double-digit increases in electricity-related energy demand since 2000, in combination with substantial endowments of diverse energy resources (Chang & Yao, 2013, pp. 150–1). The GMS adopted an "Energy Roadmap for Expanded Energy Cooperation" in 2009. Its goals are to increase energy access on the part of all sectors and communities in the subregion, but with a focus on the poor, through the promotion of best energy practices in the subregion; develop and utilize more efficiently indigenous, low-carbon, and renewable resources, while reducing the subregion's dependence on imported fossil fuels; improve energy supply security through cross-border trade while optimizing use of subregional energy resources; and promote public–private partnership and private sector participation, particularly through small and medium-sized enterprises for subregional energy development. Climate-change mitigation is an additional area of work. Specific projects focus on regional interconnection arrangements involving natural gas and regional grid infrastructure development (including improving rural electrification) and the development of regional power trade (Asian Development Bank, n.d.).

Discussions of the institutional arrangements associated with the GMS's role in regional energy development note that it has been focused on developing a framework for regional trade in power. Leaders of the six GMS states agreed on an Inter-governmental Agreement on Regional Power Trade in 2002. This was followed by the formation of a Regional Power Trade Coordinating Committee (RPTCC) to "actively coordinate the successful implementation of regional trade and to represent the countries involved in regional power trade" (Chang & Yao, 2013, p. 156). With the ADB acting as "broker for cooperative initiatives" within the GMS framework (Chang & Yao, 2013, p. 153), efforts launched with the Energy Roadmap toward furthering institutional development for energy cooperation within the GMS have continued on topics such as developing a regional framework for investment in renewables; energy policy coordination among participating countries, including strengthening energy information sharing; and establishing a regulatory framework for power trade in the region (Jude, 2013). Among the objectives of these efforts is increasing the role of private investment in energy development in the region.

It is unclear to what extent China is contributing to the institutional development of the GMS as a vehicle for energy cooperation or if it is weakening it. Participation in the GMS through Yunnan and Guangxi have served China's broad development goals for those two land-locked provinces, deepening China's economic integration with Southeast Asia through them, in part by liberalizing border trade with both Myanmar and Vietnam. China has provided financial support for development in the GMS, including through the ADB, and also took the lead in hosting the first GMS Economic Corridors Forum among the GMS members in Kunming in 2008. An analysis by Hensengerth suggests that the GMS agenda, including energy, indicates areas of transnational concern in which China is willing to cooperate. However, this reflects the advantages to China of participation in multilateral frameworks, particularly where hydropower development is concerned. Hensengerth quotes Buntaine (2007), who observes that "China has used the institutional density brought about by regionalism to its advantage by promoting cooperation that fragments economic and environmental issues." Hensengerth goes on to make the case that where derogation of some measure of sovereignty is required for China to engage in subregional cooperation, as it is in the Mekong River Commission, it has drawn the line and has opted not to participate. Finally, China's calculus on further institutionalizing GMS may be affected not only by its subregional relationships, but by its relations with Japan, which, again, with the United States, is the ADB's largest shareholder—and thus an indirect but important additional Northeast Asian participant in the GMS (Hensengerth, 2010, pp. 124–6).

The Greater Tumen Initiative

Like the GMS, the Greater Tumen Initiative (GTI) is a subregional intergovernmental grouping covering the Tumen River delta area, specifically China's three northeast provinces (Heilongjiang, Jilin, and Liaoning), Inner Mongolia, Mongolia's eastern provinces or *aimags* (Dornod, Khentii, and Sukhbaatar), the eastern sea rim of South Korea (Gangwon, Geyongsangbuk, Busan, and Ulsan), and the Primorsky Territory of Russia. Until 2009, North Korea also participated in GTI activities. The GTI was originally formed in 1995 with UNDP leadership as the Tumen River Area Development Programme (TRADP) to develop the Tumen River delta, where China, Russia, and North Korea meet. Its chief decision making body is a Consultative Commission composed of national government-level officials (thus not the provincial-level representation, as in the case of China in the GMS) at the vice-ministerial level from member countries. A GTI secretariat, staffed and funded by the UNDP, administers and coordinates GTI activities and manages GTI projects.

Regional energy development has always been an objective of the GTI; however, unlike the GMS, it is not a development bank program and, despite enthusiastic rhetorical support from participating countries (GTI, 2013a), its planning and implementation capacity has been hampered by a lack of a financing mechanism. GTI as a whole has support from the UNDP's Northeast Asian Cooperation Project, the Deutsche Gesellschaft für Internationale Zusammenarbeit (GIZ), with which it has had a cooperation agreement since 2012, the ADB, and UNESCAP. Since 2007, the GTI's energy focus has been led by an Energy Board, with an advisory grouping of technical experts known as the Expert Council. The Energy Board's main activities, which are supported by the GTI secretariat, include enhancing energy policy coordination and cooperation; reducing non-physical barriers to energy trade and investment in the Greater Tumen Region (GTR); promoting an exchange of information on energy among GTI member countries; and conducting capacity-building activities (GTI, 2014). Recent projects include early work on developing a Tumen area power transmission "ring," the development of an NEA Energy Database and Regular Energy Overview/ Statistical Yearbook, and the creation of the Energy Forum for Northeast Asia as a cooperation network among governments, the private sector, think tanks, and financial institutions. The GTI Energy Board meetings have suffered from uneven attendance—neither China nor South Korea participated in the inaugural meeting of the Energy Board (Zhu, 2012).

Northeast Asia's energy institutions as an energy regime: the balance sheet

Assessed against the core features of an energy cooperation regime, how does the complex of energy institutions in which Northeast Asian countries participate stack up? In what ways is this complex serving as an energy regime for Northeast Asia?

Assets

With reference to Table 8.2, on the assets side of the balance sheet, the picture this assessment has created of the complex of Northeast Asian institutions shows that in the functional area it has three principal strengths. For one, it includes a multiplicity of intergovernmental institutions that explicitly engage in activities involving energy cooperation across the region. This includes particular competencies through institutions for improving the quality and transparency of data at both the regional and subregional levels. This function is performed to some extent by various activities within all regional groupings, but explicitly through those structured by APEC, ASEAN+3, and the EAS, along with the GMS and GTI. In addition, with this function carried out to varying degrees by nearly all of the regional energy institutions, the institutions collectively offer a numerically rich set of opportunities for communication among states that produce energy, those that consume energy, and between the two groups. Lastly, there is a wide array of initiatives represented across the complex that seek to address the challenges associated with the negative externalities associated with energy use.

Assets in the structural category include clear membership parameters for all institutions, and substantive institutional capacity on the part of the groupings in that all, to some degree, have permanent administrative staff and budget support, as well as effective convening capacity. However, this positive assessment rests on the caveat that this chapter applies a soft definition of "procedural capacity," which gives credit to the capacity of the institution in question simply to

Table 8.2 Northeast Asian regional energy institutions

Core features	ECNEA	APEC EWG	APERC	APEC Energy Ministerial	APEC ESI	ASEAN+3 Oil Market and NGF	ASEAN+3 SOME EPGG	ASEAN+3 Energy Security System	EAS Energy Ministerials	SCO Energy Club	CAREC Energy Roadmap	GMS Energy Roadmap	GTI Energy Board
Functions													
Set rules for market openness/investment protection										\			
Stabilize demand/prices for suppliers										\			
Coordinate responses to market failures		\			\			\					
Improve quality and transparency of data	X	X	X	X	X	X		X	X	\		X	X
Coordinate communication among producers and consumers and between the two groups	X	X	X	X	X	X	X	X	X	\	X	X	X
Manage externalities	X	X	X	X	X	X	X	X	X		X	X	X

(continued)

Table 8.2 (continued)

Core features	ECNEA	APEC EWG	APERC	APEC Energy Ministerial	APEC ESI	ASEAN+3 Oil Market and NGF	ASEAN+3 SOME EPGG	ASEAN+3 Energy Security System	EAS Energy Ministerials	SCO Energy Club	CAREC	GMS Energy Roadmap	GTI Energy Board
Structures													
Membership parameters	X	X	X	X	X	X	X	X	X	X	X	X	X
Permanent technical staff	\	X	X	X	X	X	X	X	X		X	X	X
Budget support	\	X	X	X	X	X	X	X	X	X	X	X	X
Procedural capacity	X	X	X	X	X	X	X	X	X	X	X	X	X
Convening capacity	X	X	X	X	X	X	X	X	X	X	X	X	X
Country membership													
China	X	X		X	X	X	X	X	X	X	X	/	/
Japan	X	X		X	X	X	X	X	X	/	/	/	/
Mongolia	X									/	X		/
Russia	X	X		X	X				X	X	X		/
South Korea	X	X		X	X	X	X	X	X				/
North Korea	X												

\ Initiative only
X Has the function or structure; is a member
/ Observer country or indirect participation

use institutionalized procedures to make decisions to achieve its mission. Thus, given the nature of the regional institutions that serve as the umbrella organizations for the region's energy-focused bodies, procedures may be used simply to set institutional agendas and work plans, or determine budget priorities. The broader regional institutions in which many of these energy bodies are embedded are designed to safeguard state autonomy over regional governance; they use consensus-based decision making and they function to provide opportunities for a regional community-enhancing convergence among the policies of states, rather than to structure collective action for policy harmonization. As Foot (2011) and Haggard (2011) both point out in their analyses of regional governance in East Asia and the Asia-Pacific respectively, this extends to the capacity of the organizational structures within these organizations—their secretariats have limited resources and capacity to initiate policies.

Assets in the category of country membership include evidence that all states in the region, including North Korea, participate in at least one regional body with an energy focus, with broad representation in the Intergovernmental Collaborative Mechanism on Energy Cooperation in Northeast Asia (ICMEC), the EAS Energy Ministerials, and, at the subregional level, the GTI Energy Board, when all GTI member countries are in attendance. China, Japan, and South Korea also show considerable overlap because of their participation in both the APEC and ASEAN+3 structures.

Finally, while not captured on Table 8.2, the related discussion of mechanisms in the institutional inventory suggests that particular assets for potentially effective regional energy cooperation are found within ADB-led CAREC as well as the GMS. The focus of these groupings on energy infrastructure is contributing to concrete, if as yet still modest, outcomes in the area of transboundary cooperation around energy delivery. Where project financing is part of institutional capacity, the incentives for countries to work together on specific projects are no longer abstract, and cooperation appears to be possible, even amid regional tensions. More evidence is needed to make this assertion with confidence, but it would be consistent with the patterns of behavior of states in other international regimes (Barrett, 2007).

It is also worth drawing attention to the numerous efforts to address the need for emergency responses within these institutions to energy crises such as price shocks and supply shortfalls. Albeit incremental, there has been some progress toward improving the region's emergency response through formal data-sharing arrangements and encouraging the development of strategic petroleum reserves in the region, with China moving to develop a strategic petroleum reserve, as well as expanding gas storage facilities in just the past decade. While the voluntary contributions by individual states toward meeting supply shortfalls limits the capacity of CERM, if plans continue to move forward to operationalize CERM and make it an ASEAN+3 institution, it could become a mechanism with significant capacity to play a meaningful role in coordinating a regional response to emergency energy supply shortfalls.

Deficits

The region's institutional deficits in the area of energy cooperation are strikingly apparent in the table. In the functional category, while most regional institutions are linked to larger initiatives or have missions that include promoting regional economic integration, none is designed with the capacity to set binding rules either for trade or investment protection. Again, reflecting an evident regional preference, many of these structures are effectively discussion forums, limited to information sharing, agenda setting, and encouraging voluntary cooperation with recommendations and or participation in initiatives. This is not to discount these functions; given what McPherson, writing on national oil companies (NOCs), describes as a tendency toward the "capture" of the energy sector by elites, moving as much information as possible about the energy sector into the public domain is critical for mitigating mismanagement, waste, and corruption, improving accountability, and generally enabling better energy governance (McPherson, 2013, p. 152).

Nor do any of the institutions play a direct role in stabilizing prices on the energy supply side. In its efforts to develop a regional transmission and regulatory authority and role in encouraging regional governments to move toward market pricing for energy, the GMS currently comes the closest to playing a role in this category of functional activity (Yu, 2003, p. 1225).

A third area of functional deficit is that, while there are numerous dialogues and initiatives for emergency energy management and regional stockpiling, and even involving overlapping participation by countries in the region, these plans have yet to be significantly implemented.

In the structural category, as discussed in the assets section of this analysis, the table obscures what may be considered significant structural weaknesses. An international energy regime complex includes rule-making capabilities as institutions within the complex, such as the IEA and OPEC, have been granted these capabilities by their member states. The institutions in the regional energy regime complex largely lack this remit, taking decisions that are nonbinding and voluntary at best. It is unclear if the SCO Energy Club, which some analysts had expected would be granted some rule-making authority, now seems to be developing in the direction of another regional consultative body. At the same time, however, if what constitutes procedural capacity on the part of these structures is more loosely interpreted in accordance with the pattern of institutional capacity typical of East Asian regional institutions, which is as a formal process for decision making and agenda setting, often rooted in the principle of consensus, then procedural capacity appears reasonably strong.

Finally, and critically, the uneven nature of membership by countries in the region across the many regional institutions involved in energy cooperation reflects the region's geopolitical and geographical divisions. This has implications for the extent to which the institutions can function as a complex on a regional scale to enhance energy cooperation among the region's six member states. Thus, while there are multiple functionalities across the institutions as a whole, they are widely and thinly distributed across them. For example, no single regional entity has more than four of the six Northeast Asian countries as members. North Korea is represented in only one of the 13 institutions discussed, and Mongolia, a rising energy producer, is represented fully in only two of them. Russian participation is also limited, as it is not part of the ASEAN+3 grouping and engages with ASEAN only as a dialogue partner—a significant deficit, given its potential as a regional supplier of energy. This seems to support the implication of Suyuan Sun's analysis in this volume (Chapter 3) that Russia is resistant to serving as a public-good provider in building an energy cooperation regime in Northeast Asia (Table 8.2). China's and Japan's limited participation in energy cooperation initiatives focused directly on the region, such as ECNEA and the GTI Energy Board, may reflect their bilateral security tensions. It may also reflect a pattern observed in other areas of regional cooperation, in which both countries have the potential to play a leadership role, but neither country wishes the other to lead, with the result that the weaker countries are left to play the driving role (Asian Development Bank, 2010, p. 18).

In sum, the balance sheet illustrates that there is broad interest across the region in enhancing the regional environment for energy security through sharing information, interacting on energy policy issues, and cooperating through information

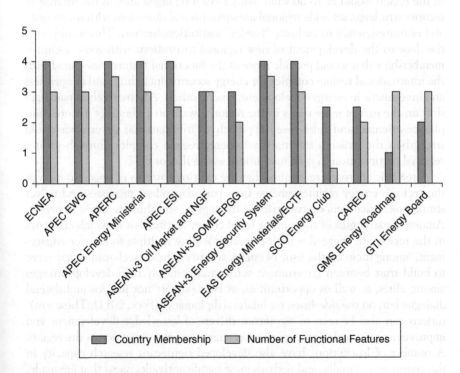

Figure 8.2 The complex of energy institutions in Northeast Asia.

sharing and exploring joint activities to develop more climate-friendly energy solutions toward improving the management of negative externalities. The balance sheet also shows, however, that the fragmentation among countries in the region linked to broader security and geopolitical issues, level of economic development, and type of economic system is reflected in the complex of energy groupings in which countries in the region participate. The barriers to regional cooperation that have affected other issue areas involving all six countries in Northeast Asia, from security to economic integration, are clearly sources of fragmentation in the area of energy as well. Cooperation on energy security fits the pattern often described as one of "shallow" cooperation found for other issue areas in the region (Haggard, 2011, p. 1). Furthermore, the relative institutional weakness of the complex as it has developed reflects preferences associated with the broader East Asian region, which has resisted pressures to move from an approach that places sovereignty above compliance with collective decisions, such that there is no derogation of sovereignty to the institutions and decisions are nonbinding.

Conclusion: strengthening energy institutions for an effective energy regime complex for Northeast Asia

Clearly, one prescription for building a more meaningful energy regime complex in the region would be to do what many have long urged and, in the interest of security writ large, set aside regional antagonisms and obsessions with sovereignty and noninterference to embrace "harder" institutionalization. This would open the door to the development of new regional institutions with more inclusive memberships that would provide more of the functional features associated with the international regime complex for energy security, including market openness and investment in energy development, among others. Alternatively, a paradigm shift on the part of more states in the region toward an embrace of a more compliance-oriented and rules-based approach to international governance could strengthen the existing international energy regime complex through greater regional participation in such institutions as the IEA or ECT.

A realistic approach recognizes that the existing patterns of fragmentation in the region's energy regimes emerge from path-dependent processes and reflect strong preferences among countries in the region, and thus are likely to persist. Among the strengths of the current set of energy institutions in which countries in the region are engaged is their role in providing multiple forums for engagement, among them on the issue of energy security. These mechanisms may serve to build trust between government actors and certainly help develop linkages among elites, as well as opportunities, as Foot puts it "not just for multilateral dialogue but, on the side-lines, for bilateral diplomacy" (Foot, 2011). These institutions can also be seen as significant drivers of knowledge development and improvements in technical expertise on energy security issues across the region. A number of institutions have also developed significant research capacity in the energy area. Finally, and perhaps most significantly, decisions that are made, whether they involve principles, definitional issues, or projects, reflect consensus among participating states. One functional challenge for building an effective Northeast Asian regime complex is that there is highly uneven participation by the region's states in the region's constituent institutions. Further research may show, however, that, given the overlap reflected in the priorities of the institutions within the regional regime complex, there is more agreement on the part of member states on critical issues than is suggested by the membership structure of the institutions alone. A simple analysis of the participation by countries in the region in regional initiatives for emergency preparedness initiatives suggests this may well be the case (Figure 8.3).

As illustrated in Figure 8.3, membership by China, Japan, and South Korea in the EAS, ASEAN+3, and APEC engages the three countries together in all major regional energy emergency initiatives, with Russia participating with them in all but the ASEAN+3 Energy Security System. Four major countries in the region thus work together on various regional energy emergency preparedness initiatives, a critical mass of countries engaged in activities focused on a common issue area. With the Cebu Declaration focused on energy efficiency and encouraging the development of renewables such as hydropower, nuclear energy, and biofuels, the emphasis of APERC on capacity development for emergency preparedness for individual member states, data development and sharing through the ESI, and incipient emergency response measures through ASEAN's initiatives, these activities are also mutually complementary. These are institutional

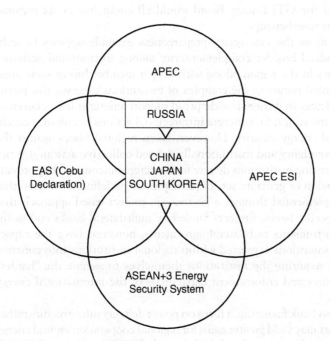

Figure 8.3 Participation by states in regional initiatives for energy emergency preparedness.

initiatives that do not deliberately interact with each but are interconnected through the countries that comprise their membership. Perhaps describing them as a regime complex for regional energy emergency preparedness is premature; however, together they represent channels of collective engagement among four major regional players in key areas of energy security cooperation.

At the same time, two countries in the region are not engaged at all in these initiatives. Increasing or "densifying" membership by Northeast Asia countries in regional institutions would strengthen interactions among them on energy issues. There are opportunities to do so. With the Ukraine crisis abetting deeper Chinese–Russian energy relations, the time may be right to persuade China to join ECNEA. In addition, energy projects under development to link North Korea to the region, including joint Mongolia–North Korean cooperation on oil trade and oil refining and dialogue about inter-Korean gas pipelines, suggest that energy cooperation could re-engage North Korea in the GTI (LaFoy, 2014). The SCO may be another institutional space in which North Korea could participate on energy issues. Mongolia is also actively pursuing APEC membership, and if its bid to become the twenty-second member of the grouping is successful, a country with considerable potential as a regional energy supplier will have been added to the grouping. Mongolia could also be engaged in the EAS and could strengthen the energy agenda of the Trilateral Cooperation Secretariat between China, Japan, and South Korea were it to take part in those meetings. These moves would mean that ECNEA, the APEC mechanisms, EAS, and the GTI Energy Board would all count five of six regional countries in their memberships.

In addition, if, as the emergency preparedness example appears to indicate, there is indeed broader complementarity among institutional activities on energy security in the region, along with deeper membership in some areas than the fragmented nature of the complex of institutions suggests, this merits attention. It indicates that there is widespread support among at least clusters of countries across the region for concrete intraregional actions to enhance conditions for regional energy security. However, given regional biases against the derogation of sovereignty and institutionally defined collective action, it is not surprising that existing institutions deliver few concrete outcomes. They provide venues for discussion or generate sets of principles or guidelines for action that may then be implemented through a bottom-up, project-based approach that would address specific issues. Projects funded by multilateral banks and facilitated by such instruments as bilateral agreements, however, have the capacity to transform intentions expressed within regional institutions into concrete actions, without requiring the institutions themselves to assume the "harder" regulatory attributes and enforcement capabilities of the international energy regime complex.

To the point on bank financing, a focus on power delivery infrastructure rather than energy inputs may yield greater gains for regional cooperation around energy security. As described, projects developed through CAREC and the GMS with ADB funding, aimed at widening access to energy across both regions through interconnections associated with the groupings, have begun to make headway. The new heavily China-backed Asian Infrastructure Bank may be a source of new financing for such projects. As analysts have observed, China's massive grid corporations are eager for regional projects; Southern Power Grid (SPG) has already developed cross-border grid interconnections with Vietnam through a contract between SPG and Electricity of Vietnam (EVN) (Taggart, 2014). Regional regulating commissions might administer transboundary regional electrical grids, structures that would add pressure to governments to enhance their cooperation over the energy inputs needed to supply the grid. As noted above, leaders of the GMS states have reached an intergovernmental agreement on power trade with a Regional Power Trade Coordinating Committee, for example. Infrastructure development could also facilitate the development of a regional "buyers' club" for oil and gas. An existing initiative to form a regional trading hub for LNG has failed to gain traction in part due to the lack of infrastructure, from pipelines to storage facilities. This may be a factor in the lack of progress on another regional effort to develop a buyers' club for LNG. Notably, regional gas and power companies have begun to engage in co-buying activities (Reuters, 2014).

All of these proposals are consistent with those proposed in the course of long-standing and ongoing dialogues within several regional energy institutions, such as in APEC's EWG and its Energy Ministerials. At the same time, for any large-scale infrastructure projects to move forward, trade and investment protections still need to be in place. In addition to the political factors previously mentioned, there is no question that the lack of regulatory capacity in Central Asia has impeded the development of regional power trade (CAREC, 2013c, p. 2). The absence of effective protections for intellectual property, as well as investment and transit, make a visionary large-scale project now under review unlikely to happen. This project, an "Asia super-grid," would harness wind and solar systems based in Mongolia for power generation throughout Northeast Asia. Proponents of the project argue that not only will it deliver power at a reasonable cost, but it will also create jobs, help reduce emissions, and contribute to regional integration (Matthews, 2012).[3] Here, bilateral agreements such as investment treaties (BITs) that include energy investment and trade may facilitate investments in the region between countries in the region, including by contributing to improving conditions for commercially viable energy investment within individual countries. Assuming that China is unlikely to move beyond observer status in the ECT, given Russia's decision to withdraw fully from the treaty in 2009,[4] these bilaterals could follow the ECT's legal protections, which extend to energy investments, trade in energy, and transit. The way in which the region has moved from bilateral free trade agreements (FTAs) toward multicountry FTAs to gradually enlarge the geographic area in which tariffs have been reduced may offer an example of how an incremental process can be used to gradually strengthen a regulatory environment supportive of economic openness and integration. Projects such as the Asia super-grid could provide the catalyst for negotiating the necessary agreements on a bilateral basis, which might be an option to a multilateral regional agreement, or to widening participation in the ECT in the region. Other schemes with similar potential include a Pan-Asian Energy Infrastructure (PAEI), which would use the concept of "joint development areas" through bilateral agreements to overcome such barriers to new energy development as those posed by conflicting territorial claims in energy-rich areas like the South China Sea to boost energy cooperation and security (Taggart, 2014). China's State Grid Corporation has also promoted a scheme for a Siberian-based regional energy grid in which it sees huge commercial potential through the deployment of its long-distance grid technology within the region.

Finally, addressing emergency preparedness is an additional area where focused activities could result in significant improvements to regional energy security. China, Japan, and South Korea have held serious discussions on bilateral and multilateral joint stockpiling arrangements, there have been proposals for a Russian stockpile, financed by Northeast Asian countries, and South Korean plans to become an oil hub for Northeast Asia through tax incentives for global oil trading companies and other incentives, as well as the development of oil storage facilities, are moving forward (Anon., 2013a).

Efforts along these lines, focused on cooperation around energy delivery systems, bilateral investment treaties, increasing collective bargaining power in negotiating deals on oil and gas, and strengthening emergency preparedness, would be valuable additions to enhancing the effectiveness of the complex of institutions in which Northeast Asian countries interact on energy issues to enhance energy security for the region. Expanding the membership of countries in Northeast Asia in regional institutions centered on energy cooperation would reduce fragmentation and contribute to deepening regional dialogue on energy security, as well as help align thinking about energy security among regional governments. These are pragmatic efforts that contribute to addressing the deficits of the energy regime complex in which Northeast Asian countries engage, acknowledging that the current complex of institutions has its current form as much because of shared regional preferences as regional antagonisms.

Notes

1 The UNDP definition of energy security is "the availability of energy at all times in various forms, in sufficient quantities and at affordable price" (United Nations Development Programme, 2004).
2 See Chapter 3, "Energy acquisition, usage, and China's engagement in Northeast Asian energy cooperation," by Suyuan Sun in this volume, for a discussion of China and the IEA.
3 Notably Bernhard Seliger, who initiated the Gobitec proposal, has urged Northeast Asian countries to form a Northeast Asian Renewable Energy Association (NARA) as a locus of political cooperation toward improved regional cooperation on renewable energy (Seliger, 2012).
4 According to some legal opinion, even having withdrawn from the treaty, Russia remains bound to uphold the proprietary rights of the oil and gas investors under Article 45 of the ECT until 2029. See Mak (2012).

References

Andrews-Speed, P. 2011. *Energy Market Integration in East Asia: A Regional Public Goods Approach*. ERIA Discussion Paper 2011-06. Jakarta: ERIA.

Anon. 2013a. Asian Energy Ministers Agree to Boost Cooperation, Joint Stockpiling of Oil. Yonhap News Agency, December 9. Online: http://english.yonhapnews.co.kr/business/2013/09/12/79/0501000000AEN20130912008351320F.html (accessed June 30, 2014).

Anon. 2013b. SCO Members Ink Memo on Creation of Energy Club. Asia-Plus, August 12. Online: http://news.tj/en/news/sco-members-ink-memo-creation-energy-club (accessed September 4, 2014).

Anon. 2014. SCO Membership in Sight for Mongolia—China's FM. ITAR-TASS News Agency, July 11. Online: http://en.itar-tass.com/world/740163 (accessed September 6, 2014).

APEC (Asia-Pacific Economic Cooperation). 2007. Agenda Item 5.1, Energy Working Group EWG33, Auckland, New Zealand, March 28–29.

APEC (Asia-Pacific Economic Cooperation). 2008. *Progress Report on the RTEIS System Apr. 2008 to Nov. 2008*. Online: www.ewg.apec.org/documents/EWG36_RTEIS.pdf (accessed September 4, 2014).

APEC (Asia-Pacific Economic Cooperation). 2014. *APEC Oil and Gas Security Exercises: Final Report*. Online: http://aperc.ieej.or.jp/publications/reports/ogse/Final_Report_OGSE_May-2014.pdf (accessed September 2, 2014).

ASEAN. 2007. *CEBU Declaration on East Asian Energy Security*. Online: www.mofa.go.jp/region/asia-paci/eas/energy0701.html (accessed September 4, 2014).

ASEAN. 2011. Joint Ministerial Statement of the 8th ASEAN+3 (China, Japan and Korea) Ministers on Energy Meeting, Jerudong, Brunei Darussalam, September 20. Online: www.asean.org/communities/asean-economic-community/item/joint-ministerial-statement-of-the-8th-asean3-china-japan-and-korea-ministers-on-energy-meeting-jerudong-brunei-darussalam-20-september-2011-2 (accessed September 4, 2014).

Asian Development Bank. 2006. *Energy Efficiency and Climate Change Considerations for On-road Transport in Asia*. ADB Department for International Development. Online: www.adb.org/documents/reports/climate-change-ea/Climate-Change-EA.pdf (accessed September 7, 2014).

Asian Development Bank. 2010. *Institutions for Regional Integration: Toward an Asian Economic Community*. Online: www10.iadb.org/intal/intalci/PE/2011/07384.pdf (accessed September 14, 2014).

Asian Development Bank. n.d. *Road Map for Expanded Energy Cooperation in the Greater Mekong Sub-region (GMS)*. Online: www.adb.org/sites/default/files/related/19810/sef-special-annex7.pdf (accessed September 5, 2014).

Barrett, S. 2007. *Why Cooperate? The Incentive to Supply Global Public Goods*. Oxford: Oxford University Press.

Bhutta, Z. 2013. Shanghai Cooperation Organisation: Pakistan Poised to Become Member of SCO Energy Club. *The Express Tribune*, December 20. Online: http://tribune.com.pk/story/647975/shanghai-cooperation-organisation-pakistan-poised-to-become-member-of-sco-energy-club/ (accessed September 5, 2014).

Boland, J. 2011. *Ten Years of the Shanghai Cooperation Organization: A Lost Decade? A Partner for the U.S.?* 21st Century Defense Initiative Policy Paper, June 20. Online: www.brookings.edu/~/media/research/files/papers/2011/6/shanghai%20cooperation%20organization%20boland/06_shanghai_cooperation_organization_boland (accessed September 5, 2014).

Calder, K. and Ye, M. 2008. *The Making of Northeast Asia.* Stanford, CA: Stanford University Press.

CAREC. 2013a. *Energy.* Online: www.carecprogram.org/index.php?page=energy (accessed September 5, 2014).

CAREC. 2013b. *Projects List.* Online: www.carecprogram.org/index.php?page=carec-projects-list (accessed September 5, 2014).

CAREC. 2013c. *Energy Sector Progress Report and Work Plan (October 2012–September 2013).* Reference Document for Session 3 of the Senior Officials' Meeting, Astana, Kazakhstan, October 23. Online: www.carecprogram.org/uploads/events/2013/SOM-Oct-KAZ/002_104_206_Energy-Sector-Progress-report-and-Work-Plan.pdf (accessed September 6, 2014).

Cha, V. 2011. Complex Patchworks: US Alliances as Part of Asia's Regional Architecture. *Asia Policy* 11. Online: www.nbr.org/publications/issue.aspx?id=218 (accessed September 6, 2014).

Chang, Y. and Yao, L. 2013. Energy and the Greater Mekong Sub-region. In D. Zha (ed.) *Managing Regional Energy Vulnerabilities in East Asia: Case Studies.* New York: Routledge, pp. 150–1.

Cutler, T. 2014. *The Architecture of Asian Energy Security.* NBR Special Report No. 46 (forthcoming 2014). Online: www.nbr.org/publications/specialreport/pdf/SR46_Cutler_advance.pdf (accessed September 3, 2014).

Dow Jones. 2010. S. Korea to Triple Energy Self-Sufficiency Ratio By 2019. Energia. gr, December 22. Online: www.energia.gr/article_en.asp?art_id=23560 (accessed September 6, 2014).

EAS EMM (East Asia Summit Energy Ministers Meeting). 2013. Joint Ministerial Statement of the Seventh East Asia Summit Energy Ministers Meeting, Bali, Indonesia, September 26. Online: www.meti.go.jp/press/2013/09/20130927001/20130927001-4.pdf (accessed September 5, 2014).

Energy Charter. 2014. FAQ. Online: www.encharter.org/index.php?id=18 (accessed September 5, 2014).

Esakova, N. 2012. *European Energy Security: Analysing the EU–Russia Energy Security Regime in Terms of Interdependence Theory.* London: Springer Science + Business Media.

Foot, R. 2011. The Role of East Asian Regional Organizations in Regional Governance: Constraints and Contributions. Carnegie Endowment for International Peace, June 7. Online: http://carnegieendowment.org/2011/06/07/role-of-east-asian-regional-organizations-in-regional-governance-constraints-and-contributions (accessed August 28, 2014).

Goldthau, A. and Witte, J.M. 2010. The Role of Rules and Institutions in Global Energy: An Introduction. In A. Goldthau and J.M. Witte (eds) *Global Energy Governance.* Washington, DC: Brookings Institution.

Goldthau, A. and Witte, J.M. 2011. Assessing OPEC's Performance in Global Energy. *Global Policy* 2(Issue Supplement s1), September: 31–9.

GTI. 2013a. GTI Cited by the Presidents of China and ROK. Greater Tumen Initiative News, June 28. Online: www.tumenprogramme.org/?info-529-1.html (accessed September 6, 2014).

GTI. 2013b. Capacity Building Training on Energy: Policies and Prospects for Regional Energy Cooperation. Greater Tumen Initiative News, July 26. Online: http://tumenprogramme.org/?info-608-1.html (accessed September 7, 2014).

GTI. 2014. Greater Tumen Initiative: Overview. Online: www.tumenprogramme.org/?list-1524.html (accessed September 6, 2014).

Haggard, S. 2011.*The Organizational Architecture of the Asia-Pacific: Insights from the New Institutionalism*. ADB Working Paper Series on Regional Economic Integration No. 71. Manila: Asian Development Bank.

Hensengerth, O. 2010. *Regionalism in China–Vietnam Relations: Institution-Building in the Greater Mekong Subregion*. New York: Routledge.

Hirst, N. and Froggatt, A. 2012. *The Reform of Global Energy Governance*. Grantham Institute for Climate Change Discussion Paper No. 3. London: Imperial College/ Chatham House.

International Partnership for Energy Efficiency Cooperation (IPEEC). 2014. About IPEEC. Online://www.ipeec.org/aboutipeec.html (accessed September 5, 2014).

Jude, A. 2013. Greater Mekong Subregion Market Coordination. PowerPoint Presentation, Sustainable Energy Training, Bangkok, Thailand, November 27. Online: www.iea. org/media/training/bangkoknov13/Session_9a_ADB_GMS_Regional_Market.pdf (accessed September 6, 2014).

Keohane, R.O. and Victor, D.G. 2010. *The Regime Complex for Climate Change*. The Harvard Project on International Climate Agreements Discussion Paper 10-33. Online: http:// belfercenter.ksg.harvard.edu/files/Keohane_Victor_Final_2.pdf (accessed September 7, 2014).

Kong, B. 2011. Governing China's Energy in the Context of Global Governance. *Global Policy* 2(Issue Supplement 51): 51–65.

Korea Energy Economics Institute. 2004. Promoting a Sustainable Energy Future in Northeast Asia, KEEI-IEA Joint Conference, Seoul, Republic of Korea, March 16–17. Online: www.keei.re.kr/main.nsf/index_en.html?open&p=%2Fweb_keei%2Fen_publish. nsf%2F0%2F8009457098E62CF94925713E002CB722&s=%3FOpenDocument%3D (accessed September 7, 2014).

Krist, B. 2014. Can Regional Connectivity Promote Development Along the New Silk Road? WITA, America's Trade Policy, July 24. Online: http://americastradepolicy. com/can-regional-connectivity-promote-development-along-the-new-silk-road/#. VBzqw0hM7dg (accessed September 16, 2014).

LaFoy, S. 2014. Greater Tumen Region Rough Logistical Nets. Rice & Iron, July 14. Online: http://nkfood.wordpress.com/2014/07/14/greater-tumen-region-rough-logistical-nets/ (accessed September 8, 2014).

Lee, J. 2013.Towards Green Energy Cooperation in Northeast Asia: Implications from European Experiences. *Asia Europe Journal* 11(3): 231–45.

Lee, J. and Novitskiy, A. 2010. Russia's Energy Policy and Its Impacts on Northeast Asian Energy Security. International Area Studies Review, 13(1): 41–61.

Linn, J.F. 2012. Central Asian Regional Integration and Cooperation: Reality or Mirage? In *EDB Eurasian Integration Yearbook 2012*, pp. 96–117. Online: www.brookings. edu/~/media/research/files/papers/2012/10/regional%20integration%20and%20 cooperation%20linn/10%20regional%20integration%20and%20cooperation%20 linn.pdf (accessed September 15, 2014).

Mak, J. 2012. Is Russia's Withdrawal from the Energy Charter Treaty of Limited Legal Significance Given That It Had Previously Failed to Ratify the Treaty? Martingdale. com, August 27. Online: www.martindale.com/energy-law/article_Josh-Mak-LLP_ 1576678.htm (accessed September 6, 2014).

Matthews, J.A. 2012. The Asian Super Grid. *The Asia-Pacific Journal: Japan Focus*. Online: www.japanfocus.org/-John_A_-Mathews/3858 (accessed September 5, 2014).

McPherson, C. 2013. National Oil Companies: Ensuring Benefits and Avoiding Systemic Risks. In A. Goldthau (ed.) *The Handbook of Global Energy Policy*. Cambridge, MA, and Oxford: John Wiley & Sons.

Meza, E. 2014. Russia Set to Join Irena. *PV Magazine*, September 4. Online: www.pv-magazine. com/news/details/beitrag/russia-set-to-join-irena_100016324/#axzz3CdreIPFC (accessed September 4, 2014).

Mitrova, T. 2010. ICM-ECNEA: Russian Perspective. *Northeast Asia Energy Focus* 7(3), Autumn.

Noor, M. 2012. Speech by Ambassador Muhamad Noor, Executive Director, APEC Secretariat. APEC Energy Ministerial Meeting, St Petersburg, Russian Federation, June 25. Online: www.apec.org/Press/Speeches/2012/0625_EMM.aspx (accessed September 6, 2014).

Orsini, A., Morin, J., and Young, O. 2013. Regime Complexes: A Buzz, a Boom, or a Bust for Global Governance? *Global Governance* 19: 27–39.

Phuong, N.T. 2013. Current State of ASEAN Infrastructure. In S.B. Das (ed.) *Enhancing ASEAN's Connectivity*. Singapore: Institute of Southeast Asian Studies, pp. 9–27.

Pron, E.M. 2014. China's Energy Diplomacy via the Shanghai Cooperation Organisation. In S. Yao and M.J.H. Talamantes (eds) *Energy Security and Sustainable Economic Growth in China*. Basingstoke and New York: Palgrave MacMillan.

Reap, S. 2014. 2nd Oil Stockpiling Roadmap Workshop and the ASEAN+3 Energy Security Forum. Agence Kampuchea Presse, February 26. Online: www.akp.gov. kh/?p=42470 (accessed September 3, 2014).

Reuters. 2014. Asian Gas Buyers Trying to Break Out of Rigid Market Structure. Reuters Africa, April 4. Online: http://af.reuters.com/article/energyOilNews/ idAFL4N0MO0V620140404?sp=true (accessed September 2, 2014).

Rozman, G. 2004. *Northeast Asia's Stunted Regionalism: Bilateral Distrust in the Shadow of Globalization*. Cambridge: Cambridge University Press.

Seliger, B. 2012. Towards a Northeast Asian Renewable Energy Association. *The Korea Herald*, July 6. Online: www.koreaherald.com/view.php?ud=20120607001045 (accessed September 4, 2014).

Shanghai Cooperation Organization (SCO). 2013. SCO Energy Club: Structure Ready for International Interaction, Not Shanghai Six's Elite Club. SCO, September 19. Online: http://infosco.biz/en/?newId=11969&domainId=sh (accessed September 5, 2014).

Sihite, E. 2013. Yudhoyono Ratifies Asean Energy Assistance Pact. Embassy of Indonesia, Athens, January 22. Online: http://indonesia.gr/yudhoyono-ratifies-asean-energy-assistance-pact/ (accessed September 17, 2014).

Small-Scale Sustainable Infrastructure Development Fund (S3IDF) and Nexant. 2005. *APEC & ASEAN: Case Studies in Regional Energy Cooperation*. Washington, DC: SARI. Online: http://pdf.usaid.gov/pdf_docs/PNADD963.pdf (accessed September 5, 2014).

Swedish Trade Council, Beijing Office. 2008. Private Sector Opportunities in the Oil Gas and Coal Sectors in Mongolia. Online: www.swedishtrade.se/PageFiles/138252/ Private%20sector%20opportunities%20in%20the%20oil,%20gas%20and%20 coal%20sectors%20in%20Mongolia.pdf (accessed September 4, 2014).

Taggart, S. 2014. A Plan to Save the South China Sea from Disaster. The National Interest: The Buzz, June 30. Online: http://nationalinterest.org/blog/the-buzz/plan-save-the-south-china-sea-disaster-10779 (accessed September 6, 2014).

Toyama, K. 2006. Enhancing Sustainability of the World Energy System. G8 Energy Ministerial Meeting, Moscow, March 16. Online: www.mofa.go.jp/policy/economy/ energy/address0603.html (accessed September 5, 2014).

United Nations Development Programme. 2004. *World Energy Assessment: Overview 2004*. New York: UNDP. Online: www.undp.org/content/undp/en/home/librarypage/environment-energy/ (accessed September 5, 2014).

UNESCAP. 2013. *Overview of ESCAP's Activities on Energy*. New York: United Nations. Online: www.greengrowth-elearning.org/pdf/ESCAP-ESCWA-ESWRSS-Presentation.pdf (accessed September 5, 2014).

Victor, D.G. and Raustiala, K. 2004. The Regime Complex for Plant Genetic Resources. *International Organization* 32: 147–54. Online: http://pesd.fsi.stanford.edu/publications/the_regime_complex_for_plant_genetic_resources/ (accessed September 6, 2014).

Vivoda, V. and Manicom, J. 2011. Oil Import Diversification in Northeast Asia. *Journal of East Asian Studies* 11(2): 223–54.

Wang, Z. and Wang, T. 2010. A Study on the Northeast Asia Energy Cooperation Mechanism. *Northeast Asia Energy Focus* 7(3): 46–56.

Weitz, R. 2014. The Shanghai Cooperation Organization: A Fading Star? *The Asan Forum*, August 11. Online: www.theasanforum.org/the-shanghai-cooperation-organization-a-fading-star/ (accessed September 4, 2014).

World Bank and AusAid. 2010. *Winds of Change: East Asia's Sustainable Energy Future*. Washington, DC: The International Bank of Reconstruction and Development/The World Bank East Asia and Pacific Region/East Asia Infrastructure Unit. Online: http://siteresources.worldbank.org/INTEASTASIAPACIFIC/Resources/226262-1271320774648/windsofchange_fullreport.pdf (accessed September 6, 2014).

Yergin, D. 2006. Ensuring Energy Security. *Foreign Affairs* 85(2): 69–83.

Yoshimatsu, H. 2014. *Comparing Institution-building in East Asia: Power Politics, Governance, and Critical Junctures*. New York: Palgrave-Macmillan.

Yu, X. 2003. Regional Cooperation and Energy Development in the Greater Mekong Sub-region. *Energy Policy* 31: 1221–34.

Zhu, S. 2012. Energy Cooperation under the Greater Tumen Initiative (GTI). Presentation, ESCAP North-East Subregional Consultation Meeting, Incheon, Republic of Korea, November 12–13.

9 Whither energy security cooperation in Northeast Asia?

Bo Kong and Jae H. Ku

This chapter distills the message from this volume's contributors to provide a comprehensive picture of the ongoing quest for energy security cooperation in Northeast Asia. After analyzing the backdrop against which the quest emerged and how it is rationalized, the chapter advances a critique of the region's endeavor and investigates why the search has remained elusive over the past decade or so. Specifically, the critique adopts a supply-and-demand framework to assess the prospect for a regional energy security cooperation regime in Northeast Asia. It concludes that member states do not demand energy security cooperation when engaging the region on energy and pursuing their discrete national energy interests. An energy security cooperation regime is further unlikely due to the region's inability to supply the necessary institutional framework. This critique then suggests moving beyond energy security cooperation and focusing rather on the existing energy complex as well as on market regimes that tackle shared concerns of energy governance in the region.

Theoretical and actual support for energy security cooperation in Northeast Asia

Over the past decade or so, the so-called epistemic community in Northeast Asia, composed of the region's publicly engaged scholars, analysts, and observers, together with various policymakers, has pursued an active search for regional cooperation on energy security. Specifically, this search has focused primarily on an attempt to create a regional regime to enhance collective energy security. Its focus on regime creation appears to resonate well with both theoretical and actual reality on the ground. On the one hand, the study of international relations has long recognized regimes as being capable of facilitating cooperation through reducing transaction costs and information imperfections and providing rules, norms, principles, and procedures that can help alter payoff structure, prolong the shadow of the future (i.e., the probability of the players to meet again or the discount parameter), enhance collective compliance, and diminish security dilemmas among states (Jervis, 1978; Keohane, 1982, 1984; Axelrod, 1984; Oye, 1985). Furthermore, regional arrangements are considered capable of rendering great service to peacemaking and peacekeeping by contributing to a deeper sense of participation, consensus, and democratization in international affairs (Boutros-Ghali, 1992).

On the other hand, this search seems to dovetail with the two profound transformations that have taken place in the region's energy domain since the collapse of the former Soviet Union (FSU). First, the region has become the center of global energy demand and witnessed a rising level of import dependence. This, to a large degree, is driven by China's transformation into the world's largest energy consumer and its diminishing ability to meet its growing demand for oil, natural gas, and coal since 1993, 2007, and 2010 respectively. While Japan and South Korea have seen their energy demand mature and slow over the past decade, both are almost completely dependent on imported energy by virtue of their scarce resource endowment. Japan's dependence on imported energy increased further due to its nuclear plant shutdown in the aftermath of the 2011 earthquake and tsunami and its Fukushima Daiichi nuclear disaster. Second, signified by Russia's comeback from the ashes of the FSU, the region has emerged as the center of global energy supply. After a decade of struggle, not only has Russia arrested its declining trend of oil and gas production, but it has also become the world's largest energy exporter. Mongolia, though it has less production and export capacity, has abundant coal and renewable energy resources, and has become a net energy exporter since 2005; it boasts a tremendous potential to become an exporter of renewable electricity, as well as a critical point of energy transit connecting Russia and the region's net energy importers. Similarly, despite its dependence on oil imports from China and Russia and its enormous power shortages, which are considered to be the main driver of the country's pursuit of nuclear power, North Korea is actually a net energy exporter and boasts significant coal and hydropower resources (IEA, 2013). Furthermore, it possesses the potential to become an oil and gas exporter should hydrocarbon reserves be established and developed in its offshore area, and the possibility to become a bridge between Russia and South Korea.

Why energy security cooperation in Northeast Asia?

Out of these two parallel trends, proponents of a regional energy security regime see an opportunity for policy coordination and for maximizing the growing complementarities between the region's net importers and exporters. A recent study sponsored by the Northeast Asia Economic Forum is an exemplar of these trends. The contributors push for greater regional cooperation on the basis of the potential economic, environmental, national security, and geopolitical dividends that would follow (Northeast Asia Economic Forum, 2005). According to this view, institutionalizing cooperation between the region's net energy importers and exporters will not only help fuel economic growth that is highly energy-intensive in China and highly electricity-intensive in South Korea and Japan, but it will also foster economic recovery and growth in economically depressed regions of the Russian Far East (RFE) and Siberia.

In addition to promoting joint prosperity, strengthening synergies with Russian gas or Mongolian renewable energy will help the region as a whole, and its major energy-consuming nations in particular, combat their environmental pollution and climate challenges. As illustrated by the 2005 Songhua River chemical spill incident, which contaminated the water flowing from China to Russia, and the commonplace complaint about air pollution spillover from China frequently registered in Japan and South Korea, the environmental problems do not recognize borders in this densely populated region.

Furthermore, this view posits that a Northeast Asian energy regime is also likely to yield security dividends because energy is now perceived as a national security issue across the region. For the net energy importers, energy has been elevated to a perceived national security issue, thanks to their growing dependence on foreign energy that often travels long distances from volatile regions prone to civil conflict, state failure, and resource nationalism—as in the case of the Middle East, North Africa, and Latin America respectively—through the long maritime supply routes vulnerable to piracy and terrorism attacks—as in the case of the Strait of Hormuz, the Gulf of Aden, and the Strait of Malacca—at wildly fluctuating energy prices, especially for oil. Likewise, for Russia and Mongolia, energy constitutes the linchpin of their quest for prosperity, power, status, and strategic leverage and is thus also regarded as a national security issue. Institutionalized cooperation, in the eyes of its proponents, is likely to help the net importers reduce their dependence on the volatile sources of imports from afar, mitigate their vulnerabilities to the choke points of seaborne energy transport, and eliminate the price premium for the Middle East crudes, while enabling the net exporters to secure access to reliable market, abundant capital, and advanced technologies from their neighboring Northeast Asian neighboring economies. For Russia, the potential benefits include diversification away from its traditional European market and less dependence on members of the Commonwealth of Independent States (CIS) for transit. Some of the recent geopolitical dynamics, including Europe's declining energy consumption in the aftermath of the 2008 global financial crisis, the looming competition with Russian gas in Europe from the growing shale gas production in North America and expanding liquefied natural gas (LNG) production capacity in Australia, and the rising tensions between Russia and the West in the aftermath of the 2013–14 Ukraine crisis, have seemed to help Russia move even closer to its Northeast Asian neighbors and accentuate the trend of Russia's pivot to the east, which occurred prior to 2008 (Wood Mackenzie, 2013).

Finally, formalized energy security cooperation is also thought to have the potential to generate broader geopolitical benefits for the region. Its proponents highlight the instrumental role that a growing natural gas trade may play in bringing nations together for long-term political and economic relationships between sellers and buyers, which in turn would go a long way toward stabilizing the region. Moving beyond a specific fuel, various scholars have identified three ways in which broad regional cooperation on energy could contribute to Northeast Asian security. First, it could reduce strategic competition for resources among net energy importers, because of their projected increases in demand and diversification needs, thus improving regional security (Vivoda, 2010); second, it could help defuse disputes over territories rich in energy, such as the East China Sea, and reduce tensions on the Korean Peninsula, by bringing North Korea into a more active, participatory role by routing cross-border natural gas pipelines across the country and meeting its energy needs, which will in turn help shift it away from its nuclear technology research (Chung, 2000; Kim, 2014); and, third, it could promote regional integration and confidence by creating a sense of international community and regional identity in Northeast Asia (Choi, 2009).

Three phases of an elusive search for regional energy security cooperation

Other than justifying their search, over the past decade or so, the proponents of a regional energy security regime have also embarked on a search for specific project proposals as anchors for their vision. This search went through three episodes of ebb and flow. The opening of the energy-rich countries in the FSU at the end of the Cold War provided the backdrop against which the first phase took place. Specifically, in the 1990s, these proposals largely focused on moving FSU hydrocarbons, especially natural gas, to the major consumer countries in the region. Those that have garnered the most attention in the region mainly include: the Asian-Pacific Energy Community concept based on the proposal of 32 Japanese companies featuring a grand pipeline grid that would extend from Yakutsk in Russia to Dampier in northern Australia, connecting Russia, China, South Korea, Japan, Taiwan, and six Association of Southeast Asian Nations (ASEAN) countries; the so-called Vostok Plan, proposed by the crumbling Soviet Union in 1991 and entailing a pipeline from Sakhalin in Russia to Japan via North Korea and South Korea; the Energy Silk Road Project, involving a Turkmenistan–China–Japan natural gas pipeline via Uzbekistan, Kazakhstan, and South Korea; the Irkutsk Region Gas Project, featuring a natural gas pipeline from the Kovyktinskoye gas field in Russia to China and South Korea through Mongolia; and the Trans-Asian Gas Pipeline Network concept, involving a gas pipeline from Russia to Japan via China or Mongolia (Valencia & Dorian, 1998).

Once surfaced, these proposals captured the region's attention and remained the focus of energy security cooperation discussions throughout the 1990s, and some are still widely discussed today. However, when regional energy demand nosedived and global oil prices collapsed during the 1997–8 Asian financial crisis, the appetite for expensive cross-border pipelines dissipated and the search for a collective energy security cooperation regime entered its second phase, characterized by a punctuated stasis and dormancy.

China's entry into the World Trade Organization (WTO) in 2001 and its ensuing rapid growth in demand for foreign energy rekindled a new round of searching for greater regional energy security cooperation. By this time, the scope of the proposed agenda had moved beyond a specific fuel and become much broader. For example, other than promoting cross-border gas pipelines to link Russia and China, the two Koreas, and Japan, the revitalized calls for Northeast Asian cooperation also centered on "joint exploration of offshore resources, clean energy and energy conservation technology sharing, oil stockpiling, and joint operations for protecting sea lanes of communication" (Choi, 2009), removal of regional energy price subsidies (Thomson, 2006), and some cross-border electricity cooperation projects, such as the "Asia super-grid" project and the Gobitec Project as mentioned in Chapter 5.

During the same period, this search for energy security cooperation in Northeast Asia has transcended the realm of analytical exploration and gained increasing traction among policymakers. Indeed, various politicians have echoed the search by putting forward a number of policy initiatives. For example, regional energy security cooperation was an integral element of the "the Northeast Asian Cooperation Initiative for Peace and Prosperity" that President Roh Moo-hyun of South Korea launched upon his inauguration in February 2003, which was designed to build the "Age of Northeast Asia," based on mutual trust and cooperation. Similarly, regional energy security cooperation also figured prominently in a key foreign policy speech Prime Minister Koizumi of Japan gave in January 2002, in which he proposed the creation of a broader East Asian community, composed of ASEAN, China, Japan, South Korea, Australia, and New Zealand. In April 2013, President Park Geun-hye of South Korea launched the Northeast Asia Peace and Cooperation Initiative and the Eurasian Initiative to address what she called "Asia's paradox"—that is, the discrepancy between the growing economic interdependence in the region on the one hand and the relatively underdeveloped political and security cooperation on the other—and to increase regional cooperation on developing alternative energy and reducing dependence on fossil fuels (Republic of Korea Ministry of Foreign Affairs, 2013).

Despite this active and consistent search over the past decade or so on the part of the region's epistemic community and policymakers, Northeast Asia has seen little multilateral regime formation in its energy domain. The overwhelming majority of the proposed multilateral projects remain at the conceptual level. Despite the rhetorical support from the region, they remain a distant option. The only two projects that have been completed are projects exclusively for the benefit of China—the first is the Central Asia–China natural gas pipeline, which is essentially the same as the proposed Energy Silk Road Project. The second project is the ESPO pipeline moving Russian oil to both China and Japan. However, it is more of an outcome of the Russia–China and Russia–Japan deal than a trilateral arrangement.

While the region does not lack energy-specific or energy-germane initiatives, such as those referenced above, none has acquired independent financial and staff resources, permanent headquarters, or the procedural capacity to forge decisions and collective action. Instead, most fall into the category of the so-called "zombie initiatives," that is, they are in suspended animation—neither entirely dead nor entirely alive (APERC, 2007). Neither is the outside region likely to midwife a Northeast Asian energy security regime. With the deepening economic integration between the region's main energy importing economies—China, Japan, and South Korea—and ASEAN comes the hope that the ASEAN+3 might be able to fill in the institutional need for energy security cooperation in Northeast Asia.

However, this hope is based on false assumptions, as the Northeast Asia–ASEAN energy relationship, shared interests notwithstanding, is becoming increasingly competitive on two accounts: First, the two groups already separately and vigorously compete for fossil fuel supplies both inside and outside Asia; and, second, as energy demand continues to grow rapidly in ASEAN economies with their deepening industrialization, urbanization and modernization, they will inevitably have less appetite for exporting their energy resources to Northeast Asia (Thomson, 2006). Consequently, a regional energy security regime remains elusive in Northeast Asia. The region remains a geographical cluster rather than a political concept. There is still a stark lack of collective identity to link the region beyond shared borders (Hemmer & Katzenstein, 2002).

Why has this search been elusive?

With this disappointing record of the decade-plus search for a regional energy security regime in Northeast Asia, there thus arise three fundamental questions: Why has this search failed to lead to substantive institution-building in the region's energy domain? What does this failure imply for future efforts to promote energy security cooperation in the region? And what are the lessons we could learn from this elusive search?

Specifically, while recognizing the desirability and benefit of energy security cooperation in the abstract, we believe this search has ignored the actual demand from member states for such an energy security regime in Northeast Asia and the ability of the region to provide such an institution. On the one hand, it has almost completely overlooked, if not dodged, the following key questions about state preference for energy security cooperation in the region, especially in an institutionalized manner: How does each state perceive energy security? Are these perceptions compatible with each other? What are the core energy security interests of each member state vis-à-vis Northeast Asia? How are they aligned with the attempt to create a regional energy security regime? To what extent do all crucial powerful actors in the region agree that institutionalized cooperation is the best way to maximize benefits of cooperation?

On the other hand, it has failed to examine the hard truths about the ability of the region to provide such an energy security regime and the need for such a provision. To be sure, there is plenty of analysis that correctly attributes the region's lack of institutional architecture in general and an energy security regime in particular to: the difficulties associated with the region's anarchical international relations; lingering Cold War legacies of no full diplomatic normalization and territorial disputes; rising nationalism and mutual distrust fueled by power rivalries, a shifting balance of power, an unapologetic Japan about its imperial history, an ambivalent United States, and a rising China suspicious of U.S. alliances and any of its institution-building efforts (Chanlett-Avery, 2005; Wada, 2006; Choi, 2009). However, this discussion of the supply of institutions in the energy domain neglects the remote feasibility of building an overarching, comprehensive energy security regime around energy, which in and of itself covers such a wide range of discrete fuels—oil, natural gas, coal, nuclear, and renewable energy—with each presenting a different set of energy security challenges for governments and firms in the region. It also leaves unaddressed whether member states are committed to, or capable of, carrying out such an institutional design task. Finally, the elusive search for a Northeast Asian energy security regime operates under the assumption that the implied approach is the most appropriate one for addressing common energy security challenges facing the region. It fails to examine whether these challenges are being, or have been, tackled by other institutions, thus removing the need to build a new regime in the region's energy domain.

Consequently, proponents of multilateral energy security cooperation in Northeast Asia have largely incorrectly equated the potential benefits of their proposed regime with the actual demand from member states. While they recognize some of the supply-side challenges, they tend to focus on the issue of attainability but push aside the issue of feasibility and necessity. As a result, they have let the potential normative value of regional energy security cooperation obscure the actual demand for such an elusive regime and the region's ability to supply it.

Varied energy security look

Despite the rhetorical enthusiasm and support for creation of a Northeast Asian energy security regime, member states of the region have revealed varied perceptions of energy security, diverse national energy security interests vis-à-vis the region, and diverging preferences for appropriate strategy with respect to their quest for energy security. Further, the politics of uncertainty resulting from ambiguous payoffs of multilateral energy security cooperation and uncertain times for the region as a whole conspire to instill tremendous reluctance among members to commit to institutionalization in the energy domain. Consequently, each member state has resorted to the reliance of self-help and bilateral means to pursue discrete energy security goals. This bilateral approach to cooperation, however, is often designed to be exclusive and comes at the expense of other competitors in the region. To the extent trilateral cooperation occurs, it is not focused on an attempt to enhance each country's access to energy physically, contractually, and commercially. Thus, the inconvenient truth of the region with respect to the effort to institutionalize energy security cooperation is that no state in Northeast Asia puts energy security regime-building at the center of its engagement with the region. In fact, it remains an afterthought at best.

First, the meaning of energy security varies greatly from country to country and this variation corresponds to each country's geographical location, geological resource endowment, relationship with the broader international community, political system, and its economic disposition (Luft & Korin, 2009). For Mongolia, and especially Russia, energy is not only one of the most important sources of revenue generation, but also a facilitating factor of their international influence and strategic leverage. For China, Japan, and South Korea, in contrast, imported energy constitutes a source of their revenue drain and their perceived strategic "soft belly." Thus, Russia and Mongolia seek security of demand and the ability to use energy to acquire and project strategic influence, while China, Japan, and South Korea pursue the security of supply and strive to prevent energy from turning into a source of their strategic vulnerability. Out of this variance emerges a high level of incompatibility and divergence both between the region's net energy exporters and importers over both what energy security entails and how it should be pursued. Whereas the net energy exporters desire higher energy prices consistent with their revenue needs, seek dominance over their energy export routes, and maintain control over how their energy resources are developed at home, the net energy importers prefer lower energy prices commensurate with their purchasing power, promote safe delivery of their energy import and secure passage of supply routes, seek out reliable and dependable suppliers, and pursue open access to external energy development opportunities.

Thus, despite the perceived complementarities between the net energy exporters and importers, they are fundamentally at odds with each other over their energy security outlook. As illustrated in Chapters 6 and 7, both Mongolia and Russia actually prefer competition rather than cooperation among their neighboring economies in Northeast Asia, as the latter circumstance will afford them strategic leverage. Thus, it should come as no surprise that, as discussed in Chapters 2 and 3, Russia is often thought to have a played a role in manipulating or intensifying competition among Northeast Asian energy importers, especially between China and Japan with regard to the ESPO pipeline. To the extent both the net energy exporters and importers share an interest in diversification, their desired outcomes do not necessarily lend direct support to greater regional energy security cooperation. This is particularly true with regard to energy interactions between China and Russia. As explained in Chapter 7, both countries wish to diversify, but Russia's goal of diversification is to move beyond China to satisfy the demand in Japan, South Korea, and the broader Asia Pacific countries, while China's effort is designed to go beyond Russia and tap into the energy riches of Central Asia. Hence, as Chapter 8 suggests, while Beijing is interested in promoting a common market, including energy, under the framework of the Shanghai Cooperation Organization (SCO), Moscow prefers its own initiatives, such as the Eurasian Union, which excludes China. Similarly, when Russia discusses energy security cooperation, it prefers to address it within the framework of APEC instead of in the Northeast Asian context.

Diversity of national energy security interests

This variation of energy security outlook dovetails with the diversity of national energy security interests each member state evinces in Northeast Asia and their preferred energy statecraft for engaging the region on energy, as illustrated in Table 9.1. A glance at this table reveals two fundamental realities about member states' interest regarding energy security cooperation: To start, the core of their national energy interests in Northeast Asia have little to do with regime creation in the energy domain. For example, one primary factor motivating South Korea to seek regional energy security cooperation is to promote the eventual unification of the two Koreas. However, given China's known worries about U.S. presence on its doorstep, China's preference is clear: to keep North Korea as a buffer zone between itself and South Korea. Similarly, while Russia seeks to expand cooperation with Japan and South Korea in the region, it never relinquishes its entrenched propensity for using energy as a strategic weapon to enhance its leverage in its foreign relations and is explicit about its intentions to diversify beyond China. In the same vein, as illustrated in Chapter 2, China cooperates actively with Japan and South Korea bilaterally and trilaterally to pursue advanced energy technologies, but has little intention to enter into any institutionalized cooperation that might limit its ability to expand energy consumption or to receive technological transfers. Nor does it have any scruples about competing head to head with Japan and South Korea for Russian hydrocarbons. Thus, the bottom line is that member states in Northeast Asia cooperate or seek cooperation purely out of self-interest, but their discrete self-interest has little to do with the collective Northeast Asian energy security interests as envisioned by the proponents of regional energy security cooperation.

Table 9.1 also reveals that the preferred statecraft for pursuing national energy interests in Northeast Asia is not regional cooperation. Instead, despite a degree of variation, all states in Northeast Asia, as Chapter 2 notes, have sought to enhance their energy security by resorting to state intervention in energy markets and energy diplomacy. State intervention threatens to pull the region apart because it elevates and politicizes the stakes of competition and relative gains. Indeed, it has fueled intense zero-sum competition among member states over bilateral deals at one another's expense; the fierce competition between China and Japan over offshore gas in the East China Sea provides a case in point. But competition is hardly confined to net energy importers alone. For example, as Chapter 6 indicates, Russia sees increased Mongolian production of coal, oil, and other energy resources as direct competition with its own production. Thus, Russia has little interest in shipping Mongolian coal through the RFE to Pacific ports. Further, the prevalent reliance on the statist approach to energy has also erected a fundamental impediment to institutionalized energy security cooperation—that is, surrender of sovereign control over a certain dimension of national energy governance, which, as discussed in Chapter 8, has been a primary feature of the collective approach to energy security cooperation as practiced under the IEA. However, as Chapter 2 explicates, energy is considered to be too important to be left to the markets in Northeast Asia. As a consequence, all member states demonstrate a strong preference for self-help and bilateralism in pursuit of their discrete national energy security interests when engaging the region, which is a far outcry from the type of collective action and group-compliance envisioned under an institutionalized approach to regional energy security cooperation.

Uncertain payoffs of regional energy security cooperation

The second set of factors that dampen demand for regional energy security cooperation in Northeast Asia stems from the great uncertainties confronting

Table 9.1 Diversity of national energy interests in Northeast Asia

	Core energy interests regarding Northeast Asia	Preferred statecraft
China	• To gain physical, contractual, and commercial access to Russian oil and gas to reduce dependence on the Middle East and Strait of Malacca. • To gain access to advanced energy technologies in Japan and South Korea to improve energy efficiency and reduce the environmental footprint of domestic fossil fuel consumption.	• Reliance on a statist approach to gain preferential access to Russian oil and gas through exclusive bilateral agreement. • Cooperation with Japan and South Korea bilaterally, trilaterally, or multilaterally to access advanced technologies.
Japan	• To gain access to Russian oil and gas to enhance geographical diversification of energy supplies.	• Reliance on a statist approach to gain preferential access to Russian oil and gas through exclusive bilateral agreement.
South Korea	• To gain access to Russian oil and gas to enhance energy supply security. • To use energy cooperation, such as the proposed Russia–North Korea–South Korea gas pipeline project as a means to persuade North Korea to abandon its nuclear program, promote mutual energy dependence between the two Koreas, and facilitate their eventual unification.	• Reliance on a statist approach to gain preferential access to Russian oil and gas through exclusive bilateral agreement.
Russia	• To spur economic and political development in the Russian Far East by unlocking its energy reserves using capital and technologies from the region. • To reduce dependence on established European markets and unreliable CIS transit states. • To step up cooperation with Japan, South Korea, and other countries in the broader Asia Pacific to diversify regional exports beyond the Chinese market. • To gain a competitive strategic and commercial footprint in the dynamic Asia-Pacific "face" of globalization.	• Controlling ownership, investment, production, and distribution of energy. • Using energy as a strategic instrument to enhance its regional commercial and strategic footprint. • Encouraging competition among regional countries eager to participate in energy development projects in Mongolia or supply the country with energy.
Mongolia	• To reduce dependence on Russia and China for imports and exports of energy. • To enhance processing of natural resources and industrial production within Mongolia. • To deepen ties with both of its two powerful neighbors, Russia and China, and develop relations with "third neighbor" countries and international organizations.	• Controlling foreign investment and acquisition of domestic energy assets. • Encouraging competition among regional countries eager to participate in energy development projects in Mongolia or supply the country with energy.

the region regarding ambiguous payoffs of multilateral energy cooperation and the tectonic shifts the region is experiencing in terms of its changing balance of power, geopolitics, and market dynamics. To start, one of the fundamental premises for the envisioned regional energy security cooperation in Northeast Asia is that key elements of energy infrastructure, such as trans-border pipelines and grids, if built, will help realize the potential complementarities between the region's net energy exporters and importers and hardwire their relationships such that broader economic and political integration may follow. However, what is often ignored is that these key pieces of energy infrastructure also represent billions of dollars of investment and will create new political realities of mutual dependence. Thus, unless anchored by certainties about investment returns, regulatory transparency, confidence about timely project execution, and perceived reliability of supplier and transit countries, none of the proposed multilateral projects in the region is likely to break ground. However, as elucidated in Chapter 5, the slow progress in upstream development in Russia, its weak legal system, political opaqueness, and growing political risks for foreign investment have not only led to fatigue and frustration on the part of the Roh Moo-hyun administration in South Korea, which upon taking office promoted the concept of building the era of Northeast Asia, but also prompted the ensuing Lee Myung Bak administration to shift its geographical focus away from Russia to Africa, Central Asia, North America and Latin America. Similarly, as Chapter 6 shows, Mongolia's propensity for nationalism and confusing policies toward foreign investment have not only failed to reduce the country's dependence on its two giant neighbors, China and Russia, but also deprived it of foreign capital, technology, and the management competence essential for achieving the country's potential as a major energy supplier in the Northeast Asia. Finally, the unpredictability of Pyongyang and its precarious external behaviors, as illustrated by its sinking of the South Korean warship Cheonan and shelling of Yeonpyeong island in 2010, and its irregular, provocative testing of missiles and nuclear weapon tests, calls into question the wisdom and practicality of any attempt to build a cross-border pipeline that passes through North Korea.

Uncertainties are also deeply rooted in the interactions of the region's net energy importers: China, Japan, and South Korea. To begin with, Russia is the common target of all three net energy importers as far as their pursuit of energy security in Northeast Asia is concerned. Further, as argued earlier, all three states have resorted to state intervention, albeit with a degree of variation, in organizing their energy markets and conducting their energy diplomacy. This statist approach predisposes them to be suspicious of the implications of their relative gains of any bilateral deals between any of them and Russia, because all three net energy importers perceive energy resources to be finite and scarce. In fact, as alluded to in Chapter 4, Japan sees the rapidly growing energy demand from the Asia-Pacific region, especially from China, as a threat to its own energy security. Thus it comes as no surprise, as described in Chapter 2, that Chinese, Japanese, and South Korean state-backed energy companies compete among each other both in Northeast Asia and elsewhere. Further, the varied strength of energy firms among the three net energy importers introduces a layer of uncertainty into the prospect of their energy security cooperation in the region. In the case of the oil and gas industry, China boasts the most competitive firms, followed by South Korea; whereas Japan, as described in Chapter 4, despite consistent state support, still lacks competitive and integrated firms that operate across varied fuel markets and the entire value chain, both at home and abroad. To a large degree, this variation of business strength reflects the different scale and sophistication of their respective internal oil industries. Nevertheless, as Chapter 4 indicates, the variation of business strength impedes cooperation between Chinese and Japanese companies in developing natural gas in the East China Sea, as China does not see the need or benefit of working together, whereas Japan has little to bring to the table.

Uncertain times in Northeast Asia

Next, the shifting sands of balance of power, disruptive energy market dynamics, and rapidly changing geopolitics, along with the resultant changes in perceptions, interests, and strategic calculations, not only add to a great sense of the uncertain times facing Northeast Asia but also create a propensity on the part of member states to hedge options and maintain strategic flexibility over their pursuit of national energy security interests in the region. A case in point is the evolution of Chinese–Russian energy relations. The rapid rise of China and the collapse of the former Soviet Union, more than anything else, illustrate the profound shift in the region's balance of power. In 1979, at the beginning of its economic reform and opening up, China's gross domestic product was only 40 percent of that of the Soviet Russian Republic, the present Russian Federation; but by 2010, China's output was four times larger than that of Russia (Trenin, 2012). This power shift helps explain Russia's paranoia, as discussed in Chapter 7, about being reduced to China's resource appendage, which in turn drives its attempt to use energy to regain its influence when dealing with China as well as its simultaneous endeavor to diversify away from China, shapes its preference to pursue energy cooperation in the broader Asia-Pacific instead of Northeast Asia, and galvanized its opposition to forming an energy club under the SCO. The so-called "super cycle" of the commodities boom between 2000 and 2008, together with China's growing dependence on foreign energy, appeared to have played into Russia's strength, demonstrated by Russia pitting China against Japan in their rivalry for the routing of the ESPO pipeline route. However, as analyzed in Chapter 7, Russia's ability to brandish its energy "superpower" stature and its state control over national energy firms, to limit options for Northeast Asian states to pursue energy security, is highly circumscribed. As far as China is concerned, Russia is merely one option for its energy supply diversification. Its influence over Russia has actually increased with its success in developing other domestic and foreign alternatives. Thus, while never giving up on Russia, China accelerated LNG imports and strengthened ties with Central Asian energy-rich countries by building an oil pipeline to Kazakhstan and a cross-border gas pipeline to Turkmenistan via

Uzbekistan and Kazakhstan; this eroded Russia's influence over the landlocked energy producers in Central Asia and enhanced its leverage over Russia.

The cyclical nature of the commodities markets, the disruptive nature of energy technology development, and the transformative geopolitics in the region conspired to further reduce Russia's leverage over China and reshaped its calculations about China. The 2008–9 global financial crisis not only ended the "super cycle" of the commodities boom that fueled Russia's resource nationalism, but also dashed its hope to attract capital from the West to unlock its energy resources in challenging terrains, such as West Siberia and the Russian Arctic. Consequently, Russia had to enter into a loans-for-oil deal with China and agreed to build the China section of the ESPO pipeline before extending it to its Far East port of Kozmino near Nakhodk—both of which were consistent with China's preference and reflected the beginning of a shift of power in Northeast Asia on the energy front. Three developments continued this shift: First, Russia's established European market saw its natural gas consumption plummet in the aftermath of the 2008–9 financial crisis; second, Western Europe has been able to diversify natural gas suppliers due to a growing ability to import LNG and to make purchases from the spot market, along with the transformation of the United States as an exporter of natural gas because of the so-called shale gas revolution resulting from technological breakthroughs; and, third, the 2014 Ukraine crisis and Russia's decision to annex Crimea not only subjected Russia to debilitating economic and financial sanctions from the West, but also intensified Europe's effort to reduce energy dependence on Russia. Meanwhile, with secure energy supplies from Central Asia, growing LNG imports from all over the world, and a concerted drive to develop shale gas at home, China finds itself in a much stronger position vis-à-vis Russia in terms of bilateral energy relations. Thus, the shift Russia is experiencing deprives it of the traditional leverage it once possessed to exploit European–Northeast Asian differences. In fact, now isolated by the West, Russia can no longer play the "European card." As a result, it finds itself tilting further to China's preferences for routing and pricing of the bilateral long-term gas trade, as in the case of the Power of Siberia—the bilateral gas pipeline that has been negotiated for more than a decade. Additionally, for the first time, Moscow also began to allow Chinese resource firms to acquire upstream access in Russia. In addition to highlighting Russia's loss of leverage vis-à-vis China, these tactical changes appear to suggest that the country's effort to respond to the West's isolation and to the shift of global gravity toward Asia may have prompted Russia to overcome its paranoia about China.

Nevertheless, Russia's pivot to Asia is likely to contribute little to the prospect for regional energy security cooperation in Asia. On the one hand, it will only vindicate China's belief in the value of self-help and reinforce its preference for bilateral cooperation as its growing economic power and geopolitical influence will afford it ever more leverage in bilateral dealings. On the other hand, it will also give Russia less incentive to favor regional energy security cooperation in Northeast Asia as Moscow worries about regional net energy importers ganging up to take advantage of its weakness. Indeed, in light of the shale gas revolution,

South Korea, as discussed in Chapter 5, is less eager to enter into a long-term natural gas contract with Russia as it anticipates a further drop of Russian gas prices with the gradual emergence of a global natural gas market due to growing LNG trade.

Provision of a Northeast Asian energy security regime

In addition to the historical legacy issues and the lack of mutual trust among member states referenced earlier, two fundamental realities call into question the supply of a regional energy security cooperation regime in Northeast Asia. First, as a policy problem, energy security stands out by virtue of its problem diversity. As explained in Chapter 4, the energy security regime extends across a range of different fuels, each of which presents governments and firms with different challenges in terms of securing energy supplies. In fact, there is no single "energy security" problem, but an array of different cooperation maneuvers in the area of oil, natural gas, coal, renewables, and nuclear energy, each with its inherent challenges. A corollary of this problem diversity is that institutionalized regional energy security cooperation can take the form of a comprehensive regime encompassing the entire range of fuels or a set of loosely linked institutions corresponding to each fuel sector. However, neither form of cooperation is likely in Northeast Asia. The centralized approach would exceed the ability and interest of all member states, while the decentralized approach would involve too much bargaining and too narrowly based issue linkages, which tend to generate institutional fragmentation instead of institutional cohesion.

The other challenge stemming from problem diversity is that regional energy security cooperation may not necessarily be the appropriate venue for pursuing collective security. This is especially true in the oil sector. Oil is a global fungible commodity. There is a global oil market and no one is independent of the market. In that sense, as far as oil supply security is concerned, who owns, produces, and ships oil does not matter; instead, what matters is that there is liquidity in the global oil market. In fact, today's oil market is so globalized, integrated, commoditized, and financialized that a supply disruption anywhere amounts to a supply disruption everywhere. Therefore, oil security has, to a large degree, become an issue of global public good. No country can singlehandedly operate beyond the global oil market and guarantee its oil supply security. Thus, while helpful, regional cooperation is hardly the solution to challenges to global oil supply security.

In contrast, natural gas is a good fit for regional cooperation, but sorting out competing priorities is too complicated to induce cooperation in Northeast Asia. Despite its gradual commoditization thanks to the increasing global LNG trade, natural gas remains a local commodity traded on regional markets that has yet to be integrated. In fact, the disparity between regional prices is unlikely to disappear anytime soon. In this respect, regional cooperation is an appropriate way to go about enhancing gas supply and demand security for all member states of Northeast Asia. However, the diverging interests, appetites, and objectives regarding the required delivery infrastructure have been key impediments to regional cooperation. Specifically, all major players in Northeast Asia are very demanding about the siting, pricing, financing, and returns of gas pipelines for different reasons. Japan and South Korea's pickiness reflects the fundamental reality that they obtain their gas supplies primarily from LNG imports instead of through pipelines, whereas China's position reveals its reluctance to lock itself into a long-term arrangement when natural gas occupies a very low profile in its energy consumption mix and it has plenty of other alternative options. In contrast, Russia, as explained in Chapter 7, until recently only had residual interest in Northeast Asia. When it is compelled to turn to this region, Russian gas has to compete with growing LNG supplies, Central Asian alternatives, renewable energy, and potential shale gas development in China.

Second, the existence of loosely coupled energy security regimes, both in the Asia-Pacific region and beyond, and the largely underdeveloped energy cooperation in the region raise questions about the imperative for the supply of an energy security regime specifically focused on Northeast Asia. Chapter 8 provides a detailed account of the energy security regime complex in the Asia-Pacific region, much of which is germane to Northeast Asia. In fact, some of the proposed agenda for energy security cooperation in Northeast Asia, such as maritime energy security, regional emergency stockpile, and joint resource development, are discussed and explored under this broad regime complex. Beyond the energy regime complex in the Asia-Pacific region, there is also a set of overlapping and fragmented institutions that constitute the regime complex of global energy governance aiming to address the environmental, security, and public health externalities of energy production, distribution, and consumption around the world (Lesage *et al.*, 2010; Leal-Arcas & Filis, 2013), all of which are also the shared concerns of member states in Northeast Asia. On many occasions the regime complex of global energy governance is a more appropriate venue, as argued earlier in the case of oil security, to address these concerns. Given the historical experience and competence of the International Energy Agency (IEA) in coordinating the release of emergency stockpiles of oil in case of supply disruption that affects every consumer of oil, it is certainly more appropriate to discuss pooling of emergency stocks at the global level than at the regional level. But the challenge there is to figure out a way to fix the anachronistic exclusion of China from the organization. Nevertheless, member states have turned to this regime complex of global energy governance when they have become bogged down in energy-related conflicts. For example, Japan has utilized the WTO to combat China's use of trade on rare earth elements and stainless steel as a tool of coercion in recent territorial disputes (Gillispie & Pfeiffer, 2012).

Other than an existing energy regime complex at the regional and global level, the frequently overlooked mechanisms of energy cooperation that already exist further undermine the need for the supply of a regional energy security regime. As highlighted in Chapter 4, despite fierce competition among member states for energy supplies in the region, particularly among the net energy importers, their state-owned energy firms actually cooperate quite frequently and extensively. For example, despite their competition for crude oil in Northeast Asia and elsewhere, in 2012, South Korea and Japan exported 26 and 27 percent of their oil products to China respectively (IEA, 2014). Thus, regional cooperation, anchored by market regimes through commercial contracts, serves as a reminder not to over-exaggerate the intensity and impact of state-to-state competition for energy supplies in Northeast Asia. It also suggests that ensuring markets work in the region's energy sector may be more cost-effective and efficient in promoting regional energy security cooperation than taking on the challenge of building a regional energy security regime.

Whither energy security cooperation in Northeast Asia?

Three central messages emerge out of the discussion of the demand and supply of an energy security regime in the region. First, the diversity of national energy security interests and the policy problem of energy security run against any effort to promote a centralized and comprehensive energy security regime in Northeast Asia. Considering the enormous uncertainties confronting the region, it is possible to go one step further and argue that even the less ambitious endeavor to promote regional energy security cooperation on a particular form of fuel is not likely to succeed. The bottom line regarding the quest for regional energy security cooperation in Northeast Asia is that it was, is, and will remain elusive. In this regard, it is time the region moved beyond the discussion of regional energy security cooperation and looked at concrete steps conducive to governing externalities of energy production, distribution, and consumption at both the regional and global level.

Second, instead of reinventing the wheel and engineering a new institutional design exercise that stands little chance of success, it is time to think about how to make good use of the existing energy regime complex that exists in the broader Asia-Pacific region and at the global level. Together, these energy complexes have long since planted the seeds of energy security cooperation in Northeast Asia.

Finally, instead of targeting state-to-state or institutionalized efforts to promote regional energy security cooperation, the region should focus more on existing regimes that prove effective in delivering cooperation. Market regimes, especially through commercial contracts, if left to their own devices, can moderate state-to-state competition and facilitate win-win cooperation. However, as explained in Chapter 7, the energy regulatory systems across Northeast Asia vary greatly and have resulted in a great sense of a security dilemma in the energy sector in the region. Thus, one promising, although very challenging, area of future effort should aim at efforts that can promote congruity among regional energy markets. This would require first and foremost less state intervention and more progress toward regulatory transparency. Once set in motion, these efforts are likely to lead to more regional energy security cooperation than the elusive efforts the region has made over the past decade or so.

References

Asia Pacific Energy Research Centre (APERC). 2007. Understanding International Energy Initiatives in the APEC Region. Tokyo: Institute of Energy Economics, Japan.

Axelrod, Robert. 1984. *The Evolution of Cooperation*. New York: Basic Books.

Boutros-Ghali, Boutros. 1992. An Agenda for Peace: Preventive Diplomacy, Peace-making and Peace-keeping. *International Relations* 11: 201–18.

Chanlett-Avery, Emma. 2005. Rising Energy Competition and Energy Security in Northeast Asia: Issues for U.S. Policy. In *CRS Report for Congress*. Washington DC: Congressional Research Service.

Choi, Hyun Jin. 2009. Fueling Crisis or Cooperation? The Geopolitcs of Energy Security in Northeast Asia. *Asian Affairs* 36(2): 3–28.

Chung, Ok-Nim. 2000. *Solving the Security Prize in Northeast Asia: A Multilateral Security Regime*. Washington DC: Brookings Institution.

Gillispie, Clara and Pfeiffer, Stephanie. 2012. The Debate Over Rare Earths: Recent Developments in Industry and the WTO Case: An Interview with Yufan Hao and Jane Nakano. The National Bureau of Asian Research, July 11. Online: www.nbr.org/research/activity.aspx?id=261 (accessed October 21, 2014).

Hemmer, Christopher and Katzenstein, Peter J. 2002. Why is There No NATO in Asia? Collective Identity, Regionalism, and the Origins of Multilateralism. *International Organization* 66(3): 575–607.

International Energy Agency (IEA). 2013. *Energy Balances of Non-OECD Countries*. Paris: OECD/IEA.

International Energy Agency (IEA). 2014. *Oil Information*. Paris: OECD/IEA.

Jervis, Robert. 1978. Cooperation Under the Security Dilemma. *World Politics* 30(2): 186–214.

Keohane, Robert O. 1982. The Demand for International Regimes. *International Organization* 36(2): 325–55.

Keohane, Robert O. 1984. *After Hegemony: Cooperation and Discord in the World Political Economy*. Princeton, NJ: Princeton University Press.

Kim, Younkyoo. 2014. Rethinking Energy Security in Northeast Asia. Nautilus Institute for Security and Sustainability. Online: http://nautilus.org/napsnet/napsnet-special-reports/rethinking-energy-security-in-northeast-asia/ (accessed September 9, 2014).

Leal-Arcas, Rafael and Filis, Andrew. 2013. The Fragmented Governance of the Global Energy Economy: A Legal-institutional Analysis. *Journal of World Energy Law and Business* 6(4): 348–405.

Lesage, Dries, Van de Graaf, Thijis, and Westphal, Kirsten (eds.). 2010. *Global Energy Governance in a Multipolar World*. Farnham: Ashgate.

Luft, Gal and Korin, Anne. 2009. Energy Security: In the Eyes of the Beholder. In Gal Luft and Anne Korin (eds.) *Energy Security Challenges for the 21st Century*. Santa Barbara, CA: Praeger Security International, pp. 1–17.

Northeast Asia Economic Forum. 2005. *Promoting a Northeast Asian Energy Community*. Honolulu, HI: Northeast Asia Economic Forum.

Oye, Kenneth A. 1985. Explaining Cooperation under Anachary: Hypotheses and Strategies. *World Politics* 38(1): 1–22.

Republic of Korea Ministry of Foreign Affairs. 2013. *Northeast Asia Peace and Cooperation Initiative*. Seoul: Ministry of Foreign Affairs.

Thomson, Elspeth. 2006. ASEAN and Northeast Asian Energy Security: Cooperation or Competition? *East Asia* 23(3): 67–90.

Trenin, Dmitri. 2012. *True Partners? How Russia and China See Each Other*. London: Centre for European Reform.

Valencia, Mark J. and Dorian, James P. 1998. Multilateral Cooperation in Northeast Asia's Energy Sector: Possibilities and Problems. In Susan L. Shirk and Michael Staniewicz (eds.) *Energy and Security in Northeast Asia: Supply and Demand, Conflict and Cooperation*. San Diego, CA: University of California, Institute on Global Conflict and Cooperation.

Vivoda, Vlado. 2010. Evaluating Energy Security in the Asia Pacific Region: A Novel Methodological Approach. *Energy Policy* 3 (9): 5258–63.

Wada, Haruki. 2006. Envisioning a Northeast Asian Community: Regional and Domestic Factors to Consider. In Edward Friedman and Sung Chull Kim (eds.) *Regional Cooperation and Its Enemies in Northeast Asia: The Impact of Domestic Forces*. New York: Routledge, pp. 38–58.

Wood Mackenzie. 2013. Russia's Pivot East: the Growth in Energy Trade with China. *Global Horizons Service—Risks & Uncertainties Insight*, September. Online: www.woodmacresearch.com/content/clientportlet/client/mccrg0003/downloads/Russias_pivot_east.pdf (accessed September 6, 2014).

Index

106, 109–11, 122–3; coal 3, 100, 101, 109, 113, 114, 117, 123; coal gassification project 110–11; and cooperation in Northeast Asia 106–13; domestic energy capabilities 102; and East Asia Summit (EAS) 184; economic assistance to 102; economy of 102, 103; electricity generation/transmission 101, 119–20, 121, 123; energy as strategic leverage/national security issue 194, 198, 199; and energy cooperation 101–6; energy dependency of 105, 106; energy interests of/preferred statecraft 201; energy resources of 114, 193; environmental issues 109, 110; exports of energy 3–4, 101, 109, 114; failure to honor contracts 117–18; fear of foreign countries/investment 104; foreign investment in 116, 121, 122; foreign policy of 102, 106–7, 122; government missteps 121; Greater Tumen Initiative (GTI) 107, 175; infrastructure 100, 108, 110, 111, 112, 113, 114–15, 121, 123; institutional representation 181; international participation of 102; and Japan/South Korea 102, 112–13; loans from China 105; nationalism of 202; and North Korea 102, 113, 184; oil reserves 118; and pipelines 4, 9, 101, 108–9; political issues 115–16; political risks of 108; pollution 109; poverty 108; rail network 105, 109, 111, 113, 114–15, 123; and regional energy cooperation 101, 114–21; renewable energy 94, 112–13, 120, 193; resource nationalism of 122, 159; resources of 3–4, 100, 121; and Russia 102, 103–4, 105, 106, 111, 119, 123, 200; solar power 100, 112, 120; sovereignty concerns of 109–10, 111, 116; as supplier of energy 9; "third neighbors" of 102, 103, 106, 123; as a transit country for Russian pipelines 4, 9; as transmission corridor 109, 114, 120–1; and United States 102, 108; uranium 100, 111, 119; use of competition 107–8, 199; wind power 94, 100, 112, 120
Mongolian Ministry of Energy 118

monopolies: Gazprom 145; Japan 69
multilateral energy cooperation 29, 46, 52–5, 58, 81, 90
multilateral energy regime-building 51–7, 196
Myanmar 56, 174, 175

national champions, oil industry 16
National Development and Reform Commission (NDRC) 45
National Energy Leading Small Group, China 57
national energy security interests, diversity of 199–201
national energy strategy, Russia 129, 131
nationalism: and energy security 16, 32; intensification of 159; of Mongolia 202; resource/of Mongolia 122, 159; resource/of Russia 17, 26–7, 127, 130, 133, 158, 204; U.S. 24
national oil companies (NOCs) *see also* international oil companies (IOCs): China 18, 19, 20, 25, 33, 38, 49, 50–1, 56; and elites 180; overseas investment of 17; state-owned 15–16
national security: and energy/Russia 194, 198, 199, 200; and energy security 12, 39, 158, 159, 162, 194; and energy supply 12, 162; Mongolia 118
National Security Concept, Russia's 2009 129
natural gas *see also* liquefied natural gas (LNG): and China 72, 145; East China Sea 22, 23, 28; and Japan 70, 72, 145; market structure of 73; and regional cooperation 205–6; reserves of in Asia-Pacific/Russia 72; and Russia 42, 134, 145–6; and South Korea 145; U.S. exports of 25
naval expansion, Northeast Asia 158
New Basic Energy Policy Act 2006, Japan 21, 96n.11
Newcom 112
new technologies, and cooperation 30
Nexen 25, 74
Nigeria 20, 24
Nippon Oil 73, 74
Noda, Prime Minister 23
North Africa, and China 39–40, 41